Good Bones

Good Bones
Glorious Relics from the Age of Reading

Essays by

Brooke Allen

TIVOLI
BOOKS

This is a Tivoli Book
Published in 2025

Tivoli Publishing LLC
P.O. Box 8
Tivoli, NY 12583
The United States of America

ISBN (paper) 978-1-966218-12-8
ISBN (ebook) 978-1-966218-13-5

Library of Congress Control Number: 2025944607

Cover design: Daniel Akst
Cover image: *Tower Reliquary with Eight Apostles and the Symbols of the
Four Evangelists,* c. 1200-1250, Metropolitan Museum of Art

To Catherine Drucker and Danuta Shanzer,
who have shared my interests
for more than fifty years.

CONTENTS

Preface

We are in the middle of a seismic cultural change, as transformative as that which followed the appearance of the printing press half a millennium ago. And just as that invention turned the Western world into a literate society, we are now transitioning into a post-literate one. Despite universal public education, thirty percent of American adults read at the level of a ten-year-old. Which is not to say that the other seventy percent read at an adult level; many of them are not much more advanced, and a significant portion are functionally illiterate.

As internet technology has swept over the world, the short-form video is becoming the preferred medium for information. Teenagers spend a mind-bending eight hours a day looking at screens; college students arrive at elite institutions without having been required to read a single book all the way through and, according to recent discoveries, do most of their writing once they arrive with the help of AI. And most adults are too immersed in their own devices to spend much time launching their offspring into the world of print. Even older people who were once avid readers now find themselves unable to lose themselves in a book as they once regularly did. There are too many digital distractions, and the practice of reading online has changed the way we read traditional texts, accustoming us to skimming and skipping around. Reading a book, a whole book, is an active mental process that requires considerable attention.

A high literary culture developed in Europe and, later, America after the advent of the printing press. The novel developed slowly; it reached its apex in the nineteenth century and was still going strong in the decades following World War II. During my own childhood, in the 1960s, mainstream America was not what anyone would call an intellectual society, but lip service was paid to the life of the mind and a large proportion of the population sought to better themselves through literature. Certain members of the publishing world—Bennett Cerf, for example, or Clifton Fadiman—even attained the status of media stars. Intellectuals sneered at Reader's Digest Condensed Books, but they introduced countless thousands to great writers, maintaining a broad cultural consciousness of who those writers were and why they mattered. And surely some of those thousands went on to read the full works.

To peruse a dense novel requires time, which plenty of people had in abundance before the advent of screens. It requires concentration, the capacity for complex thought, and a sensitivity to linguistic nuance and psychological significance. It requires the ability to recognize a theme and identify thematic patterns. It requires silence, time, and solitude. The ability to pay long attention to a written narrative is a muscle. That muscle is weakening.

There are still plenty of people who aspire to write (as we can see from the proliferation of writing workshops and MFA programs) but no one can ever write well without cultivating the practice of constant and deep reading. Reading and writing are entirely complementary, necessary to one another. As the historian Steven Mintz has written, "Writing is not merely a mode of communication, it's a process that, if we move beyond simple formulas, forces us to reflect, think, analyze and reason." And, he reminds us, "There are no shortcuts." E. M. Forster and many others have noted that you don't know what you think about a subject until you've written about it: the writing process refines, guides, and eventually alters the original thought. This kind of mental work has already been hollowed out with the arrival of AI tools like Chat GPT.

The authors I've covered in this collection, though all were famous in the very recent past, are figures that will probably disappear in the post-literate society if they have not done so already. There are many reasons for this, aside from the obvious one that their works are complex and time-consuming in an age that demands immediate rewards, and their assumption that their readers share a broad general culture which has already, just a few decades later, vanished. For one thing, there is the radical social leveling that has occurred during the twenty-first century. Humanity has been crudely divided into "elites" and "non-elites," and a considerable moral onus has been attached to the former. Aristocrats are now by definition beyond the pale (which puts a couple of my choices, the wickedly sly Lord Berners and the snobbish Osbert Sitwell, out of the running these days), while to be "of the people" bestows virtue.

But the sad fact is that the lion's share of the great fiction written before the Second World War is concerned with the refinements, signals, and codes of social class and status. A novelist like Anthony Powell, discussed in these pages, can create brilliant material out of apparently absurd social markers. To a new generation of potential readers, such concerns seem incomprehensible and abhorrent, and might label Powell as a simple snob—which he was not. But of course such niceties continue to exist in our own world, albeit in different forms. Social class divisions will be always with us, no matter how we try to get rid of them. In the meantime, magical writers like Powell and Sybille Bedford will perplex modern readers who pride themselves on their anti-elitism.

Then there is our Robespierrean practice of cancellation, whereby a single racist, sexist or antisemitic remark by even the most liberal author will get him struck from the college curriculum. Take George Sand (Aurore Dupin) for instance, who inspired many other women by the way she seized personal freedom and political engagement but defined herself as anti-feminist. Or August Strindberg, an extreme progressive and feminist who was nevertheless capable, in the knee-jerk manner of his time, of the odd politically incorrect comment. And what about Elspeth Huxley, a brilliant chronicler of the time and place she grew up in, British East Africa during the early twentieth century? A vanished world indeed. Huxley, who settled in England and never lived in Africa after her youth, supported Kenya's struggle for independence and could be described as an African nationalist, but her unwillingness to demonize the colonialists, whom she depicted as all too human, might be enough to damn her in today's morally intransigent climate.

The absence of history from modern curricula has created two or three generations of American readers who are essentially encased in their own era, unable to pick up on the myriad cultural and historical clues inscribed in novels of bygone times. Consider Samuel Butler's *The Way of All Flesh*, for instance, a take-no-prisoners attack on the entire system of Victorian mores. At the time Butler wrote this heavily autobiographical novel (between 1873 and 1884) he feared it was too shocking and scandalous to see the light of day, and its appearance had to await his death at the beginning of the twentieth century. Even then the book shook things up, to put it mildly, and encouraged generations of would-be iconoclasts to rebel. It was still a potent document during my own teenage years in the 1970s. But now, as I discovered when I tried to teach it in a college class, it is all but impenetrable to young people due to its load of cultural ephemera, particularly regarding the

Anglican church. The same could be said of the delightful poems of John Betjeman.

Even writers who were considered both important and easily accessible at the end of the twentieth century seem to be disappearing now from people's shelves. Who reads John Updike these days? Anne Tyler, an excellent middlebrow writer whom "everybody" read quite recently, is no longer much spoken of, though her novels have given pleasure to millions. Witty couplets by Ogden Nash, perhaps the best beloved of twentieth-century poets if not the most "important," are no longer quoted. Eudora Welty, a serious major novelist and short story writer, is largely associated with Southern gothic and Southern humor; she was a master of both, but of so much more as well. The same is true of playwright Horton Foote, a regional writer, yes, but regional in the way that Chekhov was regional: for all times and all places. Truman Capote is still a big name, but I have long suspected that he is famous more because of Audrey Hepburn and Philip Seymour Hoffman and the Black and White Ball and Dill in *To Kill a Mockingbird* than because people actually read his fiction. Oscar Wilde, too, is probably more popular for his wit and style, and his identity as a gay trailblazer, than for his exquisite prose.

I would add a final thought about why imaginative literature is in crisis. The novel is, above all, concerned with personal relations. That is its great subject. And we suddenly find ourselves living at a moment when personal relations as traditionally conducted are breaking down. More people live alone, fewer are acquainted with even close neighbors, many families live at great distances, and the relationships we have are mediated by technology in new and untested ways. Even when people are together they are often more attuned to their phones than to the friends sitting next to them.

The authors I've written about in these essays are just a few of the thousands of literary artists who have given aesthetic and intellectual sustenance to many readers over many years, and who are sinking into oblivion as I write. Here are a few beautiful relics, the sacred bones of a literary culture being ground into dust by technology and AI and many other distractions—and, perhaps most of all, by the bad choices of school boards and other educators over the course of half a century. Like T. S. Eliot, I have shored up some fragments against my ruins. I hope through this book to share some of these enthusiasms with others.

1. THE STRINDBERG VARIATIONS
AUGUST IN SWEDEN

I n twenty-first-century America, August Strindberg (1849–
1912) is known as a "classic" writer, but his actual works are
familiar primarily to drama students and nonprofit theater
directors. A few of Strindberg's plays—*Miss Julie, The Father,
Master Olof, The Dance of Death, The Ghost Sonata, The Stronger*
—have worked their way into the canon. As much as their excel-
lence, the fact that these works provide some powerful mono-
logues for acting students has ensured their survival there. But does
anyone outside of Sweden have any conception of Strindberg the
satirist, the radical, the rebel, the humorist, the historian, the
novelist, the feminist, the hypnotist, the painter, the photographer,
the alchemist, the wild eccentric?

The last big biography of Strindberg was Michael Meyer's in
1985, a hefty tome that concentrated largely on Strindberg the
sexist, racist, and anti-Semite, and compared his character unfavorably with that of the more conventionally liberal Ibsen, whose life
Meyer had also penned. All this was very much in keeping with the
preoccupations of academia at that time, when biographers and
professors were increasingly finding it hard to forgive great authors
for their lapses from political virtue. Strindberg, like so many men

of his time and place, took some racist, sexist, and anti-Semitic positions. But this was only part of the story, for he was also a political radical who shocked contemporaries with his progressive stands, and at significant moments in his life vigorously championed both Jews and women. He was a deeply complicated man whose prejudices and enthusiasms were as contradictory as those of the times in which he lived.

All this is clarified now in Sue Prideaux's *Strindberg: A Life*, a spectacularly revealing and readable biography of the mad genius. Prideaux, an Anglo-Norwegian who is also the author of a prize-winning life of Strindberg's famous frenemy, the painter Edvard Munch, is a sophisticated and humorous writer who, in her portrait of Strindberg, presents the whole man; she is above petty political categorization, for which the complex Strindberg is in any case not a good candidate. He was one of the most astonishing personalities of the modern age, a polymath who encapsulated many of the profound shifts in thought, art, and psychology that separated the nineteenth century from the twentieth. A man of demonic energy, in his not-too-long life he produced sixty plays, three books of poetry, eighteen novels, nine works of autobiography, ten thousand letters, and a considerable corpus of journalism. "If more of this vast agglomeration had been translated," Prideaux comments, "he would surely be more widely valued as one of the founders of modern literature and enjoyed as an irreverent commentator on the ideas of half a century."

Sadly, Strindberg's fiction has never traveled much beyond Scandinavia. His comic novel *The People of Hemsö* (1887), set on a fictionalized version of the island of Kymmendö off Stockholm where Strindberg summered in the 1880s, is in Prideaux's judgment "the great comic masterpiece of Swedish literature." Strindberg's idea, successfully executed, was to produce a story of bawdy peasantry that might have been illustrated by Breughel. His novels *The Red Room* (1879) and *Black Banners* (1907) remain classic and still effective satires *à clef*, attacking the sort of hypocrisy in high places that has in no way died out since the author's time. His short story collection *Getting Married*, whose advanced sexual politics scandalized Sweden when it was published in 1884, was still deemed by Germaine Greer a century later "an extraordinarily broad and reverberating sort of book." Strindberg's twelve history plays earned him the title of "Sweden's Shakespeare," but since few non-Swedes seem to take an interest in Swedish history they are all but unknown outside of his country. He also wrote the first "people's history" of modern times, *The Swedish People*, which, while flawed ("over-extended, hurried, under-researched and finally far too personal," in Prideaux's judgment), was groundbreaking in its approach to historical focus.

Strindberg was also fascinated by the burgeoning interest in the unconscious; an avid student of Jean-Martin Charcot, Pierre Janet, and Hippolyte Bernheim (who each had a strong influence on Freud), he brought these new ideas into his plays and other writings. His work pioneered the artistic use of the irrational and even of absurdism, with flashbacks and reruns that demonstrate the fragmentation of time and self. Perhaps unsurprisingly, he was one of Kafka's favorite authors. Sean O'Casey thought him peerless: "Strindberg, Strindberg, Strindberg, the greatest of them all . . . Barrie sits mumbling as he silvers his little model stars and gilds his little model suns, while Strindberg shakes flames from the living planets and the fixed stars, Ibsen can sit serenely in his Doll's House, while Strindberg is battling with heaven and hell."

S trindberg's autobiographical works are not to be trusted as sources for accurate biography, as Prideaux is well aware. "Strindberg left nine volumes of autobiography which are a complex mix of sticking closely to the action of his life and veering into the wildest imagined scenarios." The playwright's actual life was already fantastic enough. His own childhood was to inspire one of his better-known aphorisms: his definition of "family" as "the home of all social evil, a charitable institution for comfortable women, an anchorage for house-fathers, and a hell for children." His father, Carl Oscar Strindberg, was a middle-class spice merchant with delusions of aristocracy who took a waitress as mistress and produced two sons with her before finally making up his mind to take the socially suicidal step of marrying her. Their third son, August, was their first born in wedlock, but he was their least favorite.

When Carl Strindberg went bankrupt in 1853, the six-year-old August became a scapegoat for his father's every frustration. Strindberg writes in *The Son of a Servant*:

> Hungry and afraid, afraid of the dark, of spankings, of upsetting everybody. Afraid of falling and hurting himself, afraid of being in the way. Afraid of being hit by his brothers, slapped by the maids, scolded by his grandmother, caned by his father and birched by his mother . . . he could do nothing without doing wrong, utter no word without disturbing somebody. Finally, the safest thing was simply not to move. His highest virtue was to sit on a chair and be quiet. It had effectively been dinned into him that he had no right to exist.

The playwright's mother Nora Strindberg adhered to Pietism, a strict variety of Lutheranism emphasizing personal faith and clean living, and enjoyed the hellfire sermons of its wilder preachers. Anti-intellectual by definition—it deemed that, of all books, only the Bible was to be trusted—Pietism made a virtue of Nora's ignorance, and she saw her third son's liking for books and intellectual inquiry as theologically perilous, a punishable offense. In later life Strindberg was to write that "Pietism was then what spiritualism is now—a cut-rate philosophy claiming to offer a higher knowledge of hidden things, which was therefore eagerly taken up by women and the great uneducated and finally even made its way into the royal court." As a child he suffered acutely from its edicts, as interpreted by Nora: she "knew" she was saved, she told the boy, and that he was not.

At the age of seven August was sent to the Klara School for boys, a place he found so hateful that he thought it must have been invented as a punishment for Original Sin. The atmosphere became temporarily more civilized when one little girl, the daughter of the rector, joined the French lessons. This was Strindberg's introduction to love, and probably his first intimation that a more equal relationship between the sexes might be possible, for from that moment on he loudly advocated coeducation. He eventually moved on to the Stockholm Lyceum, but for various reasons his secondary education was not much happier than his primary schooling had been. Nora Strindberg died in 1862, and Carl, with indecent haste, married the children's governess, thirty years his junior. August received no more guidance from his stepmother than he had from his mother, and was perplexed and disturbed, as ever, by the strict mores of Lutheran Sweden. Like many other teenagers the young August was tormented by a book that, in Prideaux's words, "galloped through Sweden like the Four Horsemen of the Apocalypse, spreading terror and misery": *A Warning Against the Enemy of Youth by a Friend of Youth*, by the Pietist Karl von Kapff. "Possibly unique in extending the consequences of masturbation to politics, von Kapff suggested that the favorite practice of revolutionaries spread their poison through society." Terrified by von Kapff's admonitions, August began spending many hours in church, longing for salvation; he even contemplated taking Holy Orders, though this religiosity proved short-lived.

In 1867 Strindberg entered Uppsala University. Although by this time Carl Strindberg had built his business back up, he refused to pay his son's tuition, so that August was compelled to leave the university and take a job as a teacher at—of all places—the hated Klara School. (His father, perversely, chose to grumble at the son's consequent loss of social status.) The young Strindberg turned out to be an inspiring teacher: "I had several good history teachers later," one of his students recalled, "but never one whose lessons were so vivid as well as informative . . . Strindberg was one of the teachers we adored." But he was a poor disciplinarian, and while he had yet to find a driving purpose in life, he was quite sure that he wanted "not to be enrolled as a regular member of society."

Strindberg began toying with the idea of taking up medicine, and a kind friend, Dr. Axel Lamm, invited him to join his household while he supervised his studies. The Lamm family (which was Jewish) provided Strindberg's first experience of liberal, cosmopolitan culture, and he flourished under its aegis; the opportunity to be, for the first time, part of a happy family was particularly valuable to him, and though he eventually dropped his plans to be a doctor, the broad scientific education he received under Dr. Lamm was not wasted. His next thought was to become an actor, and in 1870 he took a job playing various non-speaking roles at Stockholm's Royal Theater. When he tried to move up in the hierarchy, he was advised in no uncertain terms to take some acting lessons, an admonition that sent him into an emotional collapse: "He wept for rage, went home and took an opium pill that he had been keeping for emergencies. Then a friend took him out and they got stupendously drunk."

I t was a turning point in his creative life. The next morning, as he lay sunk in misery, his subconscious seemed to take over. Here is his account of the experience, from his autobiographical work *Time of Ferment*:

> While thus lying on the sofa he felt an unusual degree of fever, during which his brain seemed to work at arranging memories of the past, cutting out some and adding others. New minor characters entered; he saw them mixing in the

action, and heard them speaking, just as he had done on stage. After one or two hours had passed, he had a comedy of two acts ready in his head . . . But now he had to write it. In four days the piece was ready . . . When the work was finished, he drew a deep sigh of relief, as though years of pain were over, as though a tumor had been cut out . . . [Later that evening] he wrote a four-page letter in rhyme and discovered that he could write verse . . . it seemed to him like a visitation of the Holy Spirit . . . someone or something seemed to be there which, or who, was not there before . . . he fell on his knees and thanked God for the gift of poetry.

Prideaux writes rather more dryly than Strindberg about this first creative outpouring: "When one looks at this early clutch written in the inspired rush, it must be conceded that however divine the intervention, the resulting art was of dubious merit but the fact that words continued to glimmer and swell on the God-given tide was perhaps more important than the words themselves. At last he felt chosen, blessed, directed." His first few plays, as Prideaux indicates, have not stood the test of time, but finally a verse play called *In Rome* (about the Danish neo-classical sculptor Bertel Thorvaldsen) was accepted by the Royal Theater. Its eleven performances in the autumn of 1870 financed the author's return to Uppsala University, where he now enjoyed the sort of intellectually adventurous, bohemian student life he had always craved. He learned Icelandic and studied the sagas; he composed songs and sang them on his guitar; he took up painting. His father offered to fund the rest of his education on the condition that he did not write any more plays—apparently this occupation was considered *déclassé*—but the neophyte dramatist ignored this edict, producing three more in quick succession. *The Outlaw*, written in 1871 when the author was only twenty-two, earned him an audience with the king, who presented him with a gift of two hundred riksdalers.

The result of this was Strindberg's first masterpiece, *Master Olof*, written at this time but not produced until ten years later.

Strindberg left the university in 1872 without a degree and began the drudgery of trying to support himself as a freelance writer, attempting novelettes for ladies' magazines, art criticism, translations, and editorials. He even edited an insurance magazine, which he ran into the ground after six months. He also fathered an illegitimate child whom he disowned: lingering guilt haunts two of his autobiographical novels, *The Son of a Servant* and *Inferno*, and throughout his life he suffered from a morbid horror of men's uncertainty about their biological paternity; his best and most graphic artistic expression of this fear appears in the great play *The Father* (1887).

I t was at this time that Strindberg met the woman he wished to marry. Siri (born Sigrid Sofia Mathilda Elisabeth) von Essen was the daughter of a Finnish aristocrat and the wife of Carl Gustaf Wrangel, a popular military man and a scion (though from a lesser branch) of a great family. At the time of this momentous meeting, Siri was twenty-four years old, with a two-year-old daughter. "Of Byzantine slenderness," Strindberg gushed, "which allowed her dress to fall in simple, noble folds, like the dress of St. Cecelia, her body was of bewitching proportions, her wrists and ankles exquisitely turned." Strindberg fell headlong into the sort of Madonna-worship he later excoriated: "Henceforth this woman represented to me a soul incarnate, a soul pure, unapproachable ... woman as both virgin and mother ... I worshipped her."

Launching himself into emotional Grand Guignol, Strindberg first vowed to renounce his married inamorata and staged a dramatic final parting before moving to Paris. Thirty miles south of Stockholm, as his ship passed the little island of Dalarö, the crazed lover hurled himself histrionically from the ship, fetching up at a Dalarö hotel where he decided to kill himself "by contracting pneumonia or some other fatal disease, which would keep me in bed for weeks. I would be able to see her again, kiss her hand and say goodbye for ever." The suicide attempt, clearly never a very serious one, failed, and the lover duly returned to Stockholm to continue the pursuit. The fact that Strindberg was offering her a career on the stage sweetened the deal, and, as she wrote to her mother, she had never been content with the passive Carl Gustaf anyway. "Battle and progress is my motto—Peace is not for me—I wasn't born a Woman—I was born an artist!" As she and Strindberg planned their future together, he drew up a marriage contract, far ahead of its time, that would give each partner control of his own property: he was beginning to formulate certain feminist ideals.

But his idealism, and his Madonna-worship, soon began to wilt. Siri had taken on her first stage role, in a Swedish version of *Jane Eyre*. She turned out not to have much talent, and the theatrical milieu quickly coarsened her once aristocratic manners: Strindberg was appalled to discover that "his alabaster Madonna, his pure princess, his gentle, motherly Siri turned into—an actress." She drank, swore, smoked. This was not at all the way Strindberg had envisioned his bride's artistic maturation; "he was not championing the idea of female equality so that women could behave as badly as men. The understanding in his mind had been that the elevation of women to equality would generally elevate standards." Nor did things go smoothly on the domestic front. Siri's little daughter Sigrid Wrangel died, and then Strindberg and Siri's first child together, Kerstin, died mysteriously a day after her birth. Siri lost all her money when the firm she invested in went bankrupt, and in 1879 Strindberg also declared himself bankrupt, as his father had done before him.

Fortunately his next project, *The Red Room*, was a resounding popular success, a broad-strokes satire that arrived at a moment of widespread disillusionment with Sweden's governing class and intellectual elite. The author was now widely considered a genius, but rather than basking in his fame he fled it, sinking into arcane studies, a lifelong habit: the history of aquavit, Swedish relations with China and Tartary, Central Asian geography. He studied Japanese and Chinese, and also went back to dramatic writing, producing several plays including *Sir Bengt's Wife* (1882), a considered reply to Ibsen's *A Doll's House.*

Now *Master Olof* finally appeared and made a major impression on Stockholm theatergoers. Strindberg's thousand-page history, *The Swedish People,* was finished at the same time, and he was soon planning another historical work, *The New Kingdom: Satirical Sketches from the Era of Assassinations and Jubilees.*

This last work scandalized the establishment. Narrated by a bedbug which lived in Stockholm's House of Nobility, an equivalent to the British House of Lords, "It let rip in ten shatteringly direct chapters which did not spare church, state, or big business . . . Reaction in the corridors of power was shock and a sort of surreptitious delight at the audacious truths he had dared speak." It also earned him an important new supporter: the eminent publisher Albert Bonnier, who offered to take Strindberg on and advanced him a hefty sum of money against future earnings—a bonanza to the debt-ridden author. In 1883 the Strindberg family, newly solvent, left Sweden for what would be a six-year journey through France, Switzerland, Italy, Central Europe, and Scandinavia. This trip, states Prideaux, "would transform him from an essentially Swedish writer into a European voice." Strindberg read Byron and Rousseau, and worked on a long cycle of poems called *Somnambulist Nights* while Bonnier, back in Sweden, urged him to write a novel. Strindberg pondered the plight of the professional artist:

> This is my dilemma! To be useful, I must be read! To be read I must write "art," but I consider "art" immoral. So: whether to die with a pure soul or carry on with what is for me an immoral activity! Solve that! And then, when

I've pondered and fought, along comes that black devil
who dwells in my heart, and mocks everything: the
epicurean spirit of art awakens in me, and I long for the
pleasure that producing works of art affords. And it is a
tremendous pleasure, which is precisely what makes it
immoral.

He considered a novel about nihilists, also a satirical travel
book about Europe to be called *Through the Continent of the
Whites*, a play on the African explorer Henry Stanley's *Through
the Dark Continent*. But in 1884, once more out of money, he
found himself at work on *Getting Married*, a collection of twelve
stories dealing with the difficulties facing those who seek an
honest, successful marriage in an intrinsically hypocritical society.

T he Woman Question" galvanized and polarized European
society in the late nineteenth century, and *Getting Married*
was Strindberg's contribution to it—an outrageous one, by the
standards of the time. Anti-feminists were angered by the mani-
festo's call for women to be given the same education as men, in
the same schools; to be given the vote; to be eligible for all occupa-
tions; to keep their own names; to have their own bedrooms.
Women of every political stripe were angered by their demotion
from the pedestal they had occupied throughout the nineteenth
century; Strindberg openly attacked the Madonna-worship he had
dubbed "gynolatry."

There shall be complete equality between the sexes, which
will do away with that revolting form of hypocrisy called
gallantry, or politeness to ladies. A girl will not expect a boy
to get up and give her his seat, for that is the hallmark of
the subservient slave; and a brother will not get into the
habit of expecting his sister to make his bed, or sew his

short buttons, for these are things he must do for himself . . .

False gallantry will cease of itself, and men and women will associate together as men do now. But things shall not be as at present, when men have all male banquets, which end with a toast to the ladies, while the latter sit at home eating porridge and milk.

Getting Married, it turned out, was more than just offensive; it was actionable on grounds of blasphemy, for in one of the stories the author had referred to Holy Communion as an "impudent deception." Police seized the remains of the first print run from Bonnier's office, and Strindberg worried whether or not he should return to Sweden and face prosecution. His eventual return to his homeland and his dramatic trial (thousands of spectators crowded round the courthouse, throwing up their hats when his acquittal was announced) made him a momentary hero in the cause of free speech, but his feminism had fatally soured, and he was soon plugging away at a sequel to his story collection, *Getting Married II*—a very different kettle of fish from its predecessor. He had lost his former respect for the fair sex, and began his second volume with "a scattergun volley of misogynist quotations taken from Rousseau, Aristotle, Schopenhauer, and even Annie Besant whom he detested." One of the stories was such a brutal and transparent portrait of Siri as a drunken, slovenly wife and mother that she announced she would henceforth cease to read what he wrote—a great blow to their marriage, much of which had until then revolved around Strindberg's writing life.

This tiff was symptomatic of a general breakdown in their partnership, and a corresponding heightening of Strindberg's tendency to paranoia. Suddenly he began to be tormented by suspicions: that he had not been the father of their first child, who had died; that the child might still somehow be alive, hidden by Siri; that Siri was a secret lesbian. This last notion was fueled by

Siri's close friendship with an aggressive and challenging young woman named Marie David. All these fears, as well as a new fascination with extreme psychological states (he read all the latest publications on this subject), went into his new works, including, most significantly, *The Father*.

This marked the beginning of a spurt of creativity. There was *The People of Hemsö* (1887), his comic masterpiece, and the final volume of his fictionalized autobiography, *A Madman's Defense* (1888)—a work that has been compared with those of Poe and Kafka, and whose themes presage both Freud and existentialism. In 1888 Strindberg also founded the Scandinavian Experimental Theatre, and in March 1889 three of his new plays were scheduled to be premiered there: *Miss Julie*, *The Stronger*, and *The Creditors*.

Once again Swedish censorship sprang to the defense of public morality; the police raided the dress rehearsal of *Miss Julie* and banned the play. The producers got around the ban by staging the play at a private performance in Copenhagen two weeks later, but it was not until 1984—a century after its completion—that it could finally be produced in its entirety in the author's native country. Strindberg tended to blame all this prudery on "this intellectual syphilis called Protestantism . . . [N]owhere does it wreak havoc as in Scandinavia."

The Strindbergs' personal life was becoming as scandalous as August's plays. They had finally returned to Sweden, but their life as a couple had been irreparably damaged by both Siri's unfaithfulness and Strindberg's mounting paranoia. In 1890 they applied for a divorce and Marie David, who now affected male dress, moved in with Siri and the children. Strindberg was incensed and the fur flew. Marie sued Strindberg for libel; Strindberg pushed Marie down the stairs; Marie sued Strindberg for assault; Strindberg sued Marie for trespass. None of this kept Strindberg the artist from maintaining a certain objective humor about the events, and two excellent new plays came out of the fiasco.

Strindberg's post-Siri life was, if anything, even more emotionally stormy than his married years had been, the boundary between eccentricity and madness finer than ever. In 1892 he traveled to Berlin at the invitation of Ola Hansson, a writer who shared Strindberg's interest in abnormal psychology and the connection between genius and insanity. A tavern on Unter den Linden, Zum Schwarzen Ferkel (The Black Piglet), became the hangout for Strindberg's new group of friends, a crowd who

> saw themselves as part of a great renaissance of the soul against the intellect, part of the mystical underground current rising as a counter-culture to Darwinian certainty. They were not rising up against science—but against scientism, the attitude that all phenomena were explicable . . . They wished to restore validity to the invisible and the irrational . . . They aimed to find a technique to tap the unconscious processes for art: to master and control that elusive process "inspiration." To this end they studied the structure of the brain, optics, psychiatry, mysticism, and symbolism, they paid attention to dreams before Freud made it routine to do so and, notoriously, they sought to unlock the doors of perception through excessive use of drink, drugs, and sex.

Parties at Zum Schwarzen Ferkel were colorful. Strindberg enjoyed performing on a guitar he kept deliberately out of tune so as to demonstrate the importance of chance and accident in the creative process. Under the tutelage of Edvard Munch, another denizen of the hangout, Strindberg refined his painting skills. He had already exhibited his paintings in Sweden, where one critic had complained that they looked like dirty bed-sheets hung up to dry, but in Berlin he achieved a *renommé* as a painter that he retains to this day. Another new friend of the 1890s was Paul Gauguin, whom Strindberg met in Paris when the painter was between Tahitian voyages. "Gauguin played his mandolin and Strindberg played his guitar and they planned a South Seas musical entertainment which sadly came to naught," Prideaux tells us.

In May 1893 Strindberg married Frieda Uhl, a twenty-year-old Austrian girl he had known for three months and who was already widely renowned, Prideaux says, as "a man-eater who never passed up a meal." Things began badly and got worse. On their wedding night Strindberg tried to strangle Frieda in his sleep; later that night she heard him say, also in his sleep, "She would not believe I could get such a young girl!" After a few weeks of marriage they went to England for a visit, where they began to quarrel violently. "As they walked along the banks of the Thames he harbored violent fantasies of pushing her into the river or of the rough dockers ravishing her." By October Frieda was pregnant, and wanted an abortion and a divorce. He pleaded for reconciliation. The child was born (a girl), but each partner wanted out of the marriage, which was dissolved in 1895. Frieda, who specialized in the pursuit of famous men (Augustus John described her as "the walking hell-bitch of the western world"), eventually settled in London, opening a nightclub off Piccadilly.

After his split from Frieda, Strindberg moved to Paris to devote himself to alchemy. "I will be mad," he wrote to Gauguin. He meant "to plunge himself into the Dionysian journey of submerging the conscious in the lava of the unconscious, thus continuing the journey that had started in Berlin." Alchemy, it should be stated, was not considered as mad then as it is now; in fact, as Prideaux reveals, there were some fifty thousand alchemists living in Paris at that time, and occult matters had not yet lost their aura of scientific viability. Strindberg became, at least for a time, a respected member of the scientific community.

When Edvard Munch arrived in Paris he quickly became the target of his former friend's paranoid delusions. Strindberg was convinced that Munch was trying to murder him by shooting gas through a wall while he slept; he practiced subjugating Munch to his will; he stabbed knives in the air to fight off evil spirits; he performed dances of exorcism.

Frieda Uhl's sister Marie suspected that he sometimes put on an act.

> My sister and I have often wondered if these dramatic and frequently theatrical events were not so much expressions of an occasional abnormal idea but rather experiments designed to create a good theatrical effect and, also, to test its impact on an audience. It is difficult to decide how much is fantasy, how much reality, hard as it is to imagine how Strindberg really saw the real world.

The genuine madness into which Strindberg had sunk during his time in Paris began to recede after he left the city, perhaps because he was no longer exposed to the quantities of chemicals he had breathed in during his alchemical experiments. Returning to Sweden for the first time since his departure with Siri, he settled in the provincial city of Lund. Life was calmer: here he completed *Inferno*, and between 1898 and 1901 produced a total of twenty plays, including his famous *To Damascus* (Parts I and II) and *Advent*. In 1899 he returned, after sixteen years, to Stockholm.

Strindberg might have been older and more stable, but his love life didn't reflect it. In 1900 he met the young actress Harriet Bosse. He became obsessed, believing that Harriet visited him nightly, in incubus form, for sex. Prideaux links the incubus visitations to a concurrent outpouring of creativity: "During the time that his spirit was shackled to Harriet he wrote thirty-one works, all of them worth reading, including *Swanwhite*, the only play in which the modest, prudish Strindberg lifts the skirts on his erotic fantasies, showing them to be Art Nouveau in terms of décor and stuffed with symbols anticipating Freud."

The couple married in 1901: the writer was fifty-two, his bride thirty years younger. Though they produced a daughter, the marriage was hopeless; there were sexual incompatibilities and by this time there seems to have been no living with the semi-deranged Strindberg. They divorced in 1904, but remained close friends. The incubus visitations, incidentally, continued, and perhaps they accounted for the author's final creative push, a series of four "chamber plays": *Storm*, *The Pelican*, *The Burned House*, and *The Ghost Sonata*. None of these was a success, and *The Ghost Sonata*, today a classic, was found totally incomprehensible—evidence, some said, of the playwright's madness. It ran for only twelve performances and was not shown again until four years after the author's death.

Old age was now approaching, but Strindberg was not one to go gently. At sixty he fell in love with an eighteen-year-old, Fanny Falkner, and longed to marry her, but this time the age gap was so big that the bride, star-struck as she was, balked and refused. He completed *The Roots of World Languages*—"as eccentric a book," in Prideaux's judgment, "as any he had written." And he launched a written campaign against an influential cabal of reactionary nationalists, declaring, in his words, "a war of liberation against stupidity and snobbery, and time-serving in literature and government." These fifty articles and the responses to them have become known as "the Strindberg feud," and through them he demonstrated his ongoing talent for polarizing opinion in Sweden. In his early sixties, as he developed stomach cancer and was clearly approaching death, he was called by some "a sex-philosopher, a sphinx, a vampire, a parasite, a volcano who belches not fire but filth"; by others, particularly the Social Democrats and the workers, he was honored. The Swedish Academy pointedly ignored Strindberg and awarded the Nobel Prize that year to Maurice Maeterlinck; influential fans retaliated by awarding him an "Anti-

Nobel Prize" two months before his death, which occurred in May of 1912. At his funeral the following week, ten thousand mourners followed the hearse to the cemetery. Not bad for a man who had made so many enemies.

In a review of Michael Meyer's 1985 Strindberg biography, Herbert Mitgang wrote in *The New York Times*, "I cannot imagine that a lengthy life of this man could interest anyone except a student of his writings. A biographer must ask, what did Strindberg do? And the only comprehensive, significant answer is, he wrote."

How wrong can a critic be? The answer to "What did Strindberg do?" is clearly "a hell of a lot," and though before reading Prideaux's biography I was in no way a student of Strindberg's writings, I found myself so riveted by every part of this extraordinary man's life that I immediately ordered *Getting Married*, *Inferno*, and *Occult Diary*. Nor have they disappointed me. *The Red Room* is next on my list.

Prideaux might be faulted by some for not having produced a "critical" biography. But for a one-volume, widely accessible life this might not have been possible; the sheer volume of Strindberg's oeuvre would expand such a work to impossible dimensions. That should be a goal of some much longer and more scholarly study. This one concentrates, for better or worse, on the life rather than the work—and it is a life that can hardly fail to amaze.

(2012)

2. A LIFE AS THEATER
GEORGE SAND

Benita Eisler's 2003 biographical study, *Chopin's Funeral*, reads more as a double portrait of Chopin and his lover, George Sand, than as a single biographical study of Chopin himself. It must have been hard for Eisler to resist this dual subject, for Chopin was essentially a negative and elusive character, difficult to pin down on the page, while Sand was an emotional exhibitionist who presented the drama of her life as soap opera for wide public consumption. As a personality she overshadowed and overpowered the diminutive, delicate composer. Chopin was a genius, and it is difficult and perhaps futile for a biographer to explain genius; Sand, merely talented, presents a more comprehensible case study. Also, Sand exemplified in many ways the spirit of her time and place, making her an attractive subject for the cultural historian, while Chopin, in the manner of so many geniuses, followed his own idiosyncratic path.

Eisler's new book *Naked in the Marketplace: The Lives of George Sand*, like her book on Chopin (but unlike her comprehensive volume on Byron, published in 2000), is a slight and accessible introduction to its subject. It may seem odd that Sand, the most notorious woman of her day, would need such an introduction to the informed general reader, but the world changes swiftly and there are plenty of informed readers out there nowadays who know nothing about George Sand and will be riveted by her tale. In our intellectually provincial manner, we of the twenty-first century consider ourselves to live in unusually extravagant and dramatic times. But the Romantic era in France rivaled ours not only in the variety of its roads to political self-delusion but even in its mingling of the public and the intimate, its genius for publicity, its apotheosis of *gloire*, fame, and—failing these greater goods— mere notoriety.

"Love as the ultimate virtue would become the guiding principle of her life—and the principal theme of her novels," Eisler comments. But what exactly did Sand mean by love? Nothing that involved discretion or generally civilized behavior: "She would always demand authenticity (or drama) in her relationships, at least when she was the transgressor." This ideal of "authenticity" brands Sand as a disciple of Jean-Jacques Rousseau, but as with Rousseau himself the more skeptical reader wonders how pure and authentic any emotion can remain when it is displayed in the service of self-promotion. Sand's *Histoire de ma vie* rivals Rousseau's *Confessions* in professing emotional honesty while positing a clearly idealized protagonistic self. As Eisler says, in the *Histoire de ma vie*:

> The shared pain of an unhappy couple becomes the martyrdom of the partner who owns the narrative. In Sand's retrospective view of herself, unruly sex disappears offstage. By the time she tells her story, the private Aurore Dupin Dudevant had become the public figure George Sand. Beloved in old age as "the Good Lady of Nohant," she had begun to sanitize the past; episodes of passionate abandon, followed by notoriety and scandal, were transformed into platonic or maternal relationships. One of her loves, Alfred de Musset, published his own version of their

wild affair. But who believes a mad poet? George Sand always had the last word.

Sand considered "authenticity," or at least its pretense, as her own prerogative, but she resented it when practiced by others. Chopin's final rejection of her, which was undoubtedly authentic, provoked her deep resentment. Chopin should not have been so authentic! He should have kept his authenticity to himself! "If I had made mistakes, even committed crimes," she wailed, "Chopin should not have believed them, should not have *seen them*. There's a certain point of respect and gratitude past which we no longer have the right to examine the behavior of these beings who have become sacred to us."

In any case, Sand's presentation of herself as "authentic" was just another pose: her life was largely comprised of such poses, some of which directly contradicted one another. Born to a working-class mother and an aristocratic father, Sand felt free to choose her own class identity and, as Eisler points out, "The core of her personal narrative . . . was the decision to define herself as a 'daughter of the people' and, later, the belief that her mixed heritage gave her, along with unique insight, an emblematic role as 'Representative Woman' of her time." Eisler claims that this decision robbed her of her father and his legacy. But how can this be true when Sand in fact inherited her paternal grandmother's estate and spent much of her life as its *châtelaine*, effectively assuming a feudal role in the community and ending her days as the Good Lady of Nohant?

And what about her anti-feminist pose? George Sand flouted all contemporary standards of feminine behavior: she dressed in men's clothes, claimed the maximum of personal freedom, supported her family as a writer, divorced her husband, and lived openly with her lovers; she even had a well-publicized lesbian relationship, with the beautiful actress Marie Dorval. She did, in other words, exactly as she pleased and dominated the men in her life rather than being dominated by them. Yet she disdained feminist ideals, disapproved of divorce, claimed that women were unfit to vote, and declined the opportunity to stand for office as the first woman deputy to the National Assembly, saying that women were not yet ready for political office. One thinks of Sand's doppel-gänger and heir, Colette, and comes to the conclusion that Sand, like Colette, knew instinctively that political feminism is a sexual turnoff: if she were to remain a man's woman, she would have to stress the differences between the sexes rather than the similarities, and specifically her own difference as the most feminine of crea-tures. If that meant feigning helplessness and incompetence against all evidence to the contrary, then so be it.

J ust how authentic can any life be when it is lived and played as theater, or as literature? The chilly WASP Henry James—Sand's polar opposite in temperament—described Sand's love affair with Alfred de Musset as "all rapture and all rage and all liter-ature . . . The lovers are naked in the market-place and perform for the benefit of society." Sand was an indifferent novelist: though her output was prodigious and her books were successful during her own time and far beyond, the sociology and ideology in them tend to overpower the art, and there is some truth, unfortunately, in Flaubert's brutal judgment that in Sand's prose "everything oozes and ideas trickle between words as between slack thighs." In the end it was Sand's life, not her literary output, that turned out to be her major work of art. And as with so many great works of art, the gorgeous surface only partially conceals the dark and sometimes ugly reality.

Benita Eisler approaches her narcissistic subject with surprising sympathy, tracing the roots of Sand's often cruel behavior to her childhood, which was indeed a strange one. Her mother, Antoinette-Sophie-Victoire Delaborde, was a onetime prostitute who had formed a series of attachments to officers in the

Napoleonic army. After having given birth to an illegitimate daughter, Caroline, Sophie met the aristocratic Corporal Maurice Dupin, a grandson of the great eighteenth-century officer the Maréchale de Saxe and the heir to a substantial estate in the Berry region. The two married in June 1804, only a month before the birth of their daughter Aurore-Lucile-Amandine Dupin—the future George Sand.

Maurice Dupin was killed in a riding accident when Aurore was still very small, and from that moment she became a pawn in a battle of wills between her imperious grandmother, Marie-Aurore de Saxe Dupin de Franceuil, and her no less determined mother. Soon after Maurice's death, Sophie effectively sold the little girl to her grandmother, accepting an allowance from the old lady in exchange for her legal parental rights. For the next several years Aurore lived at Nohant with Madame Dupin, enduring long visits from the disreputable and increasingly unbalanced Sophie. "More and more, Aurore's upbringing became a battleground, pitting Sophie—semiliterate, intuitive, emotionally explosive—against her mother-in-law, class-bound, rigid, and repressed." The knowledge that her mother had given her up for cash; the daily trials of Sophie's erratic behavior and growing paranoia; the growing suspicion (to be confirmed in later years) that Maurice Dupin was not her biological father: all these were hard trials of Aurore's adolescence. It is impossible not to feel compassion for this brave girl; many would have cracked under the strain.

Relief eventually came, however, when at the age of fourteen Aurore was sent as a boarder to a convent school. "I rejoiced in the convent," she later said. "I felt an overwhelming need for respite from all these inner conflicts. I was tired of being the apple of discord between two beings, both of whom I cherished. I almost wished they would both forget me." There, at the convent of the English Augustine Ladies' Order, she caught a dose of religion from which she never quite recovered, though her freethinking grandmother tried hard enough to cure her of Christianity. As the years progressed her religious impulses were diverted into social and political channels. "[T]he liberal spirit became for me synonymous with religious belief. I can never forget—I will never forget —how the Christian impulses swept me, unhesitatingly, from the first, into the progressive camp where I remain to this day," she wrote.

In the spirit of her age she embraced revolution, and her erotic ideal was the revolutionary and/or the artistic genius, preferably both combined in one person. Her husband, the Baron Casimir Dudevant, was neither, but he made a useful stepping-stone to adulthood and independence. The illegitimate son (but recognized heir) of a minor nobleman and a maidservant, Dudevant had the advantage, for her, of being "neither a fortune-hunter nor a blueblood willing to 'forgive' her dubious heritage." The two were married in 1822, and a son, Maurice, was born the following year. Almost immediately thereafter, Aurore embarked on her first extramarital affair, with the conservative Catholic jurist Aurélien de Sèze. She milked the domestic drama for maximum effect (a lifelong habit), drawing the cuckolded Dudevant into the fray and compelling him to become, of all things, her confidant.

A daughter, Solange, was born in 1828, but while she bore the name Dudevant she was actually the child of another of Aurore's amours, the atheistic, idealist scientist Stéphane de Grandsagne. But this affair was also brief, for she soon fell simultaneously in love with a new man, Jules Sandeau, and a new cause, the July Revolution of 1830. Having left Dudevant, she began a *vie de bohème* in Paris with Jules and earned a position with *Le Figaro*, the only woman on its staff. She covered the events of the Revolution with the passionate enthusiasm that marked everything she set her mind to, though in this context her gusto seems in dubious taste: "I don't have to tell you that I went everywhere and saw everything with my own eyes," she wrote to a friend. "I love the noise, the storm, even the danger, and if I were selfish, I'd hope to watch a revolution every morning, it's so much fun!"

It was at this time that Aurore began writing fiction and became George Sand, using Jules Sandeau's name as inspiration. Her first novel, *Indiana*, appeared in 1832, and there would be four more in the following three years. "A post-colonial soap opera," Eisler says, "*Indiana* is both daringly modern and maddeningly dated—a conflict that would color all its author's future fiction . . . With her first novel, the neophyte had discovered a new formula that all but guaranteed critical and commercial success: a skillful mix of controversy and convention, romance and rebellion." *Indiana* is hopelessly over-the-top by today's standards, and driven by an unconvincing idealistic utopianism. Its failings show up in rather stark contrast to the better work that was appearing in France at that time, most notably that of Sand's contemporary, Balzac. She herself, perhaps in a defensive mode, was openly contemptuous of Balzac's aesthetic, condemning his realism as mere sensationalism: "to make sure it's new, it has to be ugly."

Sand lacked real literary genius, but she was a consistently inventive writer. Her combination of dramatic and sometimes sensational story lines with subjects of topical interest, and her fascination with sociology and human nature—marriage, gender roles, social structures—kept her work popular and accessible. *Valentine*, a satire on nouveau riche farmers in her own rural area around Nohant, was a more interesting work than *Indiana;* so was the autobiographical *Lélia*, deemed by Sainte-Beuve, the king of critics, to be a great "philosophical novel."

A literary godfather to Sand, Sainte-Beuve also proved helpful in finding her a new lover: the twenty-three-year-old Alfred de Musset. The tiny, frail poet appealed, as Chopin would do, to Sand's motherly instincts—"With her," Eisler says, "the maternal and the erotic were one"—and Musset responded right on cue: "Love only those who know how to love," he declaimed disingenuously. "I only know how to suffer. Farewell! I love you as only a child can love."

The ensuing drama was indeed played, in Henry James's words, naked in the marketplace. With the gossipy Sainte-Beuve as her confidant, Sand must have known that every detail of the love affair would be common knowledge in Paris. When Musset fell ill in Venice, Sand claimed to have fallen in love with his doctor, an unassuming professional named Pietro Pagello, and even left the poet to move into the doctor's tiny apartment. But bourgeois discomfort in Italy was a little too grim: soon Sand was again fretting for Paris. She and Musset embarked on a feverish, hyperbolic correspondence about their past and future: their letters read like trilling arias. "Love something like me!" Musset exclaimed. "I tremble to think of it! You thought you were my mistress, but you were my mother. We didn't make love, we committed incest!" Their letters somehow became public, and there was plentiful gossip and slander in Paris, with some of the worst of it being eagerly spread by Prosper Mérimée and Gustave Planche, the critic. By the time Sand came home several months later, with Pagello in tow, all literary Paris was divided into "Sandistes" and "Mussetistes."

With Musset sinking into psychosis, Sand indulging in the most extravagant passions, and with the hapless Pagello stuck in the middle, the comedy played itself out very much in the public eye. The two protagonists "entertained for each other every feeling in life but the feeling of respect," as Henry James put it. Perhaps no couple even in our own publicity-mad era—not Elizabeth Taylor and Richard Burton, not Mary Matalin and James Carville, not even, perhaps, Kim and Kanye—has capitalized so thoroughly on the world's insatiable prurience.

Both writers mined the raw material of their twenty-one-month affair—even as it was happening—to produce a new kind of nonfiction fiction, the literary equivalent of *cinéma vérité*. In poetry, plays, novels, confessional, and travel writing, they both wrote revealingly of the other and of themselves in "the Affair." In most instances, the writers' attempts to fictionalize their roles expose more than any other documentation could do.

Musset produced *La Confession d'un enfant du siècle*, which became an instant classic as the bible of the "lost generation" of post-Napoleonic youth, and a play, *On ne badine pas avec l'amour*. But Sand, always the stronger of the two, was to have the last word: *Elle et lui*, written two years after Musset's death, gave the world her side of the story. Her self-canonization—she presented herself as a saint with only the purest of motives—did not deceive many readers. In later years, close study of Sand's handwriting and of the subject matter of certain letters has shown that she doctored, changed, or rewrote a number of Musset's letters and her own so as to keep them in line with her own gloss on the events.

Sand's next lover was the famous radical lawyer Michel de Bourges, whom she likened to Robespierre in intransigence and political zealotry. Their romance was not long lived, but Michel acted as her legal representative in her divorce trial, winning her all the rents from Nohant and custody of Solange. Eisler paints the astonishing scene well: "With not a flicker of embarrassment, Baroness Dudevant's lover now made a stirring case on behalf of the wronged wife (seated in full view of the court in a simple white, hooded dress) who merely sought to regain her dignity and property from a debauched and wastrel husband."

S and's meeting with Franz Liszt marked a turning point in her life. She had always worshipped genius, and Liszt was the real thing, as well as having the sort of fame and glamour that nowadays adhere only to rock stars. Sexually he was out of reach, for he enjoyed a stable relationship with the beautiful Marie d'Agoult—

though Sand tried to make Marie jealous by boasting about her own psychic bond with Liszt: she would crouch under the piano while the genius performed, she told Marie, so that she could physically experience each vibrato. But Sand acknowledged Marie's primacy with a relatively good grace and was pleased to accept the couple's invitation to join them in lodgings at the Hôtel de France in the rue Lafitte. There they entertained a remarkable series of guests, including Balzac, Victor Hugo, Sainte-Beuve, Heinrich Heine, Berlioz, Rossini, Meyerbeer, and Liszt's new rival Frédéric Chopin, whom Sand met for the first time in 1836.

Chopin and Sand soon became a couple—an odd one indeed. Chopin was "Utterly conventional and ultraconservative in his political and, especially, his social views," and his first impressions of the infamous lady writer were not flattering: "Is that really a woman?" he asked, spying George in her habitual masculine attire. "I seriously doubt it." Something in her, he said, repelled him. Perhaps it was the sexuality she always radiated, for Chopin was a prey to shame and guilt about sexual matters. In terms of character, too, the two were opposed. "The reserve and distance he maintained between himself and the world was no romantic pose; always sickly, his energy limited, he saw preserving and protecting himself as crucial to his art. And what Sand demanded was nothing less than that he abandon this wary stewardship and yield his fears of loss and of waste (connected certainly to sexual terror) to embrace her own belief that extravagance—in money, politics, friendship, work, and love—promised not death but rebirth."

The idea of these two together sounds like a recipe for certain disaster, but the relationship turned out, for a time at least, to be miraculously productive: Chopin was to create half of his entire oeuvre during the relatively short periods of his life that were spent at Nohant. Sand lavished everything she had to give on him, at least for a time: it was, she believed, "the tribute owed by talent to genius." In Paris, the two inhabited twin pavilions in Pigalle. Sand took over all housekeeping and domestic responsibilities as well as planning Chopin's triumphant concerts at the Salle Pleyel. Of course, this placed Sand once more in the maternal role. "Lover, companion, nurse, host, and now impresario—all these gifts had never been bestowed so lavishly on an artist. Freely given, they nonetheless bore a price. Chopin's world narrowed, and his dependency on George deepened." But while Chopin may have been frail and emotionally vulnerable, he did not play the child-role as Musset had so gratifyingly done; he was a complicated adult in his own right, and the hidden strength of his character would eventually rebel against his dependent position.

As an intimate friend to the entire Dudevant family, Chopin was drawn into its unseemly dramas. Histrionic narcissists do not tend to make very good mothers, and Sand was a particularly awful one. She hopelessly spoiled her son Maurice, while re-enacting with Solange the painful scenario her own mother had played out with her, withdrawing love at every crucial moment, criticizing the girl's every effort, banishing her to faraway boarding establishments, and even excluding the child from family holidays at Nohant, when Maurice and the rest of the Dudevant circle would be celebrating together. "George's displays of love were as yearned for as they were infrequent. The absent mother became the emotional lodestar of her life, the focus of Solange's sense of privation and of her most intense longings. But when Sand herself needed confirming evidence that she was the ideal mother to both children, she showered Solange (safely out of her sight) with written endearments."

Chopin's sensitivity to the girl's plight is one of the more attractive aspects of his character.

His friendship with Solange was something apart from the others. From the beginning, a nameless bond joined them: Unloved child and homeless artist, they were both exiles; wherever they found themselves, they were there on sufferance, rewarded for performing, for charming, for

summoning a sympathy that, once granted, deepened lone-
liness. Neither could satisfy the restless, voracious, imperial
mother: her dynamism, her need, her ideals of work and
love—of self, family, humanity, God, art. In her churning
wake, they would be washed up, broken, on some distant
shore, easily replaced.

And this is effectively what happened. Sand took in an impoverished young cousin to whom she showed a marked preference
over her own daughter: Augustine-Marie Briault, called "Titine,"
whose own parents were a disreputable pair. Against Chopin's
remonstrances, Sand more or less adopted Titine, hoping to mold
her not only into an ideal daughter but a daughter-in-law as well;
Titine, she decided, would be Maurice's bride. But when Titine
began to behave crassly toward her benefactress, already fancying
herself the doyenne of Nohant, Sand withdrew her support for the
marriage. Titine's father, ignoring the fact that he had pretty much
sold his daughter to the famous writer, publicly denounced Sand
for prostituting his daughter.

I t was an ugly affair in which only the discreet Chopin behaved
well—good behavior for which Sand, who had obviously been
in the wrong from beginning to end, found it hard to forgive him.
She purposely humiliated him in her 1846 novel *Lucrezia Floriani*,
which presented a thinly disguised and cruel portrait of the
composer. All remnants of domestic harmony came to an end
when Solange fell in love with the current bad boy of Paris' art
world, the sculptor Jean-Baptiste Auguste Clésinger. Sand enthusiastically endorsed the match, and when Chopin expressed misgiv-
ings about the artist's character she denounced him as an old
fussbudget who knew nothing whatever about human relations.
But Chopin's caution was vindicated when Clésinger was revealed
as a liar, extortionist, and brute only weeks after his wedding to

Solange. Sand banished the couple and forbade the unhappy Solange from ever setting foot at Nohant again; when Chopin expressed sympathy for the tragic young woman, Sand told him that unless he himself broke off relations with Solange he too would be turned away from her door.

Chopin refused to cede an inch. "Solange . . . can never be a matter of indifference to me," he told his erstwhile lover. "Your pain must be overpowering indeed to harden your heart against your child, to the point of refusing even to hear her name, and this, on the threshold of her life as a woman, a time more than any other when her condition requires a mother's care." The relationship between Sand and Chopin, which had been cooling for some time and had almost ended after the publication of *Lucrezia Floriani*, was now definitively over. "Chopin had examined and judged her. She had ceased to be sacred"—and for that, of course, he could not be forgiven. The affair, or what was left of it, was finished.

When Chopin finally succumbed to tuberculosis two years later, Sand had long since moved on. In 1848 she found revolution to be as delightful as it had been eighteen years previously. More so, perhaps, for this time it looked as though the dreams Sand and her friends had long entertained for a socialist France might be about to come true. The *roi bourgeois* was gone forever and in his place was a provisional government led by members of Sand's own circle, with the poet Alphonse de Lamartine as President of the Republic and Sand's new lover, Louis Blanc, at the Department of Labor. Sand became the "pen of the [Second] Republic," writing for the new administration's organ, the *Bulletin de la République*, and helping create a new journal, *La Cause du peuple* (of which only three issues were published). Her writings grew more and more incendiary; of particular interest, in light of what would happen in France and elsewhere over the next century and a half, was her essay in the sixteenth number of the *Bulletin* in which, clearly under the influence of Rousseau, she rejected the concept of majority rule as not representing the true will of the people (whatever that might be!) and calling for a political response, preferably violent, to express what she called the "collective will." The hijacking of these notions by totalitarian rulers of the twentieth century would not, perhaps, have distressed her; one can picture her a century later as an enthusiastic acolyte of Stalin and Ho Chi Minh.

The failure of 1848 to produce a socialist government and the accession to power of Louis Napoleon caused Sand's final disillusionment with politics (she would side against the communards in 1870-71!), and she retired to Nohant, where she assumed the role of grand old countrywoman. Her Berrichon trilogy, made up of the novels *La mare au diable, François le Champi*, and *La petite Fadette*, celebrates "the sanctity of labor, the seasonal rhythms of nature, and the virtues of love, charity, and community." She also found a man—at last!—who worshipped her as she had always felt she ought to be worshipped: the young Alexandre Manceau, though he provided the rough sex she always craved, was content in his socially subservient status and unfailingly addressed Sand in public as "Madame." He "anticipates my every wish," she wrote complacently, "putting his entire self into bringing me a glass of water or lighting my cigarette." Sand lived on, happily enough, into her seventies, achieving respectability and even becoming something of a monument, a relic of France's glorious past.

E isler's Sand is fascinating, as indeed she can hardly fail to be; but the biographer somehow does not succeed in communicating a coherent judgment on her subject. She assures us, at various points in the book, of her admiration for Sand, and when she quotes Flaubert, who became an intimate friend of Sand's only in her old age, she implies her own accord: "You had to have known her as I did, to appreciate the depth of the woman in that great man . . . and the vast love at the heart of her genius." Yet one feels, throughout *Naked in the Marketplace*, that while Eisler respects Sand's vitality, her passion, her audacity and her extraordinary capacity for work (Sand produced nearly ninety novels), the biographer cannot help being repelled by the woman herself. She is fascinated by Sand as though by a snake, but it is obvious that her real sympathies lie with Solange, with Chopin, and with the many others that the heedless egotist trod underfoot. In a really fine biography there must be an underlying emotional identification between author and subject, however different the two might appear to be. Eisler has not achieved this; but she has written a tale that will be very hard for most readers to put down.

(2007)

3. THE MOT JUSTE
TRANSLATING MADAME BOVARY

Looking inside the cover of Lydia Davis's eagerly awaited new translation of *Madame Bovary*, the reader is greeted with a quantity of praise for Davis's 2004 translation of Proust's *Swann's Way*, a work that not only earned her a MacArthur "genius" grant but also caused her to be named a *chevalier* of the French Order of Arts and Letters—the official Gallic seal of approval. Among the accolades Viking Penguin has included for Davis's Proust is one from Dave Eggers: "I think Davis's is definitive."

Definitive? Impossible: there is no such thing as a definitive translation. Not of any literary work. For translations—like art forgeries, curiously enough—are always recognizably a product of their period. They may seem neutral at first, but as the years go on, telltale features of the 1920s, say, or the 1980s, will appear. This is a problem even when the period happens to be the same as that of the original work: Victorian English has different speech patterns, different conventions, an entirely different flavor from the stripped-down mid-nineteenth-century French prose Flaubert labored over so painstakingly.

Davis has counted nineteen English *Madame Bovary* translations prior to her own. Some of them continue to enjoy great acclaim, like that of Eleanor Marx Aveling (daughter of Karl), for instance, written in 1886 and revised by Paul de Man in 1965, or Francis Steegmuller's 1957 version. And there is Geoffrey Wall's 1992 *Bovary*, which has long been available in the Penguin Classics edition but will soon be supplanted by Davis's. Numerous college professors are displeased by the fact that Penguin is dropping Wall's excellent *Bovary*. There is no need, they argue, for a new *Bovary*: it's simply a marketing ploy by Viking Penguin, who saw Davis as a hot property (so far as a literary translator can be hot!) and commissioned her to produce a new version so they could sell it all over again.

The professors may be right. The Wall version, after all, is first-rate, faithful to Flaubert's text, and admirably restrained: Wall never gave in to the temptation that has dogged so many transla-tors, a wish to embellish and "improve" the original. His respect for the material is complete, and both his choice of vocabulary and his rendition of Flaubert's unique rhythm is achieved with talent and stylistic discretion.

To translate Flaubert takes a confidence that amounts to audacity, for no author was ever so obsessed by style. "There are no noble subjects or ignoble subjects," the author reflected while writing *Madame Bovary*; "from the standpoint of pure Art one might almost establish the axiom that there is no such thing as subject—style in itself being an absolute manner of seeing things." How is such a style to be translated—and can it be? And what about Flaubert's identification of the best prose with poetry? "A good prose sentence," he wrote, "should be like a good line of poetry—*unchangeable*, just as rhythmic, just as sonorous. Such, at least, is my ambition." This immediately brings to mind the defini-tion of poetry, a fine one I think, as that which cannot be trans-lated. Is *Madame Bovary* poetry? Can it ever, really, be adequately translated?

Let's look at one passage—an important one in that it introduces Charles and Emma Bovary's visual world. It's a world that a painter, or someone like Flaubert, with a painterly eye, might find beautiful but that is, above all else, *gray*. We know that this overall grayness is vital because Flaubert has said so. "The story, the plot of a novel is of no interest to me," he claimed in a conversation with the Goncourt brothers. "When I write a novel I aim at rendering a color, a shade." In *Salammbô*, he said, that shade was a vivid purple, whereas in *Madame Bovary* "all I wanted to do was to render a gray color, the mouldy color of a wood-louse's existence. The story of the novel mattered so little to me that a few days before starting on it I still had in mind a very different Madame Bovary from the one I created."

Here is the passage, brief and spectacularly visual:

La pluie ne tombait plus; le jour commençait à venir, et, sur les branches des pommiers sans feuilles, des oiseaux se tenaient immobiles, hérissant leurs petites plumes au vent froid du matin. La plate campagne s'étalait à perte de vue, et les bouquets d'arbres autour des fermes faisaient, à intervalles éloignés, des taches d'un violet noir sur cette grande surface grise, qui se perdait à l'horizon dans le ton morne du ciel.

And how have the translators rendered it? Here is the Aveling/de Man version:

The rain had stopped, day was breaking, and on the branches of the leafless trees birds roosted motionless, their little feathers bristling in the cold morning wind. The flat country stretched as far as the eye could see, and the tufts of trees around the farms seemed, at long intervals, like dark violet stains on the vast grey surface, fading on the horizon into the gloom of the sky.

Here is the Francis Steegmuller version:

The rain had stopped; day was breaking, and on the leafless branches of the apple trees birds were perched motionless, ruffling up their little feathers in the cold morning wind. The countryside stretched flat as far as the eye could see, and the tufts of trees clustered around the farmhouses were widely spaced dark purple stains on the vast gray surface that merged at the horizon into the dull tone of the sky.

Here is Geoffrey Wall's:

The rain had stopped; it was getting light, and, on the leafless branches of the apple trees, birds were perching silently, ruffling up their little feathers against the chill wind of early morning. The flat landscape stretched out as far as the eye could see and the clumps of trees around the farmhouses showed up, at wide intervals, as patches of deep violet on that vast grey surface, which blurred at the horizon into the dullness of the sky.

And finally Davis's:

The rain was no longer falling; day was beginning to dawn, and on the branches of the leafless apple trees, birds were perched motionless, ruffling their little feathers in the cold morning wind. The flat country spread out as far as the eye could see, and the clumps of trees around the farms formed patches of dark violet at distant intervals on that vast gray surface, which vanished, at the horizon, into the bleak tones of the sky.

It's interesting to see that Davis's is actually the closest to the original. "The rain was no longer falling" renders the negativity of "La pluie ne tombait plus" better than does the positive verb "to stop," used by the other translators. "The leafless apple trees" is an exact translation of "les pommiers sans feuilles" whereas "the leafless branches of the apple trees" and "the branches of the leafless trees" are not. Flaubert's birds "se tenaient": Davis, with Steegmuller, has rendered this as "were perched," whereas Aveling and de Man used the more fanciful "roosted," in the active voice as well, and Wall also selected the active voice. "Bouquets d'arbres" does not have a really satisfactory English equivalent; Davis's use of "clumps," following Wall, seems more satisfactory than "tufts." Davis and Wall's "patches" is somehow less obtrusive than Aveling/de Man and Steegmuller's "stains." The French word "violet" presents the choice of two English translations, "purple" and "violet," which do not really mean the same thing; Davis has chosen "dark violet," and if readers of this article think all this sounds dull and nitpicking they should reflect on what different images are conjured up by "purple stains" and "patches of dark violet." All our translators seem to agree on "vast gray surface," but their interpretations of the untranslatable French adjective *morne* differ wildly. Here Davis's "bleak" with Aveling/de Man's "gloom" gets closest to the text's essence, because the definition of *morne* includes sadness: Steegmuller and Wall's "dull" and "dullness" are therefore less than satisfying.

This kind of list-making might seem to reduce translation to a technique rather than an art, but in fact it is both, and it's fair to say that Flaubert would have minded enormously about each and every one of these questions: this is the man, after all, who labored for months to produce a thirty-page scene. Even a throwaway line can have tremendous importance in the greater scheme. In the introduction to his *Bovary*, Steegmuller points to the novel's penultimate sentence, in which the narrator, speaking of the pharmacist Homais (Flaubert's "life force" character), says, "Il fait une clientèle d'enfer." As Steegmuller justly observes, "a perfectly 'correct' translation of a phrase can be inadequate, in that it fails to render an essential symbolic meaning." "Il fait une clientèle d'enfer" has been variously, and not incorrectly, translated as "His practice grows like wildfire," "He is doing extremely well," and "He has a terrific practice"—but surely, as Steegmuller points out, l'enfer (hell) isn't in the original for nothing. How do our translators render it?

Steegmuller, a little too obviously, makes it "The devil himself doesn't have a greater following than the pharmacist." Aveling/de Man: "He has more customers than there are sinners in hell." Wall, most cleverly (inserting the "hell" motif so that one hardly notices it at first) says "He is doing infernally well"—a rendition Davis echoes with "He himself has an infernally good clientele," rather stiffer and less idiomatic, though closer to Flaubert's sentence.

But then, as Paul de Man pointed out, "Flaubert himself is neither fluent nor really idiomatic (except in conversations)." This is important to remember, if the work of our translators, including Davis, sometimes appears to be less than elegantly fluid. Flaubert's method was to set a scene by the use of accretion. To quote his admirer Vladimir Nabokov, Flaubert had a "fondness for what may be termed the unfolding method, the successive development of visual details, one thing after another thing, with an accumulation of this or that emotion." Let's take for an example an early visit Charles Bovary pays to the Rouault farm in Davis's translation:

> He arrived one day at about three o'clock; everyone was in the fields; he entered the kitchen but at first did not notice Emma; the shutters were closed. Through the slits in the wood, the sun cast over the flagstones long, narrow stripes that broke at the angles of the furniture and trembled on the ceiling. On the table, flies were walking up the used

glasses and buzzing as they drowned at the bottom, in the dregs of cider. The daylight that came down the chimney, turning the soot on the fireback to velvet, touched with blue the cold cinders. Between the window and the hearth, Emma was sewing; she was not wearing a scarf, and one could see, on her bare shoulders, little drops of sweat.

This is vintage Flaubert: even without the clue provided by the name "Emma" one would recognize it instantly as his work, and that is to Davis's credit. She has reinstated the serial semi-colons, a hallmark of Flaubert's style that Nabokov noticed. (While teaching *Madame Bovary* at Cornell, Nabokov saw fit to make frequent "corrections" to Aveling's translation. He would have preferred both Wall's and Davis's, I think. It is too bad he never attempted one himself.) The jarring juxtaposition of something ugly, earthy, or vulgar with something perceived to be beautiful is typical of Flaubert's technique: here, the idyllic vision of Emma sewing (like a scene from Chardin or Vermeer) is disturbed by the image of flies walking about in the cider dregs, and drops of sweat on Emma's shoulders—not "perspiration," with which Aveling and de Man softened Flaubert's original *sueur*. Nineteenth-century ladies of course did not sweat—at least they did not sweat until Flaubert made them do so—and one of the drawbacks of early translations of *Madame Bovary* was that they were too polite and circumspect for this most brutally honest of authors. More recent translators like Davis no longer labor under this handicap.

And what about dialogue—the most difficult part of any novel to translate? How can one approach the tone of the original? How idiomatic should one be? If the original is slangy, should the translation be slangy, too? And why does slanginess in a translation date so much more badly than it does in the original? Isn't that one of the factors that actually causes a translation to "date"? If one character's speech is pompous, for instance, how can the translator make his version stylistically pompous without deviating too much from the language and vocabulary of the original? Why does translated dialogue so often tend to be wooden?

D avis does well in this department, especially with the elevated, stylized language of pretentious characters like Homais, or the speechifiers at the agricultural fair. With the novel's central figures she is rather less successful—though perhaps this is because naturalistic dialogue is not really something Flaubert aspired to produce. Let's look at a speech of Rodolphe's (in Davis's translation):

> "Ah! In fact there are two moralities," he replied. "The narrow one, the conventional one, the one devised by men, that keeps changing and that bellows so loudly, makes such a commotion down here, in a perfectly pedestrian way, like that gathering of imbeciles you see out there. But the other one, the eternal one, is all around and above us, like the landscape that surrounds us and the blue sky that gives us light."

This is how Geoffrey Wall translated the same passage:

> —Oh, the thing is there are two moralities, he replied. The little conventional one that men have made up, one that's endlessly changing and that brays so fiercely, makes such a fuss down here in this world, like that mob of imbeciles you see there. But the other morality, the eternal one, is all about and above, like the fields around us and the blue sky that gives us light.

Both these versions sound unnatural. But then so does the original, for Rodolphe was, in modern parlance, a bullshit artist, wrapping banal ideas in highfalutin' language. Davis's "bellows" seems more felicitous than Wall's "brays," though the latter is closer to Flaubert's original *braille*. It's hard to imagine anyone actually making the speech as it appears in any of the three versions, but the French one seems somewhat more possible.

There is a description in the Goncourt Journals of a conversation the brothers witnessed in 1857 between Flaubert and the author Ernest Feydeau (father of the playwright):

Flaubert and Feydeau started discussing a thousand different recipes for style and form, pompously and earnestly explaining little mechanical tricks of the trade, and expounding with childish gravity and ridiculous solemnity ways of writing and rules for producing good prose. They attached so much importance to the clothing of an idea, to its colour and material, that the idea became nothing but a peg on which to hang sound and light. We felt as if we were listening to an argument between grammarians of the Byzantine Empire.

This is precisely why the task of translating Flaubert has always been so daunting, and why it is dubious that there can ever be a definitive translation or even a wholly satisfactory one. Davis has produced a very fine one, marginally better, I think, than Wall's. Some Flaubert aficionados have been deterred by her admission that *Madame Bovary* is not actually a favorite book of hers: she has always been put off, she says, by the author's coldness and his obvious contempt for his characters and their milieu. But this alienation doesn't seem to have harmed her rendition, which displays a cool detachment not at all dissimilar to Flaubert's own.

(2010)

4. The Poet in his Dungeon
James Henry Leigh Hunt

There are certain people who have exerted considerable influence in the history of letters without having been great writers themselves: Gertrude Stein, for instance, and in our own recent past, George Plimpton. They have served as a species of facilitator, encouraging young talent, gathering writers around them, creating a cross-germination of ideas and styles. Such a person was James Henry Leigh Hunt (1784–1859). Of his more than eighty published works, only two short poems remain in general currency: "Abou Ben Adhem" and "Jenny Kissed Me," both of which turn up frequently in popular anthologies. The rest of his poetry has turned to dust, for it exemplifies the superfluities of its age: Hunt had all the affectation of Browning and the sentiment of Dickens, but the genius of neither. His passionate political journalism, famous in its day, has lost its urgency along with its topicality, and is now of interest only to the historian.

Only as a critic has Hunt retained an eminent place in nineteenth-century literature. His genius was not for original imaginative work, but for recognizing that originality in others.

But Leigh Hunt had a tremendous personality which lives on through the diaries and letters of his famous friends—Byron, Shel-

ley, Carlyle, and countless others—and in the great fictional character that Dickens made of him, Harold Skimpole of *Bleak House*.
In fact if one were to try to describe Hunt one could not do better
than to call him "Dickensian": his character and life were extravagant in exactly the manner we have come to associate with that
novelist.

Posterity has given Hunt mixed reviews as a personality and
literary arbiter. Virginia Woolf saw him as "our spiritual grandfather, a free man . . . a light man, I daresay, but civilized . . . These
free, vigorous spirits advance the world." Peter Quennell, writing
in 1940, was more damning. Hunt had admirable qualities, he
acknowledged, but

> wherever they grew upwards and outwards into his public
> life, they were apt to fritter themselves into gush and arti-
> fice. Thus, for social purposes, his real devotion to a host
> of friends was transmuted into sentimentalism and vapid
> coterie-talk, while his knowledge and intense love of art
> and literature tailed off in the attitudinizing of a suburban
> *petit maître* . . . Under Hunt's touch, fancy was whimsy,
> and beauty prettiness . . . While Hunt chirped or caroled
> amongst his busts and vases, wreathed verses in true-love
> knots or gaily hummed the *motifs* of an Italian opera, there
> were often tradesmen at the door and always growing chil-
> dren to stamp or scream in the immediate background.

After having read Anthony Holden's biography of Hunt, *The
Wit in the Dungeon*, I am more inclined toward Woolf's opinion
than Quennell's. Not that Quennell's observations and judgments
are untrue: it is just that when everything is taken into account,
Hunt's infinite enthusiasm can only be seen as a force for good. He
appreciated talent, beauty, and quality, and nurtured these wherever he found them. He might have been a bad husband and an

improvident father, but these faults should lie between him and his family, not between him and posterity.

Nicholas Roe produced a fine study, *The Fiery Heart*, but it covered Hunt's life only up to Shelley's death in 1822. The sole full-length life of Hunt until now has been Edmund Blunden's 1930 *Leigh Hunt: A Biography*, so Holden's effort is very welcome. It was an absolutely fascinating life, irresistible, one would think, to an imaginative biographer. Hunt was born the year Samuel Johnson died and died the year A. E. Housman was born; his life spanned two entirely distinct periods in English literature, the Romantic and the Victorian. As Holden says, "He was poet, critic, editor, essayist, novelist and playwright, the mentor and friend of Keats and Shelley, colleague and sparring partner of Byron and Hazlitt, intimate of Lamb and Carlyle, Browning and Dickens. Alongside Wordsworth, who largely eschewed literary London, Hunt's was the longest nineteenth-century literary life, with the widest circle of acquaintance and as large a claim as any to the shaping of literary opinions."

Even Hunt's childhood was Dickensian: his first memory was of the jail cell where his father, Isaac, had been imprisoned for debt. Isaac and his wife were Americans—Mary a Philadelphian, Isaac a Creole from Barbados—who had remained loyal to the English crown during the Revolution and were accordingly compelled to move to England, Isaac literally having been tarred and feathered for his outspoken support for the monarch. Back in England Isaac decided to devote his considerable theatrical gifts to a career in the pulpit. It was an unfortunate choice, according to his son, who felt that he "should have been kept at home in Barbados" where "he might have preached, and quoted Horace, and drunk his claret, and no harm done." Isaac Hunt passed on to his son not only his profligacy but some desirable qualities as well: a love of literature and "a remarkable capacity to remain cheerful in adversity."

The intellectually precocious Hunt attended the charity school at London's Christ's Hospital. He left at the age of fifteen without having been chosen to go on to university, but he was already an enthusiastic and promising poet whose proud father arranged for his juvenilia to be published by subscription. But this quick start seemed to lead nowhere, and "for the next four years Hunt would do little but write more derivative, unoriginal verse."

It was his older brother John Hunt, a printer, who finally provided direction. John wished to become a publisher specializing in the sort of radical journalism pioneered in William Cobbett's *Political Register*; in 1805 he launched an eight-page weekly paper called the *News*, taking his younger brother on as drama critic. In this new capacity Hunt proved a surprising success—although "How hard it goes with one who would like to have been known as a poet to concede that he has more of a hand for prose," he ruefully admitted. He began to earn a reputation as a lively commentator on the theatrical scene and a refreshingly unbiased critic, in the eyes of one contemporary "the greatest dramatic critic of that day" whose judgment "was universally sought and received as infallible by all actors and lovers of the drama."

The clever and versatile Leigh was clearly John Hunt's greatest asset, and the two brothers now embarked on a fruitful journalistic partnership. Both were liberal Whigs with a strong faith in liberty and human rights, and were prepared to risk not only their reputations but also their persons and livelihoods in these causes. Hazlitt described John Hunt as "the tried, steady, zealous and conscientious advocate of the liberty of his country, and the rights of mankind," and the painter Benjamin Haydon was just as adulatory, calling him "As noble a specimen of a human being as ever I met in my life." In 1808 the brothers launched the *Examiner*, a reformist journal "upon Politics, Domestic Economy and Theatricals," with John as the publisher and Leigh the editor and chief contributor; his byline was the "indicator" symbol of a little pointing hand, and over the years "Indicator" became his nickname and *nom de plume*.

L eigh Hunt's front-page editorials were, as Holden tells us, "almost recklessly outspoken from the first" in their defense of the Hunt brothers' favorite causes: parliamentary reform, Catholic emancipation, and the abolition of the slave trade. When reminded that slavery was indispensable to Britain's imperial ambitions Hunt famously replied that "it will be more glory to England to have abolished the Slave Trade than if she had conquered the universe." Needless to say he quickly became unpopular with the government, which made numerous attempts to suppress the brothers' publications on charges of libel—especially when Leigh, in a spirited critique of the military practice of flogging, compared the British army unfavorably with that of Napoleon.

These jibes continued in the pages of the *Reflector*, a quarterly the Hunts founded in 1811 that, along with its political content, relaunched the occasional essay, publishing now-classic pieces by Charles Lamb, William Hazlitt, and Hunt himself. The beginning of the Regency later that year provided the *Reflector* and the *Examiner* with an irresistible target in the person of the fat and dissipated Prince Regent (later King George IV), who once he had gained power immediately turned his back on his longtime Whig supporters and become an arch-Tory. Hunt's front-page "Princely Qualities" of 1812 and Lamb's anonymous poem "The Triumph of the Whale" were particularly damaging to the Prince's image.

The Tory press went completely over the top on the occasion of the Prince Regent's half-century, with the *Morning Post* extolling him as the "Glory of the People . . . the Protector of the Arts . . . the Maecenas of the Age . . . Wherever you appear, you *conquer all hearts*, wipe away tears, excite *desire and love*, and win *beauty* towards you . . . You breathe *eloquence*—You inspire the

Graces—You are an *Adonis in Loveliness*!" How could Hunt resist this? Far from being an "Adonis in Loveliness," Hunt wrote, the Prince was in fact a "corpulent gentleman of fifty . . . a violator of his word, a libertine over head and ears in debt and disgrace, a despiser of domestic ties, the companion of gamblers and demireps, a man who has just closed half a century without one single claim on the gratitude of his country or the respect of posterity."

This is going a little far even by modern standards, and the Hunt brothers were now called up on libel charges. The publicity was embarrassing to the Crown and the Tory administration, and the Hunts were offered clemency if they would agree to launch no more attacks on the royal family, but they declined and went to trial. Found guilty, they had to wait six weeks for sentencing, during which period they bravely continued their assaults on the Regent from the pulpit of the *Examiner*. Leigh Hunt remained defiant: "Rhetoric has weapons," he wrote, "which nothing can either escape or arrest. A prison will only give us double leisure to polish them."

Arguing that he was a political prisoner and therefore deserved privileges denied to mere criminals, Hunt managed to secure comfortable rooms in the prison that he could decorate to his own satisfaction and arranged that his wife, Marianne, and their young family should be able to join him there. He then proceeded to create "a salon unique in either literary or penal history":

> Its walls were papered with a trellis of roses, its ceiling painted as a cloud-speckled sky and the barred windows hidden behind Venetian blinds. While the carpenter built him some bookshelves, in came as much of his furniture as the larger of the two rooms would accommodate, plus a piano, a lute and busts of the great poets.

> His portrait of Milton hung on one wall, another of brother

John in pride of place above the fireplace. There was "not a handsomer room on that side of the water," declared Hunt himself, while one of his first and most constant visitors, Charles Lamb, mused that "there was no other such room except in a fairy tale."

The small prison yard outside Hunt meanwhile converted into a pastoral bower, providing it with green palings. The trellised plants, flowers, and small trees were real, as were a neatly manicured lawn and an apple tree which provided enough fruit for an apple tart, served by the maid who was allowed to complement the Hunt ménage. He would make a point of "dressing myself as if for a long walk; and then, putting on my gloves, and taking my book under my arm, stepped forth, requesting my wife not to wait dinner."

It soon became quite the fashion among the Whig literati to visit the poet in his dungeon. Longtime friends like Haydon, Lamb, Hazlitt, Thomas Moore, and Henry Crabb Robinson gathered frequently in the prison salon, and new friends, attracted by the renegade's glamour, came to call, including Jeremy Bentham and Lord Byron. Byron found the prisoner extremely congenial. "Hunt is an extraordinary character, and not exactly of the present age. He reminds me more of the Pym and Hampden times—much talent, great independence of spirit, and an austere, yet not repulsive aspect." Byron allowed that "He is, perhaps, a little opinionated, as all men are who are the centre of circles, wide or narrow—the Sir Oracles, in whose name two or three are gathered together —must be, and as even Johnson was; but, withal, a valuable man, and less vain than success and even the consciousness of preferring 'the right to the expedient' might excuse."

From prison Hunt continued his attacks on the Regent in his *Examiner* column, but after his release in 1815 his principal activities shifted from the political to the aesthetic, "playing Addison to Hazlitt's Steele." He championed Byron, earning for his pains a reputation as a social climber. This was unfair, as Byron himself pointed out: "When party feeling ran high against me," he later wrote, "Hunt was the only editor of a paper, the only literary man, who dared say a word in my justification. I shall always be grateful to him for the part he took on that occasion." Hunt actively promoted the careers of Shelley and of the younger, unknown Keats. His essay "Young Poets" in the *Examiner* of December was the first to recognize and comment upon "a new school of poetry": Shelley, a "very striking and original thinker," Keats and his "ardent grappling with nature," and John Hamilton Reynolds. The same issue published a new poem, Keats's "On First Looking into Chapman's Homer"; Shelley's "Hymn to Intellectual Beauty" and "Ozymandias" appeared in later numbers of the magazine.

The young poets were very grateful for such attentions. Most of Keats's biographers have agreed that Hunt's article was the making of his career, and Keats dedicated his first volume of poetry to his benefactor with this sonnet:

> Glory and loveliness have pass'd away;
> For if we wander out in early morn,
> No wreathed incense do we see upborne
> Into the east, to meet the smiling day:
> No crowd of nymphs soft voic'd and young, and gay,
> In woven baskets bringing ears of corn,
> Roses, and pinks, and violets, to adorn
> The shrine of Flora in her early May.
> But there are left delights as high as these,
> And I shall ever bless my destiny,
> That in a time, when under pleasant trees
> Pan is no longer sought, I feel a free,
> A leafy luxury, seeing I could please
> With these poor offerings, a man like thee.

Shelley and Hunt became bosom friends. They had a good

deal in common: high spirits, generosity, a passion for poetry and language, and a tendency to financial recklessness. "Hunt and Shelley shared an unconventional (to say the least) attitude to money," Holden writes, "which was to cause both lifelong difficulties. Their mutual version of the redistribution of wealth was to share money when it was in plentiful enough supply, with mutual feelings of gratitude rather than obligation."

Hunt's outspoken radicalism brought him enemies as well as friends, and he now became the target of almost insane attack by one John Gibson Lockhart, the assistant editor of the high Tory *Blackwood's Edinburgh Magazine*. Playing on his readers' basest snobbery, Lockhart attacked Hunt's circle as the "Cockney School" of poets and Hunt himself as its "chief Doctor and Professor," an "underbred" fellow rotten through with suburban vulgarity. Lockhart's venomous rhetoric still has the capacity to shock:

> One feels the same disgust at the idea of opening [Hunt's book-length poem *The Story of Rimini*], that impresses itself on the mind of a man of fashion, when he is invited to enter, for a second time, the gilded drawing-room of a little mincing boarding-school mistress, who would fain have an *At Home* in her house. Everything is pretence, affectation, finery and gaudiness . . .
>
> The extreme moral depravity of the Cockney School is another thing which is forever thrusting itself upon the public attention, and convincing every man of sense who looks into their productions, that they who sport with such sentiments can never be great poets. How could any man of high original genius ever stoop publicly, at the present day, to dip his fingers in the least of those glittering and rancid obscenities which float on the surface of Mr.

Hunt's Hippocrene? His poetry resembles that of a man who has kept company with kept-mistresses. His muse talks indelicately like a tea-sipping milliner girl.

Lockhart claimed that Hunt's friendship with the lordly Byron could only have been won through tireless tuft-hunting.

Lockhart then turned his attention to Hunt's "younger and less important auxiliaries" like Keats, Shelley, and Hazlitt, "the Cockney Aristotle." Hazlitt successfully sued for damages and eventually the assault died down, but it did permanent damage to Hunt, who is still frequently referred to as the leader of the Cockney School. Holden tells us that Lockhart's attacks "have often been used to portray Hunt as a malign influence on early Keats, and to a lesser extent on Shelley and Byron. But a recent, historicist school of thought takes them rather to confirm Hunt's role at the center of a literary and political group so ambitious and effective that conservative forces could not let it go unchallenged."

In the meantime Hunt had launched one of his most interesting ventures, a weekly called the *Indicator*. Although it lasted less than a year and a half it made a permanent mark on English literature: as Holden says, "With Keats and Shelley, Hazlitt and Lamb all among its contributors, the *Indicator* would have earned its place in literary history solely for the first appearance of the original version of Keats's 'La Belle Dame Sans Merci.'" But Hunt's own contributions were also important, for in the *Indicator* he revived and promoted the old personal essay in the style of the *Spectator* and *Tatler*.

In 1822, Shelley concocted a scheme for Hunt and his burgeoning family to join him and Mary in Italy. He, Hunt, and Byron would collaborate on a periodical, to be called the *Liberal*: the rich Byron could provide the cash, Hunt the sweat equity. Byron found the idea interesting since his publisher, John Murray, had refused to publish his most recent work. The *Liberal* seemed the answer to everyone's problems, though Shelley doubted whether Hunt and Byron would prove congenial: "How long an alliance between the wren and the eagle may continue, I will not prophesy," he said nervously.

The prospect of this voyage excited Hunt for he had long yearned to lay eyes on the fabled Mediterranean, but like so much else in his life the trip seemed cursed from the very beginning. Encountering storms off the coast of England, the Hunts were marooned for almost six months in Plymouth and then spent a miserable seven weeks in their sea-crossing. Shelley was delighted to get them settled in, but then, only a month after their arrival, he embarked on his fateful sailing trip: after ten days missing at sea, his body was washed up at Viareggio. Hunt and Byron were present at the funeral pyre, and Hunt's description of it helped to immortalize the scene for a generation of readers, writers, and painters.

The feckless Hunt was lost in Italy without Shelley, and soon his relationship with the narcissistic Byron soured just as Shelley had feared it would: as Byron's friend Edward Trelawney observed, there was "not a single subject on which Byron and Hunt could agree." The *Liberal* limped along, but Byron withdrew his support after only four issues and in 1823 departed on his own fateful trip to Greece, leaving the Hunt family stranded and broke. Sweltering in the Italian heat, at a loss as to how to support his children, Hunt began to hate the country. But after Byron's unexpected death Hunt was finally rescued from his Italian exile by an enterprising publisher on the condition that he produce a gossipy, realistic biography of Byron to offset all the gush and idolatry that was being written about him. The book that resulted, *Lord Byron and Some of his Contemporaries; with Recollections of the Author's Life, and of his Visit to Italy*, was condemned by Hunt's contemporaries as tasteless and ill-bred, but it is now generally agreed to have provided a healthy corrective to the Byromania that overtook Europe at the time.

By this time over forty, the father of eight children, and with his associates Keats, Shelley, and Byron all dead, Hunt entered a new circle and began to assume the persona that would eventually find fictional form in Dickens's Mr. Skimpole. Holden writes that "the coming three decades would increasingly see Hunt's literary character and reputation all but identified with his attitude to money"—with good reason perhaps, for as his son Thornton Hunt recollected, "he had no grasp of things material, but exaggerating his own defects, he so hesitated at any arithmetical efforts that he could scarcely count." His alcoholic wife was even less capable than he was of controlling the children or making ends meet. Thomas Carlyle, a new friend, described their household vividly:

> His house excels all you have ever read of—a poetical *Tinkerdom*, without parallel even in literature. In his family room, where are a sickly large wife and a whole school of well-conditioned wild children, you will find half a dozen rickety old chairs gathered from half a dozen different hucksters, and all seeming engaged, and just pausing, in a violent hornpipe. On these and around them and over the dusty table and ragged carpet lie all kinds of litter —books, paper, egg-shells, scissors, and last night when I was there, the torn half of a quartern-loaf.
>
> His own room above stairs, into which I alone strive to enter, he keeps cleaner. It has only two chairs, a bookcase and a writing-table; yet the noble Hunt receives you in his Tinkerdom in the spirit of a king, apologizes for nothing, places you in the best seat, takes a window-sill himself if there is no other, and there folding closer his loose-flowing "muslin cloud" of a printed nightgown, in which he always writes, commences the liveliest dialogue on philosophy and the prospects of man (who is beyond measure "happy" yet); which again he will courteously terminate the moment you are bound to go.

Always short of cash, plagued by indifferent health and numerous obligations, Hunt could no longer afford to brave the libel courts, and he tried to confine himself to what Holden calls a "cheerful sentimentalism." He proved as firm and supportive a friend to the rising generation of writers as he had to their elders, encouraging, among others, Browning, Dickens, Thackeray, Carlyle, Tennyson, Bulwer-Lytton, Landor, Rossetti, and Macaulay. He continued to write criticism and poetry, and also tried his hand at the drama, penning one "torrid melodrama," *A Legend of Florence*, that scored quite a hit. He campaigned rather abjectly for the job of Poet Laureate but lost out twice, first to Wordsworth and then to Tennyson.

Hunt became particular friends with Dickens, who provided much-needed financial support by contributing the proceeds of plays and public readings to him. But Hunt's demands always exceeded reasonable bounds, and Dickens finally became irritated by his improvident friend. His brutal lampoon of Hunt in *Bleak House*, then, should not come as a complete surprise to those aware of the novelist's personal failings.

In the case of Hunt/Skimpole, Dickens was even more than usually delighted with his own mimetic prowess.

Skimpole . . . I suppose he is the most exact portrait that ever was painted in words! I have very seldom, if ever, done such a thing. But the likeness is astonishing. I don't think he could possibly be more like himself. It is so awfully true that I make a bargain with myself never to do so, any more. There is not an atom of exaggeration or suppression. It is an absolute reproduction of a real man. Of course I have been careful to keep the outward figure away from the fact; but in all else it is the Life itself.

The novelist's friends, reading early drafts, were nervous about the obvious resemblance, with John Forster objecting that it was "too like." Dickens responded by directing "Phiz," his illustrator, to make Skimpole short and tubby so as to differentiate him as far as possible from the tall and willowy Hunt, but otherwise he altered very little in the portrait. When Hunt read it and declared himself "pained and perplexed," Dickens denied everything hotly. Skimpole, he wrote, "is not you, for there are traits in it common to fifty thousand people besides." In any case, he continued—transparently giving away the truth—"I did not fancy you would ever recognise it."

Why did Dickens do it? Why depict Hunt, essentially a benign and good-spirited man, as an unscrupulous sponger and fraud? The real response is probably the simplest: he did it because he could. Hunt was a superb comic figure who had been handed to Dickens on a silver platter, and it would have been hard to resist the temptation. As for making Skimpole a sort of con man, Dickens simply drew out and exaggerated one strand of Hunt's character for the thematic purpose of the novel.

Skimpole sadly turned out to be Hunt's most lasting claim to fame, though it was certainly not his greatest one. At the time of his death in 1859 he was the grand old man of English letters (if, as Holden points out, rather a moth-eaten one), but most of the obituaries seemed obsessed by his fictional alter-ego. It colored his image for posterity too, stressing the comic side of his character (which was certainly evident enough) and turning attention away from the very real services he performed for English literature as critic, editor, journalist, poet, nurturer of talent, and fighter in the cause of freedom of speech. For too long now he has been seen merely as a chapter in the lives of his more famous friends. Holden's biography fills a real void—which is seldom the case, any more, with literary biographies—and it is also smooth, well-written and often funny, full of apt quotations and anecdotes.

Hunt was both noble and ridiculous, in almost equal measure.

Keats glorified him in the grand style as "wrong'd Libertas"; but perhaps we should let Thomas Carlyle have the last word. Hunt, he wrote,

> turned up at his house often, always neatly dressed, was thoroughly courteous, friendly of spirit, and talked—like a singing bird. Good insight, plenty of a kind of humour, too; I remember little warbles in the turns of his fine voice which were full of fun and charm. [His talk was] often enough (perhaps at first oftenest) Literary-Biographical, Autobiographical, wandering into Criticism, Reform of Society, Progress, etc. etc.—on which latter points he gradually found me very shocking I believe—so fatal to his rose-coloured visions on the subject. An innocent-hearted, but misguided, in fact rather foolish, unpractical and often much-suffering man.

(2006)

5. SERVANT OF THE PEOPLE
SAMUEL BUTLER DELIVERS A SHOCK

Few people read Samuel Butler's *The Way of All Flesh* any more, but it would be hard to exaggerate the influence it once exerted over entire generations of angry young men and women. It was published in 1903, a year after its author's death, and burst onto the cultural scene like a cry of rage from beyond the grave. The book was very much of its moment, an intrinsic part of the Shock of the New, early twentieth-century style: this was the period in which seminal works by Sigmund Freud, George Bernard Shaw, H.G. Wells, Pablo Picasso and other groundbreakers were astounding the world. The long Victorian age was decidedly over, and *The Way of All Flesh* seemed to celebrate that fact with unbridled glee.

But in fact Butler had written the book decades earlier, between 1873 and 1884. He had deemed it too shocking for publication, as indeed it probably was at the time in spite of the fact that Thomas Hardy and Henrik Ibsen, Butler's contemporaries, were doing much to shake up the pretenses and pieties of that era. Butler's novel was a systematic attack on the entire Victorian social system, written in a laceratingly mocking tone. The Church, the family, the class system; nothing escaped Butler's wicked satire.

Shaw, an enthusiastic booster of the eccentric author, called *The Way of All Flesh* "one of the great books of the world." E. M. Forster, as great an iconoclast as Butler despite his gentler manner, thought that "if Butler had not lived, many of us would now be a little deader than we are, a little less aware of the tricks and traps in life, and of our own obtuseness." Butler was one of the great liberators of his era, as were Shaw and Forster themselves. In the words of his biographer Peter Raby, *The Way of All Flesh* was "an uneven, extraordinary and unforgettable book, evoking strong emotions of recognition and horror, and shattering forever the sacred English totem, the idea of the family."

It is written in the form of a comic, didactic Bildungsroman. The all-but-omniscient narrator, Overton, is a longtime friend of the Pontifex family and a mentor to young Ernest Pontifex, the novel's protagonist. In Overton and Ernest together Butler has created a dual self-portrait: Ernest is himself as an unhappy youth, Overton as a satisfied middle-aged man, at ease with himself and his way of life, looking on with tolerant amusement as poor Ernest flounders among the manifold "tricks and traps" his world has set for him.

The history of the Pontifex family encapsulates what Butler sees as the decline of English society in the nineteenth century. Ernest's great-grandfather, born in about 1730, was a humble countryman but possessed a spirit and intellectual curiosity characteristic, in Butler's world-view, of the Age of Enlightenment. His son George, Ernest's grandfather, has made a fortune and in the process became a conventional man of the world, stingy in business and autocratic with his family. ("When a man is very fond of his money," Overton comments, "it is not easy for him at all times to be very fond of his children also.") George aims to make his sons gentlemen and prides himself on the expensive schools they attend, but "he did not see that the education cost the children far more than it cost him, inasmuch as it cost them the power of earning their living easily rather than helped them towards it, and ensured their being at the mercy of their father for years after they had come to an age when they should have been independent."

George pushes his ineffectual son Theobald into a career in the church, in spite of the young man's feeble protests. Not that the boy was a religious skeptic; England was going through an evangelical phase in the mid-nineteenth century, and "It had never so much as crossed Theobald's mind to doubt the literal accuracy of any syllable in the Bible. He had never seen any book in which this was disputed, nor met with anyone who doubted it."

Bullied into an uncongenial profession, Theobald grows into the personification of everything Butler and his fellow skeptical freethinkers hated about the Victorian Anglican church. He marries the daughter of a fellow clergyman, not because either of them loves or even much likes the other but because he needs a housekeeper and she, one of several impecunious sisters, can see no alternative. (The brilliant episode in which Christina and her sisters play a game of cards to decide which of them will get first dibs at Theobald is one of the great comic scenes in modern literature, displaying Butler's view of bourgeois marriage as a fraud and a sham.) Once married and established, Theobald becomes as great a domestic tyrant as his father was. His own life has been ruined by society's rigid rules and expectations; why should his children get off any easier? Young Ernest, like Theobald, is destined for the Church.

George had felt something akin to spite for his son Theobald; now Theobald shows the same spite toward his own children. Butler's originality lay in his vision of the family as largely antipathetic to and destructive of individual fulfillment, and the brutal forthrightness with which he declared this belief is still capable of shocking. "Why should the generations overlap one another at all?" he asks at one point in the book, clearly in his own voice.

"Why cannot we be buried as eggs in neat little cells with ten or twenty thousand pounds each wrapped round us in Bank of England notes, and wake up, as the sphex wasp does, to find that its papa and mama have not only left ample provision at its elbow, but have been eaten by sparrows some weeks before it began to live consciously on its own account?"

Overton/Butler mocks the creed in which his generation was raised. The general idea, he says, was that "We were put into this world not for pleasure but duty, and pleasure had in it something more or less sinful in its very essence." If anything was fun or delicious, it had by definition to be a sin. It was true that "Tobacco had nowhere been forbidden in the Bible, but then it had not yet been discovered, and had probably only escaped proscription for this reason."

Ernest falls prey to every illusion his society propounds. A colleague who persuades him to sink his time and money into an idealistic evangelistic project turns out to be a crook. His brief and disastrous marriage to a woman of the lower classes only serves to convince him that contrary to what his pious education has taught him, the poor were not intrinsically worthier than the rich. "Of course some poor people were very nice, and always would be so, but as though scales had fallen suddenly from his eyes he saw that no one was nicer for being poor, and that between the upper and lower classes there was a gulf which amounted practically to an impassible barrier." After numerous misadventures the hapless Ernest finally succeeds in breaking free of his education, which in the end he is able to acknowledge had been "an attempt, not so much to keep him in blinkers as to gouge his eyes out altogether."

Like his creator, Ernest eventually becomes a writer. Describing his literary output Overton claims that "Every man's work, whether it be literature or music or pictures or architecture or anything else, is always a portrait of himself, and the more he tries to conceal himself the more clearly will his character appear in spite of him." This is particularly true of *The Way of All Flesh*. Not that Butler made much attempt at concealment: he was clearly a didactic character, like Overton, and more than a bit of a crank. His collected works filled twenty volumes, and included eccentric tracts like *The Authoress of the Odyssey*, an attempt—rather influential in its day—to prove that Homer was a woman. But today only *The Way of All Flesh* and *Erewhon*, a satire of English life disguised as a utopian fantasy, are read—and they are not read very often. *The Way of All Flesh* is indisputably his masterpiece. In this hugely entertaining novel Butler said many things that were at that time unsayable and even unthinkable. And in spite of the revolutionary social changes that have occurred over the last hundred years and more, a great deal of what he said is still unsayable, and still needs saying.

(2007)

6. The Man in Full
Oscar Wilde

I n Nancy Mitford's *The Pursuit of Love*, the young narrator, Fanny—this is circa World War I—asks her Aunt Sadie what mysterious crime Oscar Wilde had committed. Sadie, greatly flustered, admits that she never actually knew, but that whatever it was, it was dreadfully bad, worse than murder.

O tempora! O mores! A century later, and Wilde has risen to the rank of secular saint, a queer martyr. In the 1997 biopic *Wilde*, Stephen Fry played the role on a single note of dignified forbearance, showing the disgraced author enduring the humiliations and rigors of his prison and post-prison years with high-minded stoicism. No doubt the real Oscar Wilde was dignified some of the time, and certainly he deflected pain with graceful humor on many occasions, but that was not his characteristic pose: just as often, he wept, drank and wallowed in self-pity. And as Matthew Sturgis demonstrates in his exhaustively researched, enlightening and lively biography of Wilde—a "definitive" biography if there ever was one —Wilde behaved with consistent recklessness and self-indulgence. The fact that many of his sexual conquests were underage ought at least to raise some eyebrows in today's world, and surely would do so if Wilde had been heterosexual, but such behavior does not seem to have dulled the moral sheen that has been accorded him through our modern tendency to "celebrate" queer lives.

Once there were seven deadly sins. Which did Wilde indulge in? Lust? Of course. Gluttony? Ditto. Avarice? It was not a ruling passion, but luxuries cost money and thus money had to be found: "I couldn't really have anything but Chippendale and satinwood—I shouldn't have been able to write." His sin was not to hoard but to spend too freely—and to spend other people's money as freely as his own. Envy? No, he seemed free of this vice; he very much enjoyed being Oscar Wilde as long as that venture was going well. Pride? Not of the theological or spiritual variety, but he possessed arrogance aplenty. (Success "did not make him humble," Sturgis comments; "it made him insufferable.") Sloth was not a habitual problem, although the trauma of prison seemed to break his capacity for concentrated work. Wrath? No, not at all; he could not even sustain it against the persons who harmed him the most, Lord Alfred Douglas (the beautiful blond Bosie) and Bosie's father, the Marquess of Queensberry.

On the contrary, Sturgis's chronicle repeatedly demonstrates that whatever his sins, and they were manifold, Oscar Wilde was above all a nice man: generous when in funds, thoughtful, of a "conciliatory nature." His charm was of the rare variety that makes others feel appreciated and listened to; friends recalled him as "smiling, eager, full of life and the joy of living and, above all, given to unmeasured praise of whatever and whoever pleased him." Bernard Berenson found him "the kindest man imaginable."

Why, one might ask, do we need another biography of Wilde? He has already received three major treatments—by Hesketh Pearson (1946), H. Montgomery Hyde (1975) and, most recently and notably, Richard Ellmann (1987). Sturgis, an expert on the fin de siècle who has penned engrossing biographies of Walter Sickert and of Wilde's partner in decadence Aubrey Beardsley, cites deficiencies in Ellmann's chronicle, including inaccuracies (a point that has long been made by Wilde's grandson and keeper of the flame, Merlin Holland) and a tendency to take the mythology that has accrued around Wilde at face value.

Also, he points out, a great deal of new material and research has appeared in recent decades, such as the complete transcript of the trial of Wilde's libel action against the Marquess of Queensberry, and detailed witness statements. (Indeed, we learn rather more than we wish to know about Wilde's sexual practices from the testimony, provided from Wilde's own trial, of fetching young waiters and toothsome bellboys.) Previously unknown letters have also been unearthed, and specialist studies published. Sturgis felt that by integrating all this material into the story, he could "return Wilde to his times and to the facts. To view him with a historian's eye, to give a sense of contingency, to chart his own experience of his life as he experienced it." In this he has succeeded remarkably well. *Oscar Wilde: A Life* does not portray a modern hero, or a gay martyr, or a misunderstood genius: It is the story of the man in full, with flaws and fine qualities almost equally balanced.

"Somehow or other I'll be famous, and if not famous, I'll be notorious," the young Wilde declared. As Sturgis illustrates, a feeling for self-dramatization came to him very early, and was encouraged in the *conversazioni* held by his equally striking mother (known throughout Ireland as the poet "Speranza") in the family's Dublin townhouse. As Sturgis follows Wilde through his first twenty-five years we are made privy to the emergence of "Oscar Wilde," a deliberately cultivated persona; Wilde "sought to become the very essence of Aestheticism" and to turn his life, as he famously said, into a work of art.

In the creation of his chosen persona he drew inspiration from some powerful mentors: the art critic John Ruskin, whose lectures Wilde attended at Oxford; another Oxford don, Walter Pater, whose *Studies in the History of the Renaissance* Wilde called "the golden book of spirit and sense, the holy writ of beauty," and whose gatherings of male undergraduates were conducted in "an atmosphere that delicately blurred the border between pedagogy and pederasty"; and James McNeill Whistler, who eventually turned on the younger man when he started outplaying him at his own aesthetic games.

Wilde's affected languor was, at least in his early days, mostly a pose; in private he studied hard at university, and labored to develop his epigrammatic, apparently nonchalant literary style. Sturgis remarks on "the gap between the calculated exaggerations of his public persona and the patent intelligence of his private self," and a journalist who interviewed the young Wilde was not the only person to divine, behind the mask of the mincing aesthete, "a shrewd, sensible, practical fellow."

Edmond de Goncourt, who met Wilde when he was thirty years of age, described him as "au sexe douteux," but Wilde himself probably didn't know this at the time; he appeared genuinely in love with his bride, Constance Lloyd, and reveled in family life. It was not until a few years later, when he was seduced by the teenage Robbie Ross (who would prove Wilde's staunchest friend during the older man's lifetime and nurture his literary properties after his death), that he began to define himself as a homosexual, or, as he would have put it, a votary of Uranian love. Sturgis puts this into historical perspective: "Although to most Victorians, sex (of whatever description) was considered as something that people did—an individual act—rather than as the expression of a person's 'sexuality,' there is no doubt that Wilde's new experiences gave him, in his own eyes, an enhanced and altered status." He was, in other words, at the vanguard of what would become a fixation on sexual "identity" in the 20th and 21st centuries. The memorable speech he made during his trial for gross indecency, in which he characterized "the Love that dare not speak its name"—the love experienced by Plato, Michelangelo, Shakespeare—as not shameful, but noble, made a tremendous impression at the time and marked, it now seems clear, a turning point in the evolving modern perception of sexuality.

Sturgis does not pretend to be a critic—one of his gripes

against Ellmann is that he approached his biography as a literary critic rather than a historian—and he does not essay any overarching judgments. Instead he delivers the judgments of Wilde's own day. "The Ballad of Reading Gaol" turns out to have been by far the most popular of Wilde's works during his own lifetime, a fact I found surprising. The opinions of Wilde's more perceptive contemporaries can make us think. George Bernard Shaw, for instance, felt that "in a certain sense Mr. Wilde is to me our only thorough playwright. He plays with everything: with wit, with philosophy, with drama, with actor and audience, with the whole theatre." Roger Fry, writing a generation after Wilde's death, remarked that "he has a way of being right, which is astonishing at that time, or any for that matter." Robbie Ross with prescience predicted that Wilde's works would eventually come to "excite wider interest than those of almost any of his contemporaries."

Few others could have thought this at the time. The master's last years were sad ones, despite the success of "Reading Gaol." Upon his release from prison, exiled from England with very meager resources, the regretful Wilde pledged himself to a life of dignity and continence. But the new routine was too depressing. No more opening nights or fashionable dinners; instead, he had to stick to a bohemian existence that was, as Ross noted, "entirely out of note with his genius and temperament." And his writing life was over. "I find the architecture of art difficult now," he commented sadly. Constance, who had been kind to him since his release and had even considered reuniting with him, was so embittered by his offhand behavior to her that she cut him off, forbidding him any further access to his two beloved sons.

So it was back to absinthe and rent boys, and sending begging letters to distant friends—and among these, even the most generous grew tired of shelling out without hope of repayment. The author Frank Harris, who threw Wilde a lot of good money after bad, finally had enough, telling him that "everyone grows tired of holding up an empty sack." And when Wilde died, at the age of 46 (of an inner-ear infection that spread to the brain), the predominant feeling of his friends seems to have been relief. There was a "sense that an intractable problem had been solved."

Wilde's grave, along with those of Jim Morrison and Frédéric Chopin, is the most popular attraction at Père Lachaise Cemetery in Paris, beating out the likes of Balzac, Proust, Sarah Bernhardt, Colette and Molière, and is frequently smeared with lipstick kisses by modern acolytes. His ashes reside there, under the great memorial sculpture by Jacob Epstein, together with those of his dear friend Ross. The two men had enjoyed planning some such ending for their remains. "When the last trumpet sounds," Wilde announced at the time, "and we are couched in our porphyry tombs, I will turn and say, 'Robbie, Robbie, let us pretend we do not hear!'"

(2021)

With *The Wildes*, the novelist Louis Bayard has posed himself a considerable challenge. First, much of the story is told from a woman's perspective: not an easy exercise for many male authors but one that Bayard has already, with his novels *Courting Mr. Lincoln* (2019) and *Jackie & Me* (2022), performed with success. More daringly, he has set himself the task of writing dialogue for Oscar Wilde, of all people, the most quotable wit of the past couple of centuries. This sort of imaginative work, in which actual historical figures are endowed by a modern author with thought and speech, is very hard to pull off, but Bayard has contrived to make Wilde sound like Wilde and Bosie sound like Bosie, as well as to flesh out credible and sympathetic inner lives for Wilde's gentle, long-suffering wife, Constance, and his sons, Cyril and Vyvyan.

Bayard covers three decades in the Wildes' lives, but he avoids the well-trodden turf of Oscar's trials on charges of "gross inde-cency" for his relationships with men. Instead, *The Wildes* is constructed in several "acts," moving back and forth in time among various moments. These include a fraught 1892 family holiday in Norfolk; a later 1897 interlude in which Oscar was in exile and Constance and the children took a different name; the period during World War I when Cyril fought in France; and a 1925 episode with a middle-aged, reflective Vyvyan. It concludes with a richly if fancifully imagined alternate past for the family and those who loved them.

The Wilde family pulled a curtain as far as possible over their lives after the trial, destroying most of their personal correspon-dence, but a few letters survive, which Bayard works deftly into his text. "The air is full of the music of your voice," Oscar wrote in an early missive to his wife, "my soul and body seem no longer mine, but mingled in some exquisite ecstasy with yours." But by the novel's opening in 1892, sexual relations between the couple have ended: Oscar, vaguely citing a social disease caught from a long-ago run-in with a prostitute, limits physical contact to a chaste nightly kiss outside Constance's bedroom door. In the meantime, a "pro-cession of narrow-chested young men, each younger than the last," shows up to visit Oscar at the Norfolk farmhouse that the Wildes are renting. "Tell me if I've met this one before," Constance asks when Oscar announces the imminent arrival of the twenty-one-year-old Lord Alfred Douglas.

"You're holding up splendidly," their friend Arthur Clifton murmurs to Constance, "under the circumstances." But does she understand the circumstances? From the perspective of the twenty-first century, the ignorance and innocence of women of Constance's class about homosexuality seem incredible. She is certainly disquieted by Oscar's visitors, especially the egregious Bosie, but the truth dawns on her only slowly, and even then she can't quite wrap her mind around the dire possibilities. When the facts can no longer be denied, she behaves like a conventional

Victorian wife, although she was in fact open-minded and progressive. Upon Oscar's public disgrace she obliterates all traces of the Wildes' family life, changes her surname and her sons' to Holland (a family name), sends the boys to boarding schools, and flees to anonymity in a rented Italian villa. A few years later she is dead, the victim of an incompetent doctor and a botched operation, leaving the boys parentless. The disgraced Oscar was legally prevented from seeing his sons.

It had been a loving family, despite Oscar's extracurricular activities. Bayard's Constance realizes this and regrets the loss, remembering Oscar, playing with his boys, as "a profoundly happy man, wishing only that others might be the same . . . But the world made him choose—and she herself made him choose . . . because human hearts, arranged as they are, cannot comprehend such a capacity."

The badly damaged Cyril commits his life to honing his masculinity: As he wrote (in an actual letter) to his brother, Vyvyan, there would be "no cry of decadent artist, of effeminate aesthete, of weak-kneed degenerate." He would perish in a sniper's duel on the Western Front, though not, in Bayard's version of events, without a healing flash of understanding and redemption.

Vyvyan would go through his long life (he died in 1967) trying to comprehend his past and his family dynamic and to reimagine a family history in which they could all have stayed together: "That's all we ever wanted, Mother and Cyril and I. Father, too, I know that in my heart."

Oscar Wilde's attractiveness and his flaws were equally outsize, and Bayard conveys them both admirably. Oscar is a shameless showboater; Constance "has seen more times than she can count how he composes himself for his public. The cigarette, the green carnation. The blasé mien of his curtain speeches, the whole air of half-disdaining the attention he has with no small effort attracted." He is also a peerlessly entertaining and affectionate father and a consummately generous friend. Constance's good qualities—solid kindness and dependability—are complementary to his.

A meaningful thread in the novel, one that touches on the cultural impact Oscar exerted, is played out in a short scene Bayard composes. Constance maintains that there can be no art without morality. "Whereas I," announces Oscar, "have always kept those two dodgy specimens in separate rooms and forbidden them to speak." Which of the two is correct? Wilde's exaltation of "art for art's sake" caught the fancy of his historical moment, but Bayard would appear to go along with Constance's stated opinion that "the things that people do to each other—*with* each other—matter. On the page as in life." *The Wildes* in fact constitutes a morality play that encompasses an alternate history, a contemplation of how we might live were we to imagine humanity's possibilities rather than give in to its limitations.

(2024)

7. THE OLD PARROT
W. SOMERSET MAUGHAM

He was a traveler, adventurer, cynic, sophisticate and bon vivant. W. Somerset Maugham, the most successful writer of his time and maybe the most glamorous as well, set a dazzling standard for worldly glory that younger writers impotently envied. "Willie," the diarist Chips Channon observed of the elderly writer, "has been everywhere, met everybody, tasted everything."

His beginnings had not been promising. His parents had both died by the time he was ten years old. Maugham was sent from Paris, where his father had been an honorary legal adviser to the British Embassy, to an unsympathetic English uncle, "a very narrow-minded and far from intelligent cleric . . . severe, pedantic and bigoted," according to one of the novelist's elder brothers. Maugham's early experiences are mirrored in the career of Philip Carey in *Of Human Bondage*: the lonely and deracinated boy (Maugham had never visited England before his parents' death) was sent to a chilly boarding school where he was handicapped not only by his poor English but by a painful stammer.

Jeffrey Meyers is a staggeringly prolific writer who has turned out, in a decade, biographies of Hemingway, Orwell, Conrad,

Lawrence, Poe, Gary Cooper and Edmund Wilson. It would seem impossible that he could, at this pace, produce work of real depth, and in fact the first third of *Somerset Maugham* is both cursory and banal. Meyers recites events flatly and without engagement; when he does go in for character analysis, he resorts to the most timeworn psychological clichés—speaking of Maugham's stammer, for instance, he comments that "it made him a victim and intensified his introspection, turned him away from people and toward his artistic vocation." But as Maugham ages he comes to life in Meyers's pages. Meyers succeeds, too, in showing how Maugham, even at the height of his fame, never really succeeded in banishing the nervous child from his psyche.

Artistically, Maugham was not an early bloomer. He spent five years as a medical student in a London hospital and began writing during his short periods of free time. His early fictional experiments with naturalism and historical fiction were not particularly auspicious, and, as Meyers remarks, "very few authors have ever achieved success after writing so many poor books."

It was in the theater that Maugham first found his voice, writing plays that would culminate in *The Circle*, *Our Betters*, and *The Constant Wife*. At one time he had four plays running simultaneously in London, the first time any playwright had achieved this feat. His facility and skill in the craft were remarkable. As a rule it took him just a week to write each act, with a week to revise the whole.

This facility, combined with the disciplined regime Maugham had perfected during his years as a medical student, also bore fruit in a stream of novels written in a smooth and assured tone. His breakthrough book, *Of Human Bondage* (1915), is still considered by many to be his best. Maugham's experiences as a secret agent in Russia during World War I (his mission, truly an impossible one, was to keep the Kerensky government in power and Russia in the war against the Central Powers) inspired the marvelous *Ashenden: Or, the British Agent* (1928), which had an immeasurable influence on popular fiction, paving the way for Graham Greene, Eric Ambler, Ian Fleming and John le Carré. Fleming would later congratulate Maugham, and himself, on being "the only two writers who write about what people are really interested in: cards, money, gold and things like that."

Maugham's love of travel, especially to China, Malaya, Borneo, Samoa and Tahiti, brought him a world of new material and even began to define him as a writer—"adultery in China, murder in Malaya, suicide in the South Seas," as Graham Greene flippantly remarked. *East of Suez* (1922), *The Painted Veil* (1925), and *The Casuarina Tree* (1926) were the results, along with the classic short story "Rain" (1921) and *The Moon and Sixpence* (1919), Maugham's fascinating fictional exploration of the career of Paul Gauguin and, by wider implication, of the necessary ruthlessness of all artists.

M augham's private life was as turbulent as his professional one was controlled. As an older man he remarked of his youthful self that "I was a quarter normal and three-quarters queer, but I tried to persuade myself it was the other way round. That was my greatest mistake." The mistake resulted in his disastrous marriage to Syrie Barnardo, a tough, demanding woman. The two were hideously incompatible and separated before long but they fought over money and their daughter's upbringing for many years. Maugham's real spouse for nearly 30 years was Gerald Haxton, a handsome, rackety American. "He did all the things Maugham never dared to do," Meyers writes; "getting drunk and using foul language, lying, sponging and gambling, homosexual cruising and pimping."

In 1915 Haxton had been charged with gross indecency and registered as an undesirable alien in Britain, so he and Maugham had to make their home elsewhere. They chose the Riviera, purchasing a large house near Cap Ferrat which they named the

Villa Mauresque. Maugham turned the comfortable residence, formerly the property of King Leopold II of Belgium, into a pleasure dome that soon became the epitome of glamour between the wars. Embellished with Maugham's magnificent art collection, staffed by a bevy of servants who catered to the guests' every need, the Villa Mauresque was, in the words of one of its denizens, a "Garden of Eden filled with the hissing of snakes."

Here Maugham could thrive as he had never done in England. He planned his career adroitly, retiring from the theater as early as 1933; the fashion-driven stage, he observed, was a young man's game, and a playwright of 50 could not hope to keep up with its rapidly changing trends. He wrote his last novel, *Catalina*, in 1948 and in 1959, at the age of 85, stopped writing altogether. His books sold in huge numbers—tens of millions of copies during his lifetime alone, with *Of Human Bondage, Cakes and Ale* (1930), *The Moon and Sixpence* and *The Razor's Edge* (1944) perennial best sellers—and he drove a hard bargain with publishers. "He'll always begin by saying, 'Of course, I know nothing about business,'" one of his editors recalled, "but before the conversation is over he will have got . . . everything he wants—which, incidentally, is plenty."

Little by little he aged into the hooded mandarin etched on the world's memory by the great Graham Sutherland portrait. "That old, old parrot," as Christopher Isherwood described him, "with his flat black eyes, blinking and attentive, his courtly politeness and his hypnotic stammer." Maugham died in 1965 at the age of ninety-one. He suffered a long and sad decline, playing out a Lear-like drama with his daughter and Alan Searle, Gerald Haxton's successor. His ashes were interred at King's School in Canterbury, where he had, many years earlier, been an unhappy schoolboy.

For all Maugham's popularity, the real prize eluded him: he was not considered a great writer, and though he kept aiming for the artistic heights represented by Joseph Conrad, his hero, and Henry James, whom he rather despised, he never reached them.

What characterizes a great writer, perhaps, is what is left out—what must be read between the lines—and on this level Maugham falls short. His reflexive cynicism and aloofness also tainted his work; Raymond Mortimer claimed that no other major writer, not even David Hume or Edward Gibbon, had been so detached. Finally, his lack of a distinctive style was held against him, and loudly lamented by the most influential critic of the day, Edmund Wilson. (It was a lack, incidentally, that Maugham cultivated, believing that when an author could be immediately identified by his style, style had degenerated into mannerism.) But Maugham's strengths were very considerable. As William Plomer once felt it necessary to remind highbrow readers, "To be a man of the world, to be acquainted with all sorts of different people, to be tolerant, to be curious, to have a capacity for enjoyment, to be the master of a clear and unaffected prose style—these are great advantages."

Meyers's account of Maugham's life is sympathetic but brisk and unreflective, at times more like a school text than a fully fleshed-out portrait. It adds little, really, to Robert Calder's fine biography, *Willie* (1989), or to Ted Morgan's earlier *Maugham*. Still, Maugham's story is eminently entertaining, a weird mixture of Horatio Alger and Noel Coward, and it does no harm to hear it again. He was a prickly, difficult, demanding person—Meyers should get full marks, by the way, for never using the obvious word, "bitchy"—but in the end he commands respect and even a guarded affection.

(2004)

8. INTO AFRICA
ELSPETH HUXLEY

P ossibly because the men were all outdoors shooting animals and clearing land, the best-known chroniclers of the romantic, improbable lives led by white settlers in British East Africa have been women: Isak Dinesen, Beryl Markham, and Elspeth Huxley. Dinesen's *Out of Africa* is, considered in purely literary terms, the best book on the subject, but she was a self-mythologizer and, according to those who knew her and her world, essentially dishonest. Beryl Markham's autobiographical *West with the Night* has achieved a popularity out of all proportion to its merit: while Markham's life was thrilling by any standards, her prose is artificial and unconvincing, written in a sort of second-rate Hemingwayese.

Huxley (1907–1997) was less visionary and musical than Dinesen, less given to high lyricism than Markham, and more truthful than either. In forty-eight works of fiction and non-fiction—she was both a novelist and a political authority, one of the acknowledged experts on colonial and post-colonial policy—she explored Britain's African empire and its disintegration, of which she was an astute and passionately interested eyewitness. *The Flame Trees of Thika* (1959), a charming novel based on her childhood memories of British East Africa (B.E.A.) before the First World War, is a minor classic, giving a glimpse of Africa in its last, fleeting moment of primeval splendor and a matchless child's-eye view of the courage and folly of its white settlers. "One of the mild surprises of advancing age," she reflected, truly, "is to discover that part of one's lifetime has turned into history, a process which one generally assumes has come to a halt about the time that one was born."

Huxley's biography—a life that encompassed the entire history of Kenya Colony as well as substantial portions of its pre- and post-colonial story—has now been written by C. S. Nicholls, herself a white Kenyan. It makes for interesting if rather dry reading, no match for Huxley's own clear, colorful prose which has fixed indelible images in many a reader's imagination. Unfortunately for Nicholls, Huxley inherited the stoic ethos and stiff upper lip of her caste, which considered displays of feeling to be unbecoming. She habitually suppressed her deeper emotions; the only feeling she allowed herself to show was irritation. This masked her inner life and has made her an opaque and elusive biographical subject. "As for soul-baring, I'm bad at it," she admitted.

I myself lived in the one-time so-called "White Highlands," on and off, between 1973 and 1989. When I first began visiting Kenya, early in the 1970s, the settler society described by Huxley still existed in a recognizable if watered-down form, but by the end of my visits there it had all but disappeared. The spread of the telephone throughout the 1970s, and the television set a decade later, dragged the white community out of its anachronistic and cheerfully self-imposed isolation. On another level, a certain self-consciousness set in with the international propagation and, ultimately, the marketing of anything that could be labeled "colonial" or "Raj." Ralph Lauren's clothing designs, evoking a fevered fantasy of deluxe safaris led, perhaps, by Bror von Blixen for the benefit of Teddy Roosevelt, were one manifestation of this trend.

Another was the popularity of the bogus *Out of Africa* film with its improbable fashions: Meryl Streep braving the red African dust in frivolous white linen. (Real memsahibs of Isak Dinesen's generation dressed, according to Huxley, rather differently, in "hideous clothing which was far too hot and bulky for the climate. This consisted of ill-fitting gabardine breeches, partly concealed by short, wide, flapping khaki skirts, and a khaki coat and boots.") The final Disneyfication of Kenya—the moment it became clear that whatever might be left of the "real thing" had ceased to be real —occurred when an entire issue of *Architectural Digest* was dubbed "The Kenya Issue" and devoted to glossy houses, many owned by the grandchildren and great-grandchildren of original settlers, worked over by architects and designers and decked out with African art. A far cry from the pre-World War I sitting rooms described by Huxley, with green velvet sofas and even pianos incongruously standing in whitewashed rondavels, on floors of puddled clay.

That the recent apotheosis of this "settler chic" has occurred in the midst of politically correct anti-colonialism has been possible, of course, because the erstwhile white masters lost their sting along with their power. As Huxley observed in the years following Kenyan independence, "The colonist hyena [is] emerging from the shadows into which the comrades drove him in the bad old imperialist days. Now that western imperialism (though certainly not other forms) has receded into history, the white colonist can be seen not only with his manifest failings, but with virtues it is no longer blasphemous to recognize." And "far from being black-hearted villains, [the white settlers] are becoming nostalgic old things deserving of affection rather than abuse, like steam railway locomotives."

Huxley's parents, Josceline (Jos) and Nellie Grant, arrived in Africa in 1912. Though they both came from grand families— Nellie, née Grosvenor, was a cousin of the Duke of Westminster, while Jos was descended from a governor of Bombay—they had little money of their own and, impractical optimists, saw a glowing future in Africa's fertile White Highlands. Upon their arrival in Nairobi Jos purchased five hundred acres of virgin bushland, suitable, he was told, for growing coffee, some fifty miles up-country near the little outpost of Thika. Thither the couple repaired, accompanied by oxcarts loaded down with eccentric impedimenta that included an Escoffier cookery book and a dressmaker's dummy.

It is hard, confronted as we are each day with pictures of an Africa being torn apart by guns, drugs, and internationally financed warlords, to realize how isolated the interior still was only a century ago. At night, local Kikuyu warriors edged nervously up to the Grants' camp, attracted by the apparent magic of a safari lamp. "They were like bronze statues endowed with life and moved tautly, as if on springs, ready to bound forward or back. One felt that just as they vanished into the void like antelopes when alarmed, they might spring forward when angered and thrust with spears; they were triggered men." Huxley's work is imbued with a feeling of loss as "progress" destroys this world, running through Africa "at breakneck speed . . . an elemental force, like wind or sun or lightning, that doles out good and evil more or less impartially."

Elspeth sailed out to join her parents at the age of six; her memories of these early, pioneering days, with whites and Africans living parallel and mutually incomprehensible lives that intersected only on certain levels, are rendered in exquisite prose in *The Flame Trees of Thika* and its sequel, *On the Edge of the Rift*. Jos, a dreaming Micawber, and Nellie, a brilliantly entertaining woman of high energy but not, perhaps, very practical, make wonderful characters in Huxley's fictionalized memoirs but must have been infuriating parents; everything they touched failed, and Huxley had to provide financial help from the moment she was old enough to earn a living.

Huxley remained obsessively fixed on Africa throughout her writing life, but as an adult she never deviated from her decision to live elsewhere. After studying agriculture at Reading University and, for one year, at Cornell in the United States, she settled in England. At the age of twenty-four she married Gervas Huxley, a businessman and the cousin of Aldous and Julian Huxley. Like her mother before her, she was the dominant partner in her marriage; Gervas was a gentle, diffident man. But as in many such cases he seems to have served as a protective buffer between his wife and her somewhat abrasive mother. "Nellie and Elspeth," one friend recalled, "both powerful women, argued and fought all day long, comments like how dare you say that, give reason for your theory, voices rose as more gin poured in." (They quite enjoyed their clashes, however, and in 1980 Elspeth collected her beloved mother's letters and published them, with great success, as *Nellie: Letters from Africa*.)

Huxley's first book was *White Man's Country* (1935), a two-volume biography of Lord Delamere and in effect a history of the settler movement of which he was the political leader. Her sympathies, at this point, lay with her own people, the settlers; but they were to change over time, and though she never demonized the imperialists, by the 1950s she had come to believe that independence was not only inevitable but necessary. "Of course it's hard on individuals," she wrote, thinking of her many friends who lost their farms—their life's work and only capital—in the forced land sales of the new nation. "Of course it has its personal tragedies. No man on earth can stop these great waves of history from sweeping away good and bad together. They not only can't be stopped, they shouldn't be. It's right, you know, it's right that people should be free." This in spite of the fact that she disliked and mistrusted Jomo Kenyatta, and knew that the new African rulers would probably not turn out particularly well: "human beings," she wrote, "are the same whatever their colour and level of so-called civilization—that is to say, on balance, bloody."

Huxley's non-fiction has, of course, dated: Africa has moved on, with a rapidity that even she, canny though she was, could not have foreseen. Her novels, though, continue to charm, with their thoughtful vision of the traumatic and often absurd juxtaposition of African and European cultures. Her upbringing had made her keenly aware that while human nature does not much differ from one culture to another, ways of perceiving the world emphatically do. European ideas of ownership and land-tenure, large-scale agriculture, and other innovations must have shaken the African worldview to its roots. The Kikuyu, as Huxley wrote in *The Flame Trees of Thika*,

> walked about their country without appearing to possess it —or perhaps I mean, without leaving any mark. To us, that was remarkable: they had not aspired to recreate or change or tame the country and to bring it under their control . . . If water flowed down a valley they fetched what they wanted in a large hollow gourd; they did not push it into pipes or flumes, or harass it with pumps. Consequently when they left a piece of land and abandoned their huts (as eventually they always did, since they practiced shifting cultivation), the bush and vegetation grew up again and obliterated every trace of them, just as the sea at each high tide wipes out footprints and children's sandcastles, and leaves the beach once more smooth and glistening.

Huxley was a bit of an oddball, an artist and an intellectual (though she would have been too modest to describe herself as such) in a violently anti-intellectual culture. White Kenya, even when I knew it a couple of generations after Huxley's youth, was disproportionately populated by people who nowadays would be labeled as having ADD: action, of nearly any sort, was to them far preferable to reflection. Huxley gave these people clear voices with which to explore their lives and the colonial project itself. Here, for example, is a conversation between several characters from *The Flame Trees of Thika*: Robin and Tilly, based on Jos and Nellie; Lettice and Hereward Palmer, their neighbors; and Alec Wilson, a clerk from London who has taken up farming in Africa.

"Whenever I look at a Kikuyu woman toiling up a hill with a baby and a load of produce on her back weighing about a hundred pounds, [says Lettice Palmer], I feel guilty."

"How ridiculous!" Hereward exclaimed. "They are only natives. Do you expect to lower yourself to their level?"

"I sincerely hope I shall never have to try."

"Surely," Tilly put in, "the idea is that they should rise to ours."

"Do you suppose," Lettice mused, "that one day they will become adept at water-colour sketches and German Lieder?"

"It seems unlikely," Robin reflected, watching a procession of three women, bent under their loads . . .

"Surely that's the whole point of our being here," Tilly remarked. "We may have a sticky passage ourselves, but when we've knocked a bit of civilization into them, all this dirt and disease and superstition will go and they'll live like decent people for the first time in their history." Tilly looked quite flushed and excited when she said this, as if it was something dear to her heart.

"That is not the whole point of my being here," Alec Wilson put in, during a pause that followed. "I didn't come to civilize anyone. I came to escape from the slavery one has at home if one doesn't inherit anything. I mean to make a fortune if I can. Then I shall go home and spend it. If that helps to civilize anyone I shall be delighted, but surprised."

"Of course it will help indirectly," Tilly said. "They must have an example," Hereward agreed.

"Do you think that we set an example?" Lettice inquired.

Nicholls's biography will please those who are already interested in Huxley, or in colonial Kenya, but it is no substitute for Huxley's own books, especially *The Flame Trees of Thika, On the Edge of the Rift,* and *Love Among the Daughters,* her semi-autobiographical trilogy. Her sound sense and intellect, combined with humor and a descriptive gift that at times rises to the poetic, leave readers with a rich vision of a life that, whether for better or worse, has disappeared forever.

(2003)

9. WITHOUT PEER
LORD BERNERS

Mark Amory's biography of Lord Berners has called him "the last eccentric." The adjective seems a little drastic; one hopes that even Cool Britannia will be able to produce the occasional oddball here and there. But if not the last eccentric, Gerald Tyrwhitt, who succeeded his uncle as 14th Baron Berners in 1918, was certainly among the more colorful ones of his generation, memorably portrayed in Nancy Mitford's *Pursuit of Love* as the fey and whimsical Lord Merlin, whose whippets wear diamond necklaces and who dyes his flock of pet pigeons every color of the rainbow.

A man of many talents but no real genius, Lord Berners was known as "the English Satie." (Erik Satie took exception to the comparison, referring to Berners scoffingly as "a professional amateur.") Berners wrote ballet music for Diaghilev and opera with Gertrude Stein; he painted capably in the manner of Corot; he was the author of several pleasantly campy novels, including *Far From the Madding War*, *The Camel* and *The Girls of Radcliffe Hall*, in which he represented his young male circle of homosexual friends as naughty schoolgirls and himself as their repressed headmistress.

In 1934, Berners published a brief volume of autobiography, *First Childhood*, to which he produced a sequel, *A Distant Prospect*, eleven years later. Funny, unsparing, sharp yet fundamentally good-spirited, the two books carry him from his birth in 1883 to his departure from school at the age of sixteen. Out of print for many years, they are now available in handsome paperback editions.

Superficially at least, Berners's account of his boyhood follows the standard pattern of patrician reminiscence: a childhood surrounded by old retainers in a grand country house, and the evocation, in its description, of a vanished world; the shock of transition from this paradise to a Spartan prep school full of grubby boys and sadistic masters; pleasure and romantic friendship at Eton. And Lord Berners, being the quintessential aesthete, follows another standard pattern as well, that of the artistic child born into a philistine aristocracy in which blood sports were thought to be man's highest calling and "the word 'imagination' was always used in a depreciative sense."

But although he covers familiar territory, Berners writes in an engagingly fresh and amusing voice. Better still, there is nothing even remotely sentimental about his re-creation of the Victorian past. It seems clear that he was far happier as an adult consorting with the likes of Cecil Beaton, Frederick Ashton and Igor Stravinsky than he ever was among the dull, fox-hunting gentry, the solidly respectable furniture, and the mounted antlers, warthog tusks and fox masks of his childhood home.

"With regard to heredity," Berners claims, "I am unable to discover any very evident genealogy for my own character." He is especially funny on his paternal grandmother, Lady Berners, whom he calls Lady Bourchier. (For some reason, he has chosen to disguise his family members behind absurdly transparent pseudonyms.) Lady Bourchier was a baroness in her own right but "everything else in her own wrong," as Berners's father quipped. In appearance, she was "not unlike Holbein's portrait of Bloody Mary with just a touch of Charley's Aunt." Extremely religious and "violently low-church," she described herself in *Who's Who* as "distinctly low" and held household prayer services for her domestics, "declaiming scriptural exhortations in a voice that seemed to hold out very little hope of salvation for the lower classes."

B erners' parents lived semi-detached lives almost from the beginning: his father was a worldly, cynical naval officer, his mother a pleasant but exceedingly conventional countrywoman, almost comically defined by the prejudices of her caste. Consider, for example, a conversation Berners recalls between his mother and his tutor, Mr. Prout:

> My mother hardly ever discussed politics, or she might have discovered that Mr. Prout was a "horrid radical." Once when he spoke of the "idle rich" she said, "Oh, but, Mr. Prout, all the rich people I know are always very busy. They always have a lot to do."
>
> "I don't count hunting or shooting," Mr. Prout replied, "or going to parties."
>
> "Why not?" my mother asked, and the subject was dropped.

Intellectual pursuits were not encouraged at home and neither was young Gerald's enthusiasm for Chopin. Instead, his mother sought to inculcate manliness—a virtue, Berners writes, "in which one had to be laboriously instructed. Like so many other virtues, it did not seem to correspond with the natural instincts of the human being."

At the age of 9 or so, Gerald devised a booby trap by which a plank flew up and smacked his Swiss governess on the bottom as she eased herself onto the toilet seat; he was smartly packed off to boarding school. Elmley (in reality, Cheam) was a highly respected institution, but Berners makes it sound as lurid and raffish a place as Llanabba Castle in Evelyn Waugh's *Decline and Fall*. The headmaster immediately strikes an ominous note by promising, on Gerald's first day, to "make a man of him"; the boy's years there are predictably unpleasant, culminating in Gerald's ruining a budding romance with an older boy by throwing up all over him.

Gerald's Elmley career ends on a sour note as he is caught hurling a Bible across the room by the headmaster. ("The Bible! . . . The Bible, sir! You have thrown the Bible—and on Sunday too! Stand up on the form!") He then moves on to Eton. Berners writes of Eton with a deep appreciation for its beauty, but his recollections are blessedly free of the haze of romantic nostalgia that makes so many memoirs of the place a little ridiculous. He enjoyed himself thoroughly, made two significant friends (an unwashed intellectual and a vapid dandy) and conceived a passion for Wagner.

Looking back on Eton, however, Berners was unimpressed by the education he received there. It was not just the relentless obsession with organized games or the fact that any and all artistic endeavor was regarded with deep suspicion. The teachers themselves (two of whom were nicknamed Jumping Jesus and Creeping Christ) were mediocre, with the notable exception of the revered A. C. Benson. Eton's philosophy, Berners claims, was to nurture "character" at the expense of intellect. At Eton, he concludes, "I had learned nothing, less than nothing, a minus quantity. I had lost what little knowledge I had of foreign languages. In history, geography and science I had been confused rather than instructed. I left Eton with a distaste for the Classics and, what was more serious, a distaste for work itself."

Here, sadly, Berners's autobiographical writings come to an end. He lived on until 1950, but for an account of his adult life, so full of bizarre incident and odd characters, one must turn to Mark Amory's *Lord Berners: The Last Eccentric.*

(1998)

10. THE GAY BLADE
OSBERT SITWELL

One of the meanest and truest things that have been said about the Sitwells was F. R. Leavis's comment that they belong not so much to the history of literature as to the history of publicity.

The three Sitwell siblings, Edith, born in 1887, Osbert, five years her junior, and Sacheverell, five years younger still and known to family and friends as Sachie, were among the earliest examples of that twentieth-century phenomenon, the person who is famous for being famous. In his gossipy and pleasantly readable new biography of Osbert Sitwell, Philip Ziegler estimates that at the height of Osbert's success, for every one person who had read his books there were ten who knew something of him and his family. Today the ratio would probably be more like one to a thousand. Some educated people know who Osbert Sitwell was, but you don't often see anyone curled up with one of his books, not even *Left Hand, Right Hand!*, the five-volume autobiography that was so extremely popular during the mid-twentieth century.

The cover design for the new biography is telling, for "Philip Ziegler" is printed in letters at least twice the size of those in "Osbert

Sitwell." This is perhaps as it should be: Ziegler, the clever and graceful biographer of William IV, Melbourne, Diana Cooper, Mountbatten, Edward VIII, and Harold Wilson, has proved over the course of his career to be a far better writer than Sitwell ever was. Mediocre poetry and fiction, moderately amusing travel writing, light journalism, and autobiography: Sitwell's work has not stood the test of time. It is hard to credit that in his day some very intelligent people believed him to be one of the foremost writers of his generation. Today's readers are liable to be alienated by his work's aristocratic plumminess, what Ziegler aptly describes as its "clotted-cream lyricism," and to see the point of Michael Holroyd's complaint that "at its most elaborated and elongated his prose reads like that of Sir Thomas Browne, after being translated into French by Proust and subsequently rendered back into English by Henry James."

Ziegler is fully aware of his subject's second-rateness, and even admits to having at first doubted whether Osbert was worth a book. (He refers to him throughout as Osbert, not out of familiarity but to avoid confusing him with the other famous members of his family; I will follow suit.) "Often over the past few years," he says, "I have wondered if I were writing only for my own entertainment and for a handful of kindred spirits who are happy to grub around among such disregarded fossils . . . Yet at the end, I am satisfied that Osbert is worth a book; not so much for what he did as for what he was."

England between the wars enjoyed a sort of literary silver age. Evelyn Waugh, Graham Greene, Henry Green, Aldous Huxley, Anthony Powell, Christopher Isherwood, W. H. Auden, John Betjeman, Nancy Mitford, and Cyril Connolly were all in their heyday; they knew one another, corresponded, commented extensively on one another's work, characters, and sex lives. Osbert Sitwell was not a heavy hitter within this society, but he was one of its more colorful figures: pompous, bitchy, exhibitionistic, and a ready purveyor of scathing wit.

Ziegler cannot help liking Osbert, and treats him with an endearing protectiveness. For instance: "About halfway between the two world wars, Osbert found his poetic voice. It was not a very loud voice nor necessarily one well calculated to resound down the centuries, but it was individual, authentic, and in its own way curiously beguiling." While openly acknowledging Osbert's egotism, irritability, and snobbery ("Osbert attached immense importance to his royal connections . . . [H]e never missed a chance to hobnob with royalty and rarely failed to refer to such intimacies when an opportunity arose or could be contrived"), it is clear that Ziegler became very fond of his subject during the course of his research.

Osbert was proud of his aristocratic ancestry, a fact of which anyone who has labored through the first volume of *Left Hand, Right Hand!* must be aware. It was indeed "imposing, if not quite so splendiferous as he, and still more his sister Edith, were accustomed to assert," writes Ziegler. The family had been landowners for over six hundred years; the magnificent but cold and gloomy ancestral seat, Renishaw, was built in the seventeenth century. Their fortune came from manufacturing, a regrettable fact discreetly glossed over in *Left Hand, Right Hand!*; the baronetcy was a gift from the Prince Regent to an ancestor of Osbert's who rejoiced in the Wodehousian name of Sitwell Sitwell. On his mother's side Osbert was descended from the Dukes of Beaufort, hence from the Plantagenets: to Osbert and his siblings, this "was a subject of infinite satisfaction."

Osbert's father, Sir George Sitwell, was an eccentric, but not nearly so grotesque as the caricature in Osbert's autobiography. Thousands of readers laughed at Sir George as limned by Osbert, but "few," Ziegler writes, "stopped to consider what bitterness must lie behind this pillorying of a parent, or whether it was proper for a son to decry his father with such gusto." An egotist of gigantic proportions, selfish, tyrannical, and detached, Sir George could not have been an easy father, but then Osbert, as selfish as his father and far more malicious, was not an easy son. Kenneth Clark found Sir George "nicer and sadder than Osbert allowed in his ungenerous portrait"; Sachie wrote that "He wasn't nearly as comic a figure as [Osbert] made him appear. He was a much nicer person. I think he was much nicer than Osbert." Ziegler obviously shares Sachie's opinion, and deplores the large portion of Osbert's life that was wasted in pointless guerrilla warfare against a father who would dearly have liked to be his friend.

Osbert survived at Eton, but didn't shine; a contemporary remembered that "he spent most of his leisure at Westbrook's, the Eton florists, arranging flowers." He left in 1909, at the age of sixteen, unsure just what to do next. He expressed a tentative interest in the Diplomatic Service, but Sir George leaned more toward the military, and Osbert was sent to a crammer. He failed the entrance exam for Sandhurst ("in those days no easy matter," as he ruefully admitted), then failed it again. He eventually joined the 11th Hussars, but finding the cavalry uncongenial, for he detested horses, machinery, and guns, transferred to the Grenadier Guards. When war was declared in 1914 he went to France with his regiment.

Osbert's experiences in the trenches turned him into a lifelong pacifist. It was during the war that he began to write poetry, and it was war poetry very much in the spirit of what his friends Siegfried Sassoon and Wilfred Owen were producing, though hardly of the same quality. "If not blazing a solitary trail," Ziegler writes with characteristic diffidence, "Osbert was at least in the forefront of the new poetic movement." Back in England, he honed his modernist credentials by attacking the so-called Georgian poets. Typically, Osbert the polemicist chose to ignore the many pieces of first-rate work which had been published in the *Georgian Poetry* volumes, and his clever modern dismissiveness did not find favor every-where: T. S. Eliot, for example, expressed contempt for "the poets who consider themselves most opposed to Georgianism and who know a little French."

It was during World War I that the Sitwells began to operate as a team: to be precise, at a poetry reading in Lady Colefax's drawing-room in December, 1917. The cultivation of a group identity turned out to be a brilliant ploy. Each Sitwell in his own way was striking, but together they made an indelible impression. As the years wore on and their work and lives diverged, they would come to resent their corporate identity: in 1949 Edith scolded, "We do not like to be treated as if we were an aggregate Indian god, with three sets of legs and arms, but otherwise indivisible. We have all three suffered very much from this. It vulgarizes and cheapens everything and deprives all the work of its importance."

But as Ziegler demonstrates, they had no one to blame but themselves, and in their triumphant publicity tours to the United States after the Second World War—at about the same time Edith registered her complaint—they continued to capitalize on their attractions as a trio. There, Ziegler writes, "they were confident that they would give a good account of themselves but had some doubt whether the Americans were worthy of them and whether they would be properly appreciated." In the event, they were appreciated beyond their wildest expectations; they basked in the adulation.

Osbert was a homosexual of a masculine, repressed type. In youth, as an eligible bachelor, he had had a "nasty fright" when he was briefly pursued by Violet Keppel, later Violet Trefusis: "By Jove, I wish he'd accepted her!" her husband, Denis Trefusis, remarked when told of the incident many years later. Osbert was fearful and extremely circumspect about his sexuality, often registering his disapproval of those who came across as too gay. "Once he and Harold Nicolson were side by side filling in embarkation cards before a Channel crossing. 'What age are you going to put,

Osbert?' asked Nicolson. 'What sex are *you* going to put, Harold?' Osbert retorted."

The person Osbert eventually chose as a life-companion was David Horner, a tall, beautiful young man of "corroding frivolity" a few years younger than himself, a junior member of the ancient Horner family of Mells Abbey. Horner had little money of his own, but had recently been left a fortune by an older friend. He banked the cash and lived more or less off Osbert until very nearly the end of their days, some forty years later. "If Osbert thought he was getting value for money," Ziegler writes rather stiffly, "and did not begrudge supporting the partner he loved, there is no reason a biographer should be more censorious." He can't help it, though: Horner, "a big gay butterfly, fluttering around and drawing honey from all the flowers," according to Osbert's secretary, emerges as the evil sprite of this story, a compulsive troublemaker who purposely did a great deal of damage to Osbert's relations with his siblings and his friends. He also, says Ziegler,

> reinforced Osbert's baser prejudices. He was a snob . . . He was a racist . . . He was an anti-Semite, of a violence which made Osbert's previous tendencies seem almost benevolent. His wit was almost invariably unkind . . . His impatience and fretfulness were notorious . . . All of these were frailties which Osbert shared and all of them became more marked as time wore on.

Sir George Sitwell died in 1943, and Osbert inherited the title and estates. "I *love* being a baronet," he gloated with characteristic frankness. "It's the most heavenly new toy." He also loved being in control of the family fortune, and rather unexpectedly—for he had been a life-long spendthrift—he managed it very well, leaving it in a substantially improved condition to his heir, Sachie's son Reresby, upon his own death twenty-six years later.

As early as 1949 he began to notice tremors in his hands, the first signs of Parkinson's disease, which was to blight his last years and turn the one-time dandy into a cripple pathetically dependent on the ministrations of others. Surprisingly, the irascible Osbert showed courage and real gallantry as the dreadful disease progressed. Travel, which had always been meat and drink to him, he kept up to the bitter end. "Getting in and out of gondolas will prove a difficult proposition," he told a friend, apropos of a trip to Venice in 1967. "More amusing for bystanders than for me."

Osbert died in 1969. His career had been a triumph of willpower and oomph over the limitations set by mere talent. As a writer, he was never up to much, and although Ziegler claims that *Left Hand, Right Hand!* is an "unequivocal masterpiece," in my opinion he is very much mistaken. Perhaps his affection for Osbert has clouded his judgment. One of the attractive elements of this biography is the way that Ziegler tries and fails to repress his own emotional responses: his dislike of Edith, for example, his virulent distaste for David Horner, his almost perverse good will, in spite of all their faults, towards Sir George and Osbert.

For there is no doubt that Osbert was not a very admirable human being: even his closest friends felt, and were infected by, his constitutional malice. Siegfried Sassoon, who knew him extremely well, found it difficult to be his friend.

> Something in his character makes it impossible for me to feel kindly towards him. His neurotic spite and jealousy are ill-concealed by his 'social charm'. He seems incapable of serenity, or of tolerance of his contemporaries. His portrait should be a restless reflection in a valuable gilt Chippendale mirror. Peacock *en casserole* should be his staple diet. How tiresome he can be with his everlasting chatter about his antiquarian father; and his disreputably aristocratic mama; and his untidy financial affairs. Perhaps I am severe on him, but he is always merciless to everyone but himself and his brother and sister.

One feels that Osbert Sitwell must indeed have often been a tiresome person, and a treacherous one; it is Ziegler's considerable achievement to have made his biography funny, compelling, and even charming while never pretending that Osbert was more or better than he was.

(1998)

11. THE DEVIL'S DISCIPLE
PATRICIA HIGHSMITH

I t's a well-known principle that if you admire certain writers' work, maybe you'd be better off not meeting them in the flesh. Good writers are often surprisingly unpleasant people —no one can quite figure out why, but it's true. And never has there been a writer I'm so glad not to have known (though I very much enjoy her fiction) as Patricia Highsmith (1921–95). She was a predatory lesbian, in addition to being a professional home breaker; a nasty drunk; an emotional sadist; and an equal-opportunity bigot who seems to have detested every group except the American and European *gratin*. Arabs, Jews, the French, Catholics, evangelicals, Latinos, blacks, Koreans, Indians both dot and feather . . . the list goes on and on.

Richard Bradford, Highsmith's most recent biographer, observes her carryings-on, in his book *Devils, Lusts and Strange Desires*, with a sort of horrified fascination. "Compared to Highsmith, the likes of Casanova, Errol Flynn and Lord Byron might be considered lethargic—even demure. She seemed to enjoy affairs with married women in particular, but breaking up lesbian couples was a close second." "An insatiable appetite for things, and people, stolen from or denied to others, seemed to have become her *modus operandi*." She had an urgent and insatiable need for high drama ending in ruined lives, and if a relationship did not provide her with such fodder she soon moved on.

The question of mental illness of course arises, though Highsmith was never diagnosed. Bradford cites a psychiatrist, unacquainted with the writer, who passed her in a hotel corridor and noted that her facial expression was one he had never witnessed outside of an insane asylum. She herself speculated that she might have been bipolar, but to me (amateur psychologist that I am) her behavior seems more in keeping with borderline personality disorder. But we will never know.

What makes all this interesting, aside from the reader's prurience and the perverse fascination involved in watching a train wreck in progress? It is, Bradford demonstrates, that Highsmith's personality is so closely interwoven with those of her characters, her pathologies so allied with theirs, that a knowledge of her life truly expands the imaginative exercise of reading the fiction—which is not always the case with biographies. But how much do we actually know, and how much of what she tells us can be trusted? From adolescence on she recorded her life, thoughts, and fantasies in a series of "cahiers," now assembled in the Swiss Literary Archives at Bern. Bradford has clearly spent a long and frustrating time in those archives, trying to differentiate truth and fantasy, fact and fiction. He admits that the attempt was often vain —but that fact in itself tells us much about Highsmith's odd psyche. "As well as writing books featuring invented characters," he tells us, "she decided that her own life should become the equivalent of a novel, a legacy of lies, fantasies and authorial inventions." She apparently did this for several reasons: to create a life she desired rather than the one she lived, shaping her own life as fiction; to transpose her own experiences imaginatively into those of her characters; and, mischievously, to confuse scholars and biographers, poor saps like Bradford who, she knew, would scrutinize her papers after her death.

Much of her childhood and early life can be ascertained, however. Was there anything there to have caused the extreme behaviors of later years? Probably so, as it turns out. She was born in 1921 in Fort Worth, to Jay Bernard Plangman and Mary Coates Plangman. When Mary got pregnant, the Plangmans, who were looking forward to a new life in New York, attempted an abortion (with turpentine!) but botched it; Jay inexplicably revealed this incident to Patricia in later years. The birth of the child (whom neither parent wanted) hastened the collapse of the marriage, and the Plangmans split up six months later. Mary got remarried two years afterward, to Stanley Highsmith, an illustrator and photographer, who adopted the child.

Patricia claimed to have childhood amnesia, a state that is usually connected with childhood trauma, and in fact she suspected that she had been sexually abused at her grandmother's house. Bradford suggests, however, that the amnesia might possibly have been invented as a method for Highsmith to place her life within her own artistic control: "one has to wonder," he writes with justifiable frustration, "if Highsmith intuited [invented?] childhood amnesia as a means of rewriting her past." Certain salient facts, however, still stood out to her. "My [sexual] character was essentially made before I was six," she recalled, and from the age of eight or so she had entertained "evil thoughts of murder of my stepfather": "I learned to live with a grievous and murderous hatred very early on."

Patricia spent much of her childhood shuttling back and forth between Texas and New York City; at one point the Highsmiths temporarily split up and Patricia was left with her grandparents in Fort Worth for a year while her parents worked things out. Then it was back to New York and the Julia Richman High School, where one of her major crushes was one Judy Tuvim, later to achieve fame as the charming movie star Judy Holliday. In 1938 she enrolled at Barnard College, where she cut quite a swath "dressed as a character in a noir movie"; "My vision of her," remembers one contemporary, "is with a cigarette hanging out of the corner of her mouth. And the camel hair coat, the high white collar and I think she wore an ascot. I mean she was stylish." A year into college she joined the Young Communist League. Not that she was ever very political; Bradford's assumption is that she posed as a communist for attention, as it was not a persona adopted by many of the nice Barnard girls. "Quite soon, though, she grew tired of this new performance."

It was at this time that she commenced her lifelong career of social climbing, befriending luminaries like Janet Flanner, Ludwig and Madeleine Bemelmans, and Berenice Abbott. Most of all she lusted after the rich, the glamorous, the WASP. Like her most famous character, Tom Ripley, fixating on the glittering, golden Dickie Greenleaf, Highsmith was always fascinated by such creatures of fantasy: "she only truly desired women who came from the kind of social, cultural and intellectual ranking to which she aspired." She even stalked them. When she was working as a temporary saleswoman at Bloomingdale's one Christmas season, for example, she was deeply struck by a mink-clad blonde and tracked her down to her home. Unlike the situation in her 1952 novel, *The Price of Salt*, which was inspired by this incident, she and the strange woman would never actually meet, let alone have a romance. (Times being what they were, Highsmith had to publish *The Price of Salt* under a pseudonym; much later, after its true authorship had been finally revealed, it was adapted as the 2015 movie *Carol*.)

As Bradford points out, "there are eerie resemblances between the real-life stalker, Highsmith, and her horrid creation, Bruno" (the psychopath in *Strangers on a Train*). Highsmith, he continues, "spent much of her life as a writer siphoning the emotional catastrophes she prompted, encountered, and experienced," using alcohol as a way of heightening her already provocative behavior. The two most memorable characters in her fiction, Tom Ripley and Charles Anthony Bruno (whose name was changed to Bruno

Anthony in the Hitchcock film), are almost certainly memorable because of the author's personal identification with their obsessions: like Bruno, who wishes profoundly for his father's death, Highsmith fantasized for years about murdering her stepfather, and, like both Bruno and Tom, she equated murder with love. "Murder," she wrote, "is a kind of making love, a kind of possessing."

Devils, Lusts and Strange Desires is not a critical biography, but the connections between Highsmith's life and works are made clear. In the years after college Highsmith began writing, supporting herself primarily by penning scripts for the Sangor-Pines Comic Shop. (Bradford suggests that the spare comic-book style might have had some influence on her prose.) She drew well, and even considered becoming an artist rather than a writer. In 1944 she moved to a pleasant villa in Taxco, Mexico (Bradford rightly wonders where she got the funds to pay for it), and wrote a novel, *The Click of the Shutting*, which was "irredeemably bad" but whose plot foreshadowed the central relationships in *Strangers on a Train* and *The Talented Mr. Ripley*. The first of her twenty-two published novels, *Strangers on a Train*, appeared in 1952.

From this point on, with an assured income, Highsmith spent much of her time abroad: in Positano (which she wonderfully recreated as Mongibello in *The Talented Mr. Ripley*); in France, although she hated the French; in Switzerland, where she died of lung cancer and aplastic anemia in 1995, mourned by few. She had always been dreadful: once she had looked on as a distraught lover washed down an overdose of Veronal with several large martinis, then left her there on the bed and went out to dinner with friends, returning at 2:00 a.m., finally deigning to call an ambulance when she failed to wake the hapless Ellen from her coma. But as Highsmith aged, her vision grew even darker, perhaps because, as she remarked in a cahier, she regarded the vast majority of humans as "morons." One of her lovers mused: "If she hadn't had her work, she would have been sent to an insane asylum or an alcoholics' home . . . It took a while for me to figure this out, but all those strange characters haunting other people, and thinking and writing about them—they were her. She was her writing."

Devils, Lusts and Strange Desires is certainly an engrossing book, though it leaves a rancid taste in the reader's mouth. But why was it written? There are already two Highsmith biographies out there: Andrew Wilson's *Beautiful Shadow: A Life of Patricia Highsmith* (2003) and Joan Schenkar's *The Talented Miss Highsmith: The Secret Life and Serious Art of Patricia Highsmith* (2009). Bradford's introduction doesn't provide a justification, and one suspects that, 2021 marking Highsmith's centenary, he approached, or was approached by, Bloomsbury to produce a volume in honor of the occasion. Bradford, a British academic, is a prolific writer who specializes in literary biography, having authored lives of John Milton, Philip Larkin, Alan Sillitoe, both Kingsley and Martin Amis, Ernest Hemingway, and George Orwell. Trying to separate fact from fiction in the Swiss archives might have made Highsmith the most difficult subject he'd taken on. His most serious handicap in the attempt is his obvious unfamiliarity with the American scene: he compares the lifestyle of the characters in *The Philadelphia Story* with "those of the degenerate Regency Aristocracy," calls Manhattan's 103rd Street "midtown," says that Astoria "is a suburb of New York," and that Barnard College is "in Central New York, adjacent to Broadway." Simply asking an American reader to have a look at the book prior to publication would have cleaned up this sort of thing.

But at his best, Bradford can demonstrate real psychological savvy. Speaking of Highsmith's avowed anti-Semitism, for instance:

> I suspect . . . that Highsmith as the foul anti-Semite was in part an invention. Like Ripley she reflected horrible

elements of her creation honestly enough but she deliberately exaggerated them as an excercise in provocation and
self-loathing. Highsmith knew that those closest to her
were appalled by her views and her expressions of them,
which is why she continued them. She was genuinely anti-
Semitic, but in the same sense that Ripley was a genuine,
real murderer.

The key word here, I think, is "self-loathing." Was she born
this way, or had the conditions of her early life created the pathol-
ogy? For all his assiduous archival detective work, Bradford has not
succeeded in finding the answer.

(2021)

12. Love and Separateness
Eudora Welty

A s you have seen," wrote Eudora Welty in the final paragraph of her memoir, *One Writer's Beginnings* (1984), "I am a writer who came of a sheltered life. A sheltered life can be a daring life as well. For all serious daring starts from within." Her choice of the word "daring" is an interesting one, for on looking back at her long career it is daring, above all, that turns out to have been the outstanding trait of this quiet Mississippi lady whose extra-literary life was in the normal sense of the words neither daring nor adventurous. Born in 1909 in Jackson, Mississippi, the much-loved eldest child of an affectionate, cultivated, middle-class family, she lived, except for a few years at the University of Wisconsin and at the Columbia University Business School in New York, all her life in Mississippi, spending her last years (she died in 2021) at the family home built by her father in the 1920s.

But in the practice of her art, Welty was as stylistically daring as any American of this century. Possibly more so, for even the great innovators like Hemingway and Faulkner, once they found "their" voices, refined and developed them rather than sailing off again into uncharted territory as Welty did. Having perfected an entirely individual type of verbal farce with her early stories "Petrified Man" and "Why I Live at the P.O." (still her best-known and most frequently anthologized work, if not her best), she was simultaneously producing tales in a manner that can loosely be called Southern Gothic. As she matured she turned away from both genres in favor of a complex, layered style that allowed her to synthesize her many gifts.

Not all her attempts were successful; indeed they include a few really spectacular failures. Some of the early experiments in the Gothic mode, such as "Asphodel," "The Purple Hat," and "Clytie," are downright bad, relying as they do on a puerile faith in the power of the grotesque *qua* grotesque. Many of these and the other early stories that make up the volumes *A Curtain of Green* (1941) and *The Wide Net* (1943), while they remain popular and critically respected, do not have the sustained mastery of the particular that marks Welty's best work; their narratives tend to buzz around the story's essence impotently, unable to capture it and making do instead with mere hyperbole, here as always a makeshift and inadequate tool.

But for all the flops and near misses, there are at least an equal number of quite brilliant pieces and even a few that can confidently be called great. "Petrified Man," a series of conversations in a Southern beauty parlor over the course of several days, contains dialogue that is, to use a degraded word literally, inimitable. Take the following exchange between Leota, the beautician, and her regular customer Mrs. Fletcher about Leota's new boarder, Mrs. Pike:

> She flicked an ash into the basket of dirty towels. "Mrs. Pike is a very decided blonde. She bought me the peanuts."
> "She must be cute," said Mrs. Fletcher.
> "Honey, 'cute' ain't the word for what she is. I'm

tellin' you, Mrs. Pike is attractive. She has her a good time. She's got a sharp eye out, Mrs. Pike has."

How much we know about the awful Mrs. Pike after just these few words! How much we can deduce about her meager and inadequate soul! "Petrified Man" shows a perfectly pitched comic sense, and a surprising confidence and command of the language for so young a writer.

If "Petrified Man" shows one side of Welty's talent, the sombre and poetic "Livvie" shows another. Livvie, a young black woman, has been married to old Solomon since she was sixteen, imprisoned in his isolated cabin while he slowly lapses into feeble senility. The story shows the moment of her liberation and awakening as a strange young man appears and gives her love, life, the world. Here is an episode in the development of what were to become, over the course of Welty's career, really extraordinary descriptive gifts:

> Her hand took the lipstick, and in an instant she was carried away in the air through the spring, and looking down with a half-drowsy smile from a purple cloud she saw from above a chinaberry tree, dark and smooth and neatly leaved, neat as a guinea hen in the dooryard, and there was her home that she had left. On one side of the tree was her mama holding up her heavy apron, and she could see it was loaded with ripe figs, and on the other side was her papa holding a fish-pole over the pond, and she could see it transparently, the little clear fishes swimming up to the brim.

Both the sensuality and the odd note of fantasy—the chinaberry tree "neat as a guinea hen"—would continue as central elements of Welty's fiction, developed from stories like "Livvie," which works, and "A Curtain of Green," which oddly misses its mark, into the richer and riper loam of the subsequent stories that make up *The Golden Apples* (1949) and *The Bride of the Innisfallen* (1955). In "Ladies in Spring," we see the same qualities carried to an almost Dylan Thomas-esque pitch:

> After the bus put him down, he ran cutting across under the charred pines. The big sky-blue violets his mother loved were blooming, wet as cheeks. Pear trees were all but in bloom under the purple sky. Branches were being jogged with the rush and commotion of birds. The Cokers' patch of mustard that had gone to seed shone like gold from here. Dewey ran under the last drops, through the hooraying mud of the pasture, and saw the corrugations of their roof shining across it like a fresh pan of cornbread sticks.

As a rough generalization, it could be said that in her early work Welty tended to keep genres separate—Gothic, comic, and serious, descriptive stories—and that as she matured she united the different strands in a single, complex whole. *Delta Wedding* (1946), her second novel, demonstrates the development. While the novel as a whole shows a clear debt to Virginia Woolf, particularly the Woolf of *To the Lighthouse* and *The Waves*, there are individual elements that are uniquely Weltian. *Delta Wedding* is the group portrait of a large extended family, the Fairchilds, prosperous landowners long established in the Mississippi Delta. The occasion for the clan's gathering is the wedding of sixteen-year-old Dabney Fairchild to Troy Flavin, the overseer: enough of a mésalliance to inject some bracing discomfort into the proceedings, but not enough to cause anyone real misery. The narrative is an exercise in point of view, rather like *The Waves*. The bride herself; her more introverted elder sister, Shelley; her mother, Ellen, the quiet matriarch; her father; the beloved Uncle George; Troy; their little cousin Laura, visiting from Jackson: each adds his or her own wave to the narrative flow.

Not all the characters are particularly memorable, but the presence of a few fresh and rudely alive ones marks *Delta Wedding* as a work no one but Welty could have produced. There is the bossy old Dr. Murdoch, for example, an instantly recognizable small-town character (he made his appearance under a different name in "The Wide Net"). Better yet is the Fairchilds' regal Aunt Tempe, who upon arrival looks "quickly around the parlor, as though to catch it before it could compose itself" and offers her cheek to be kissed "in a temporary manner like a very expensive possession." "'The overseer,'" she announces, "nodding as if to imaginary people on both sides of the room, the tiniest smile on her face."

The scene in the parlor with Aunt Tempe and the rest of the family is comedy of the highest order, on a par with other great set pieces in Welty's fiction like Judge McKelva's funeral in *The Optimist's Daughter* or the near-drowning in *The Golden Apples*. It is in the smooth combination of the absurd with the lyrical and even the tragic that Welty, when she succeeds, does so most stunningly. The story "Kin," from *The Bride of the Innisfallen*, displays this delicate combination to great advantage. Dicey, a young woman who left Mississippi with her parents at the age of eight, is back visiting her Aunt Ethel and her cousins; her cousin Kate is her particular friend. Kate and Dicey, Aunt Ethel forcefully suggests, should go to Mingo—the "home place," the old family house—to visit their ancient Uncle Felix and "Sister Anne." Exactly how, they ask, is Sister Anne related to them?

> Aunt Edith looked patiently upwards as if she read now from the roof of the tester, and said, "Well, she's a remote

cousin of Uncle Felix's, to begin with. Your third cousin twice removed, and your Great-aunt Beck's half-sister, my third cousin once removed and my aunt's half-sister, Dicey's—"

"Don't tell me!" I cried. "I'm not that anxious to claim kin!"

"She'll claim you! She'll come visit you!" cried Kate.

Sister Anne, it transpires, is vaguely distasteful to Aunt Edith and her children, for the simple reason that they consider her common—although by the unspoken laws of their own class it would be *lèse majesté* to own to such snobbish distinctions. They scorn her pretensions—her writing to them, for instance, on a gilt-edged card—and they cannot resist probing her sensitive spots. All this is rich in the sharp, occasionally cruel humor of which Welty is a past master. But the story is much more than that: aside from being, like so much of Welty's work, a reflection on the comforts and claustrophobia of community, it is also a tale of memory, change, and loss. Behind the present, rather degraded Mingo, Dicey can remember the "real" house, and the "real" Uncle Felix of her childhood, and it is the extremely skillful combination of past and present that is the story's central achievement.

Welty is the author of five novels: *The Robber Bridegroom* (1942)—which is actually more fable than novel—*Delta Wedding* (1946), *The Ponder Heart* (1954), *Losing Battles* (1970), and *The Optimist's Daughter* (1972, first published in a different form in *The New Yorker* in 1969). Their quality is as uneven as that of the short stories; in fact only the first and most of all the last— an exquisite, almost perfect work—are really satisfactory as novels. *The Robber Bridegroom*, a playful historical romance of the Old Natchez Trace in the eighteenth century, combines folk elements, fairy tales, history, tall tales, and the ideal of Arcadia. It has had its share of passionate admirers including, most notably, Alfred Kazin; it has also had its detractors, the most persuasive being Lionel Trilling. Reviewing the book in *The Nation* upon its publication in 1942, Trilling put the narrative's easy charm in its place: its "lucidity," he wrote, "its grace, and its simplicity have a quality that invalidates them all—they are too conscious, especially the simplicity, and nothing can be falser, more purple and 'literary' than conscious simplicity." And how often, to be honest, do children's stories for adults really succeed? It is one of the hardest tones to strike, one of the hardest genres to pull off.

The Ponder Heart is another children's story for adults, more successful than *The Robber Bridegroom*: funnier, less fanciful, heightened at every moment by Welty's brilliant ear for language and idiosyncratic turns of speech; but still a little too conscious, too artificial, to amount to more than a *jeu d'esprit*. Uncle Daniel Ponder, the novel's ostensible focus, is a retarded gentleman, although true to the mores of his community the word "retarded" is never used, least of all by the narrator, the sensible Miss Edna Earle Ponder. (Circumlocution and gentle euphemism are characteristic of the culture to which Welty belongs and which she portrays so acutely. In her charming memoir *One Writer's Beginnings*, she recalls of her own mother that "she never in her life called anyone a fool, though she never bore one gladly, but she would say, 'Well, it appears to me that Mrs. So-and-So is the least bit limited.'") The action of *The Ponder Heart* centers around Uncle Daniel's marriage to a trashy girl, Bonnie Dee Peacock, and its inevitably disastrous outcome. It is all funny, smart, and technically accomplished, but the result is merely a comic tale rather than a novel—not, I think, that Welty ever meant it to be anything more.

Even for what it is, *The Ponder Heart* is marred by two weaknesses to which Welty was not immune: sentimentality and, worse, cuteness. In an unpretentious squib like *The Ponder Heart*, these flaws detract from the whole but need not ruin it. In work that pretends to high seriousness, though, they are fatal, as was the case with *Losing Battles*, the longest and most ambitious of Welty's novels. It was greeted with excessive praise when published, probably because of its length, scope, and the fact that Welty had not published a book in fifteen years. There was much ooh-ing and aah-ing over a novel that is at best mediocre, at worst both self-indulgent and self-congratulatory: Reynolds Price, for instance, deemed it "an almost frightening gift . . . of such plenitude and serene mastery as to reveal with panicking suddenness how thin a diet we have survived on."

Welty must have set too much store by her own reputation as a master of dialogue and idiom, for nearly all of this lengthy book is in the form of an extended conversation as three generations of a Mississippi hill family exchange stories and reveal, in their collective manner, the patterns and cycles of their lives. But the dialogue is disgustingly folksy and conscious; none of the many voices can be differentiated from one another; the themes are obvious and uninteresting. Worse, the narrative has a smug confidence in the virtue of its own statements and values that neutralizes the work's integrity. *Losing Battles* was nominated for a National Book Award and received almost unanimous accolades; in the long run it will turn out, I believe, to be the least regarded of her books.

The Optimist's Daughter is the most adult of Welty's novels, and also the most disciplined. A remarkably skillful interweaving of biographical with fictional material, this short but potent book carries great emotional weight. Laurel McKelva Hand, a forty-five-year-old widow who has long lived in Chicago, goes to New Orleans to be with her father as he undergoes an unpleasant eye operation. Laurel's mother has been dead for several years, and Judge McKelva has recently remarried a vulgar, stupid younger woman, Fay—a less cartoonish, although more vicious, version of Bonnie Dee Peacock in *The Ponder Heart*.

Judge McKelva does not recover properly after his surgery; instead he sinks into an inexplicable decline and finally dies. The two women take the body and return to the home that for Laurel is full of memories of her mother and father but to which Fay no longer welcomes her. Friends and neighbors visit and mourn; the funeral is organized and got through with only minor disasters; and Laurel prepares to leave the house forever, taking final leave not only of her parents but also of the young husband with whose death, twenty years earlier, she has never come to terms.

If Eudora Welty has not generally been accepted as one of the century's heavyweights, it is probably because she has been thought too regional and too feminine. Are these charges justified? Femininity, in a Southern writer, might actually be something of an advantage, since Southern society—at least among the middle and upper classes—is a matriarchal one, as Welty always recognized. Beginning with one of her first published stories, "Lily Daw and the Three Ladies" (1937), it is clearly the women who run things. In towns it is the monolithic and not-to-be-defied "ladies" who rule. In plantation life the same still holds, but the dynamic is different, as one of the characters in *Delta Wedding* reflects:

> In the Delta the land belonged to the women—they only let the men have it, and sometimes they tried to take it back and give it to someone else . . . All the men lived here on a kind of sufferance! . . . It was as if the women had exacted the place, the land, for something—for something they had had to give. Then, so as to be all gracious and noble, they had let it out of their hands—with a play of the reins —to the men . . . And of course those women knew what to ask of their men. Adoration, first—but least. Then, small sacrifice by small sacrifice, the little pieces of the whole body!

I think it can be said then that yes, Welty is a feminine writer; but it has yet to be demonstrated that this quality puts her at any disadvantage with her chosen material. To the taunt of regionalism, however, she was distinctly sensitive, and she addressed it with spirit in a 1956 essay entitled "Place in Fiction":

> It is by the nature of itself that fiction is all bound up in the local. The internal reason for that is surely that feelings are bound up in place. The human mind is a mass of associations—associations more poetic even than actual. I say, "The Yorkshire Moors," and you will say, *Wuthering Heights*, and I have only to murmur "If Father were only alive—" for you to come back with "We could go to Moscow," which certainly is not even so . . . Location pertains to feeling; feeling profoundly pertains to place; place in history partakes of feeling, as feeling about history partakes of place. Every story would be another story, and unrecognizable as art, if it took up its characters and plot and happened somewhere else. Imagine *Swann's Way* laid in London, or *The Magic Mountain* in Spain, or *Green Mansions* in the Black Forest. Jane Austen, Emily Brontë, Thomas Hardy, Cervantes, Turgenev, the authors of the books of the Old Testament, all confined themselves to regions, great or small, but are they regional? Then who from the start of time has not been so?

She has a point; for myself, I find Welty no more or less a regionalist than William Faulkner, Philip Roth, or Evan S. Connell: that is to say, they are all regionalists, but that quality can hardly be considered their most important one. Being accused of mere regionalism is the price Welty has had to pay for the exquisite skill with which she so frequently has caught the essence of the South: its beauty and ugliness, its charm, whether shallow or true, its narcissistic smirk, its spoken and unspoken hatreds, its "Southern look—Southern mask—of life-is-a-dream irony."

Welty's mother came from the West Virginia mountains, her father from an Ohio farm. She was always, then, something of an outsider in the Deep South of which she became one of the fore-most observers; the slight distance between her own vantage point and the landscape she depicted might well have contributed to the fine sharpness of her focus. Distance was, indeed, a necessary tech-nique of which she was highly aware. During the Depression she worked as a photographer for the Works Progress Administration, traveling through Mississippi to record the lives of local people. As she began writing fiction she consciously applied the photographic techniques of distancing and framing to her stories.

When her parents married in 1904 they decided to make their home somewhere unknown to them both. After some research into the matter, Christian Welty presented his wife with a choice between the Thousand Islands region and Jackson, Mississippi; Chestina chose Jackson. What sort of a writer (for surely she would have been a writer no matter what) might Eudora Welty have become if her mother had made the other choice? Would we now consider her a regional novelist of the North Country? What aspects of that region might she best have captured on the page?

If Welty is a specifically Southern writer, she is one not so much in her flair for character, place, or incident as in her peculiarly Southern obsession with family and community. All of Welty's best fiction deals on some level with these tortured subjects, as does that of so many Southern writers—*North Toward Home*, by Welty's fellow-Mississippian Willie Morris, can be seen as especially pertinent to her work.

There is more tolerance, in the Southern communities of which Welty writes, for eccentricity, stupidity, drunkenness, want of ambition, and general weirdness than exists elsewhere in Amer-ica. The tolerance is extended only, however, on condition of a certain measure of surrender to the community, a surrender that amounts merely to a willingness to be measured and defined by that community's standards. Thus in the town of Morgana, the setting for all the stories that make up *The Golden Apples*, the German piano teacher Miss Eckhart is forever a foreigner, more out of her own choice than the town's.

Missie Spights said that if Miss Eckhart had allowed herself to be called by her first name, then she would have been like other ladies. Or if Miss Eckhart had belonged to a church that had ever been heard of, and the ladies would have had something to invite her to belong to . . . Or if she had been married to anybody at all, just the awfullest man —like Miss Snowdie MacLain, that everybody could feel sorry for.

Morgana didn't ask so very much of its citizens, after all: "They only hoped to place them, in their hour or their street or the name of their mothers' people. Then Morgana could hold them, and at last they were this and they were that."

This is a price that most people, in the end, are willing to pay for the privilege of belonging. But what of those who refuse to pay it and, like Kipling's cat, choose instead to walk by themselves? In *The Golden Apples* there is one such character, Virgie Rainey. A Morgana insider by birth, she has a musical gift that sets her apart from her fellows. But she resists any role the town might try to cast her in, just as she resists the ambitions treasured for her by Miss Eckhart, who in Virgie has found a justification for her own vocation as a teacher. Virgie's strength is in her resistance. And after all, "They had all known Virgie would never go, or study, or practice anywhere, never would even have her own piano, because it wouldn't be like her . . . Perhaps nobody wanted Virgie Rainey to be anything in Morgana any more than they had wanted Miss Eckhart to be, and they were the two of them still linked by people's saying that."

What Virgie earns from her heroic stand is something more valuable, to her, than a musical career or even a sense of belonging;

it is a simple acknowledgement of her as different, as an individual, as someone who cannot be held and labeled by the town.

Laurel Hand in *The Optimist's Daughter* is a gentler soul than Virgie, and makes her break from her home town of Mount Salus in a gentler way. Nevertheless, it is a break. Married and widowed young, living in Chicago and working as a fabric designer for the past twenty years, she still thinks, to a large degree, of Mount Salus as home. After her father's funeral she slips effortlessly back into her place among the ladies of the town. They, too, feel that she is home, and urge her to move back to Mount Salus.

"Why not indeed?" said Miss Adele. "Laurel has no other life."

"Of course I must get back to work," said Laurel.

"Back to work." Miss Tennyson pointed her finger at Laurel and told the others, "That girl's had more now than she can say grace over. And she's going back to that life of labor when she could just as easily give it up. Clint's left her a grand hunk of money."

"Once you leave after this, you'll always come back as a visitor," Mrs. Pease warned Laurel. "Feel free, of course, but it was always my opinion that people don't really want visitors."

The ladies' blithe assumption that Laurel has no other life, their manner of implying, throughout Laurel's time in Mount Salus, that what goes on outside of their town is somehow fictional and certainly not of much account, is infuriating, yet it also defines the security and sanctuary such a community provides.

Laurel leaves; Welty herself, of course, stayed on in Jackson.

Robert Penn Warren once identified Welty's twin themes, correctly I think, as love and separateness. Love in her work, though, can be very broadly defined, and, as Edna Earle states in *The Ponder Heart*, "There's something I think's better to have than love, and if you want me to, I'll tell you what it is—that's company." The demands of the individual against the demands of the group: it is a particularly Southern theme, and perhaps a particularly feminine one as well. But the truth is that everyone, in every culture, is prey to these conflicting demands. Welty, who depicted them with such intelligence, more than earned her place as not just a regional but a universal artist.

(1999)

13. ANOTHER DAY,
ANOTHER DOLOR
OGDEN NASH

L ight verse used to be a vital part of American culture, high and low. It was by no means the exclusive turf of "real" poets: anyone could, and did, turn their hand to it. A birthday, wedding, or anniversary was always an excuse, if excuse were needed, for enthusiastic amateur versifying.

What brought this charming custom to an end? My grandmother, born in the late Victorian era, was an avid practitioner of the art; so were many of her friends and contemporaries. Nowadays the only person I know who still cranks out the occasional humorous ode or epithalamium is an ancient uncle, who has an ear for an eccentric rhyme. ("I'll wet my whistle; sit down with Cammy;/And watch Green Bay take on Miami.") Even children, who used to be encouraged to mark holidays and public events with celebratory poems, have succumbed to the minimalistic William Carlos Williams red-wheelbarrow aesthetic, forsaking the rhymed doggerel of the past—though I was pleased to see that in a recent issue of *The Chronicle of the Horse* where little girls were invited to eulogize their ponies, they did so in a decidedly retro fashion: one poem, I remember, began with: "My pony, Snickers, is snobby and rude/And he has a very bad attitude."

The high priest of this sort of fun was of course Ogden Nash (1902–71). He took the low humor of much light poetry and consistently raised it to the level of true wit, in Alexander Pope's formulation: "What oft was thought, but ne'er so well expressed." As a young and enthusiastic reader of poetry, good and bad, he had reflected that "if someone who knew the rules of versification, began writing bad poetry deliberately and consciously instead of unconsciously" it might "turn out to be fairly amusing." The result was stuff like the following (from "Spring Comes to Murray Hill"):

I sit in an office at 244 Madison Avenue
And say to myself, you have a responsible job, havenue?"

The difference between Nash's version of bad poetry and the real thing was his thorough internalization of rhythm. F. Scott Fitzgerald pointed this out in a letter to his daughter, who had been attempting some Nashian verse of her own. "Ogden Nash's poems," he told her, "are not careless, they all have an extraordinary inner rhythm. They could not possibly be written by someone who in his mind had not calculated the feet and meters to the last iambus or trochee. His method is simply to glide a certain number of feet and come up smack against his rhyming line." Thus a couplet like the following:

I wonder if the citizens of New York will ever get
    sufficiently wroth
To remember that Tammany crooks spoil the broth.

When the U.S. Postal Service issued a commemorative Nash stamp on the poet's hundredth birthday, it was nice to see that he looked exactly as one would have wanted him to: droll rather than handsome, clever eyes glinting from behind outsized spectacles. Now, with the publication of Douglas M. Parker's biography, I find that he lived, too, as one would have hoped: he was decorous, exceedingly gentle and polite, a loving family man thoroughly imbued with the Protestant work ethic. If one sometimes detects a faint odor of melancholy both in his poems and his letters, this aberrance is always kept strictly under control, for in the WASP ethos to which Nash faithfully adhered, melancholy is a symptom of self-indulgence and not an artistic treasure trove to be cultivated or explored.

Nash came from a family that was distinguished and well-to-do. His great-great-grandfather had been the Revolutionary governor of North Carolina, and the family gave its name to the city of Nashville. Nash spent his childhood in Savannah, Georgia and on a large estate in Rye, New York, but the family had to give this up after the business collapse of Nash's father. He attended St. George's School in Newport, Rhode Island, where he came under the influence of at least one wonderful teacher, Arthur Roberts: Roberts's grounding in correct usage enabled Nash, he later wrote his former mentor, to "hit upon the conscious employment of incorrect usage for my own devious ends," and it was "the love for the mother tongue that you instilled in me which enabled me to tease it and flirt with it to the limits of decency." Nash dropped out of Harvard after a single year and returned briefly to St. George's as a French master.

In 1922, with the Jazz Age in full swing, Nash arrived in New York, still with no inkling that he could make a living by writing. His first job was as a bond salesman; after a year and a half on the job, he had still sold only one bond—to his grandmother. He next turned to writing streetcar advertising, which he stuck with for a full two years. Believing that children's literature would offer the best possibility of actually getting into print, he and his roommate Joe Alger collaborated on a story called *The Cricket of Carador*, which was accepted for publication by Doubleday, Page & Company. Dan Longwell, the head of Doubleday's advertising department, took a shine to Nash and offered him a position as his assistant. Nash moved up in the ranks, becoming an editor of a Doubleday subsidiary called the Crime Club, and eventually a higher-level editor.

Nash focused his poetic experimentation during this period. He quickly decided that he did not have the makings of a serious poet. "There was a ludicrous aspect to what I was trying to do; my emotional and naked beauty stuff just didn't turn out as I had intended." Possibly; then again, one suspects that the sort of self-exposure involved in writing serious poetry was completely inimical to Nash's guarded character. Inspired by the light poet Samuel Hoffenstein and by a volume of animal verses by Roland Young, Nash tried his hand at the form. His success was immediate, as testified by a very early verse:

> The turtle lives twixt plated decks
> That practically conceal its sex.
> I think it clever of the turtle
> In such a fix to be so fertile.

Nash's development as a poet was intimately entwined with his courtship of Frances Leonard, whom he met late in 1928 and married two-and-a-half years later. It was a love match and a happy marriage, but possibly not always very easy: Frances could be dauntingly chilly and moody. Reading Nash's letters to his wife (collected by his daughter, Linell Nash Smith, and published in 1990 under the title *Loving Letters from Ogden Nash: A Family Album*), one gets the impression that Nash usually approached his wife hat in hand, anxious to please and propitiate. His brilliant little poem "A Word to Husbands" contains, as well as the best general matrimonial advice ever given, a clear enough picture of his own home life:

> To keep your marriage brimming,
> With love in the loving cup,

Whenever you're wrong, admit it,
Whenever you're right, shut up.

In one of his rare non-humorous poems, Nash celebrated his wife's changeable temper:

Praise the spells and bless the charms
I found April in my arms.
April golden, April cloudy,
Gracious, cruel, tender, rowdy;
April soft in flowered languor,
April cold with sudden anger,
Ever changing ever true—
I love April, I love you.

Fair enough, but reading between the lines one suspects that March might have been the more appropriate month to have chosen. Parker has written his biography with the cooperation of the two Nash daughters, so it's easy to understand why he doesn't venture very far in this direction.

Nash's long association with *The New Yorker* began in January, 1930, when they published "Invocation," a satirical jab at Senator Smoot of Utah, who in his earnest effort to protect the American public from imported pornography had assembled an impressive personal collection of the banned items:

Senator Smoot is an institute
Not to be bribed with pelf;
He guards our homes from erotic tomes
By reading them all himself.
Smite, Smoot, Smite for Ut.
They're smuggling smut from Balt. to Butte.

Nash is not widely thought of as a political writer, but he

frequently produced pointed rhymed commentary on current events and outrages, much as Calvin Trillin did decades later. Another gem of a political poem from that period is "Peekaboo, I see A Red":

> The results of the activities of the D.A.R. might not be
>   so minus—
> Were the ladies not troubled by sinus.
> Alas, every time they try to put people who don't agree
>   with them on the stand as defendants
> They find themselves troubled by the sinus of the
>   Declaration of Independence.

Nash's association with *The New Yorker* was an extraordinarily fruitful one; not only did the magazine help to shape his style, but he personally did a great deal to define the tone of the magazine as it developed. Ogden Nash was as integral a part of Harold Ross's *New Yorker* as James Thurber or Dorothy Parker. But it is possible to wonder whether Nash's talents might have developed rather more broadly if he had not been kept within the perimeters of the *New Yorker* sensibility by his editors. Katharine White, who was to be his principal editor at the magazine until her final retirement in 1958, rejected an early Nash short story, "Preface to a Wedding Trip"—which Dorothy Parker thought the best story she had read in years—because she found the characters and situation too vulgar. She also turned down his poem "Are Sects Necessary," which makes fun of the fastidious Protestant contempt for Catholicism: "Their righteousness runs too high a steeple;/I prefer the purple papal people." "Mr. Ross says he really just can't come out so wholeheartedly for the Catholic church," commented Mrs. White. "I wonder if you couldn't change the poem, making it against all sects and anti-everything." (Nash declined that suggestion, and included the original poem in his first collection.) All this emphasizes the fatal flaw in *The New Yorker*, a sort of prissiness and gentility that limited its aesthetic and limited, too, Nash's growth.

The poet's relationship with the magazine heated up when Ross, having run into Nash in a speakeasy, offered him a position as managing editor. Although Nash was not aware of it at the time, the job was essentially un-doable: no one ever measured up to Ross' impossible demands. Colleagues at the magazine referred to each successive occupant of the post as "the new Jesus"; by most counts, Nash was the twenty-fifth "Jesus" in six years. Nash was under no illusions about his own qualifications for the job, as he later related to Thurber. "I don't need to tell you that in many ways [Ross] was a strangely innocent man and he assumed that my presence in a speakeasy meant that I was a man about town. He was, I believe, still in mourning over the departure of [Ralph] Ingersoll, who had apparently been the ultimate in men about town, and was looking for a suave and worldly editor. He hired me practically on the spot." Nash lasted three months in the job, then moved on to an editorial position at Farrar and Rinehart.

E ventually Nash's success enabled him to leave office work and make his living as a freelancer. The money he earned from poetry was augmented, occasionally, by his forays to Broadway and Hollywood. His most gratifying showbiz venture was as the lyricist for the Kurt Weill musical *One Touch of Venus*; after this triumph he was bitten so hard by the theatrical bug that he tried several more stage ventures, all of them more or less disastrous, while as a contract screenwriter in Hollywood he underwent the degrading treatment, mindless assignments, and eventual depression that was the lot of all first-rate literary writers who tried to peddle themselves to the studios. He would later say that his stint in Hollywood "almost destroyed" him.

Other projects that supplemented the income he earned from his more than two dozen volumes of poetry (much of it originally published in *The Saturday Evening Post*, his major outlet aside from *The New Yorker*) included giving lectures, writing verses for Hallmark cards, limericks for *Playboy*, and advertising copy: he would sell just about anything but drew the line, he said, at writing a jingle for a constipation remedy. "If they want anything on pellagra, leprosy or syphilis I'm their man, but I'm afraid constipation is eliminated, if that isn't a contradiction in terms." He was especially brilliant on the subject of the countless petty irritations of modern life: Clifton Fadiman aptly dubbed him the Laureate of the Age of Friction. ("Progress was all right once," Nash remarked, "but it went on too long.") How much further he could have taken this theme if he had survived into the digital era!

Nash's verse may look ageless and timeless from the perspective of the twenty-first century, but that was not the case during his own lifetime: like so many writers who achieve a certain age, he lived to see himself go out of date. With the death of Harold Ross in 1951 *The New Yorker* was taken over by his deputy, William Shawn, whose sensibility was very different from that of his predecessor.

Nash died in 1971; he did not have to undergo the indignity of slipping further out of fashion, and his final poem was published posthumously in *The New Yorker*, along with a memorial tribute. The obituaries were adulatory, with *The Washington Post* describing him, succinctly and truly, as a "serious man who wrote funny." With Nash as with most of the world's great funny men, humor was not a pure substance but a composite one, a colorful mass of striations in which we can pick out not only comedy but pathos and even a sense of tragedy. But let Nash say it himself. Humor, he believed,

> is not brash, it is not cheap, it is not heartless. Among other things I think humor is a shield, a weapon, a survival kit . . . How are we to survive? Solemnity is not the answer, any more than witless and irresponsible frivolity is. I think

our best chance lies in humor, which in this case means a wry acceptance of our predicament. We don't have to like it but we can at least recognize its ridiculous aspects, one of which is ourselves.

Parker has done a tremendous service by writing this readable and workmanlike biography—the first biography of Nash, amazingly enough. His tale, within the inevitable constrictions attendant on writing an "authorized" life, is well told. But he and Dana Gioia, who has written the introduction, fail in their effort to persuade the reader that Nash was in some way "a product of modernism," a "populist modernist." To try to squeeze him into this category along with such uncongenial peers as Carl Sandburg and Vachel Lindsay seems, in the end, pointless. Almost perfectly free of influence and the anxiety that comes with it, he was what he was. And isn't that enough?

(2005)

14. WHIM OF IRON
JOHN BETJEMAN

The obsession of academic critics with differentiating "major" writers from "minor" ones, and summarily dismissing the latter, serves the interest of no one but their fellow-academics and actively harms not only those authors they deem minor, but also that large majority of the public who reads novels and poems purely for pleasure, with no scholarly or careerist motives. Within the academy, "major," at least since the heyday of Eliot and Pound, has tended to mean "difficult"— possibly because difficulty requires a need for expert interpretation and therefore justifies the existence of professional explicators. Kipling and Trollope, for example, so popular during the Victorian era as to have become an integral part of England's cultural fabric, are not only ignored in modern universities but actively denigrated.

This has also been true of postwar England's bestselling poet, John Betjeman (1906–84). The euphony of his words, the immediacy of his images, his mastery of traditional meter and rhyme schemes, in short the pure accessibility of his work has guaranteed its exclusion from "serious" studies of twentieth-century poetry. He simply did not fit into the modernist tradition, and his hugely successful career as a television personality and expert on the sort of architecture that had hitherto been considered pure kitsch did not raise his stock in academic circles. The 1993 edition of *The New Princeton Encyclopedia of Poetry and Poetics*, for instance, made no mention of Betjeman in all of its 1,383 pages. Neither did the 626 pages of *A Companion to Twentieth-Century Literature* (2001).

Technically, Betjeman did not advance beyond Tennyson, Praed, or Newbolt. For him, as Philip Larkin wrote (admiringly), "there has been no symbolism, no objective correlative, no T. S. Eliot or Ezra Pound, no reinvestment in myth, of casting of language as gesture, no Seven Types or Some Versions . . . " (Larkin allowed, however, that Betjeman did have a White Goddess: "in blazer and shorts.") His subject matter was almost aggressively retrograde; William Plomer smiled at the thought of "a new generation which is used to verse garnished with pylons and bombers and Arms for Spain and anti-Nazism and Hampstead surrealism" being "shocked by a poet who alludes to pink may, laburnum, tinned peas, cigar ends, church bells, gym shoes, deviled whitebait, hockey girls, picnics, racing-stables, and old City dining-rooms." And what other poet of his era would seriously have applied a Wordsworthian sense of wonder and joy to an utterly banal activity, as he did so beautifully in "Seaside Golf"?

> It lay content
> Two paces from the pin,
> A steady putt and then it went
> Oh, most surely in.
> The very turf rejoiced to see
> That quite unprecedented three.
>
> Ah! Seaweed smells from sandy caves
> And thyme and mist in whiffs,
> In-coming tide, Atlantic waves

Slapping the sunny cliffs,
Lark song and sea sounds in the air
And splendour, splendour everywhere.

Minor Betjeman might have been, but the poets who were his contemporaries, at least in England, thought him valuable and unique and banished the futile major/minor distinction to the irrelevance it has always deserved. To Edmund Blunden, Betjeman's work was "of the kind which makes the question of major and minor poets seem quite academic, at least while one reads and responds." Even Edmund Wilson, king of American critics, opined in the 1950s that "Since Dylan Thomas's death [Betjeman] is, I suppose, the best poet in England—a minor poet, perhaps, but a very, very good one." The fact that "minor" and "best" are not mutually exclusive terms might come as a surprise to academically trained readers.

Bevis Hillier, for one, entertains no doubts as to Betjeman's place in the canon, for he has dedicated more than twenty-five years of his life to writing a biography that is not only definitive but likely to remain so forever: it is hard to imagine anyone ever trying to top this three-volume, 1,530-page whopper. Even those who love the written word, and love Betjeman, might shy away from this doorstop. Betjeman himself suggested to Hillier that the proposed volumes would probably sell very well in old people's homes, and indeed one does wonder just how many individuals (as opposed to libraries) will buy this sequence: probably only true fanatics, sadly, so that it is doubtful whether it will win the poet many new readers.

Still, sheer volume of detail can sometimes wear down a reader's resistance, and this is such a case: after one has read eight or nine hundred pages, why not go on forever? And when an author expends himself on this sort of leisurely history, wonderful items turn up that might never appear in a more tightly controlled narrative. Where else, for example, could one find Osbert Lancaster's fabulous "Ode on the Wedding of Thomas Driberg, Esq., MP," from which I will quote a stanza? (Driberg was a well-known homosexual.)

> But hark, the Bishop's on his toes
> To ask if anybody knows
> "Just impediment or cause."
> There follows then an awkward pause.
> In every heart an anxious fear
> Of what we half expect to hear.
> Strike the organ! Beat the bell!
> The Past is silent! All is well!

Or Sir John Drummond's description of his backstage conversation with Barry Humphries (a.k.a. Dame Edna Everage) about the aged Betjeman's terminal illness:

> All [the talk] was a normal part of our shared concern for a much loved friend. But, though he can apparently do the voice when wearing male clothes, he cannot stop using the voice when got up as Edna, and I found it quite intolerable to be talking about the imminent death of one of my most cherished friends with this shrieking virago. I have always had more than a soft spot for Dame Edna . . . but in these circumstances she was too much and I excused myself apologetically.

There are countless such gems in this work. Many people are said to have known "everyone," but in Betjeman's case this is almost literally true, and while Hillier often gives minor figures in the poet's life unduly thorough treatment, there is enough gold to justify most of the dross.

.   .   .

John Betjeman, like so many writers, both loved and hated the social milieu from which he sprang, in his case the well-uphol-stered Edwardian middle class. The Betjemanns (the final, embarrassingly Germanic "n" was removed from the name by the poet himself) were unredeemedly bourgeois. Worse, they were "in trade," albeit a luxury trade: G. Betjemann & Sons were cabinet-makers. When John's father Ernest took over the business, its most popular item had been, surreal as this may seem, something called "the Betjemann patent tantalus," an apparatus for locking decanters of drink away from the servants—a detail which might have come straight out of John's favorite *Diary of a Nobody*. Ernest built the firm into a provider of very high-end craftsmanship that catered to Asprey's, Harrod's, and "the maharajah market."

The poet spent his early childhood in semi-suburban Highgate before his upwardly mobile parents moved to Chelsea. "The Betje-manns' stucco [Highgate] villa was about half-way up the social graph: the ideal vantage-point for gaining a nice sense of English social distinctions. Snobbery is a branch of applied sociology, and in this discipline John proved instinctually adept." His memories of one particular children's party are especially poignant. From "False Security":

> Can I forget my delight at the conjuring show?
> And wasn't I proud that I was the last to go?
> Too overexcited and pleased with myself to know
> That the words I heard my hostess's mother employ
> To a guest departing, would ever diminish my joy,
> I WONDER WHERE JULIA FOUND THAT STRANGE
> RATHER COMMON LITTLE BOY?

In Highgate he soaked up the ambiance that had provided inspiration to Marvell, Coleridge, Hopkins, and Housman; at Highgate Preparatory School, one of his teachers was the young

T. S. Eliot. Later he was sent as a boarder to the Dragon School in Oxford, where he came under the tutelage of the influential head-master A. E. ("Hum") Lynam. "Hum's preoccupation with reli-gion and the school services, I realize now, greatly affected me. Here was this great, but never remote and always kind man, inter-ested in religion." Thus began Betjeman's life-long love affair with English churches. Thus, too, began his love for Oxford: not so much the university with its dreaming spires as the dowdy, Gothic Revival North Oxford with its "ill-paid dons, suburban gardens, petty gossip, tinned peas, toothbrushes airing on the window-sill." (This is also the territory, some might remark, of Barbara Pym, who claimed to have been influenced more by Betjeman than by her fellow-novelists.)

Note the importance, in the above random list, of props and places almost as stage sets. Harold Acton would later call Betjeman "a genius of the *genius loci*, either pastoral or suburban," and many have considered him primarily a poet of place. Betjeman objected strongly to this formulation.

> I am not a pure poet of place. I bear no resemblance to Bloomfield or Clare and very little to Crabbe and only a little to Cowper but much more to him than the other three. This means to say that I write (and I know this) primarily with people in mind and relate the people to the background. When I am describing Nature, it is always with a view to the social background or the sense of Man's impotence before the vastness of the Creator.

That is, he clearly sees and communicates the places he describes, but always with a corresponding understanding of the lives lived in these places. This quality applied equally to his profes-sional forays into architecture. As Osbert Lancaster put it: "almost alone among contemporary writers on art, he is capable of whisking a building or a town out of the sterilized oxygen-tent in which the professional antiquarians have placed it . . . He is aware not only of the Saxon mouldings round the font but also of the tin bowl from the chain stores which the churchworker has left on top."

Betjeman knew from a very early age that he wished to be a poet, and educated himself accordingly. This may be one reason, as Hillier speculates, that his poetry is technically so old-fashioned: he learned his craft in childhood, with Victorian models, while his contemporaries began as university students, with modernism. Lord David Cecil reminded Hillier, "You have no idea how original it was for John to be writing in the style of Tennyson and other Victorians when his friends were all pastiching Eliot." The primary poetic influence of his childhood was indeed Tennyson, and it would be fair to say that Tennyson was the primary poetic influence of his mature years as well. From "Indoor Games near Newbury":

> Rich the makes of motor whirring,
> Past the pine-plantation purring
> Come up, Hupmobile, Delage!
> Short the way your chauffeurs travel,
> Crunching over private gravel
> Each from out his warm garage.

At the age of fifteen Betjeman was sent to Marlborough, an institution Spartan even by the standards of other English public schools of the era. One of the poet's contemporaries described it as "the most awful barbarous place, and it was extraordinary that people were willing to pay large sums of money to subject their children to it." Full emphasis, of course, was given to the classics, with little attempt to render the study palatable—much less, as in subsequent argot, "relevant." Beverley Nichols, who was at the school just before Betjeman, said that Greek was taught at Marl-borough "as though it were not merely dead but as though it had never lived at all," and Betjeman conceived a loathing for the Greek master, one A. R. Gidney, that he nursed for half a century and that rivaled his later great hates for his Oxford tutor, C. S. Lewis, and the art and architectural historian Nikolaus Pevsner.

The future poet Louis MacNeice was a fellow-pupil, and his memories show Betjeman as he left childhood's chrysalis and became the "character" that would soon be let loose on the world: "John Betjeman at that time looked like a will-o'-the-wisp with Latin blood in it. His face was the colour of peasoup and his eyes were soupy too and his mouth was always twisting sideways in a mocking smile and he had a slight twist in his speech which added a tang to his mimicries, syncopating the original just as a slightly rippling sheet of water jazzes the things reflected in it. He was a brilliant mimic but also a mine of information and a triumphant misfit."

Oxford, to which Betjeman repaired in 1925 only after twice failing the math and Latin exam required for entrance, greeted the misfit with open arms. Whenever possible he escaped the company of the uncongenially hearty C. S. Lewis and came under the benign influence—as so many of his distinguished contempo-raries did—of the eccentric and iconoclastic dons Maurice Bowra and "Colonel" George Kolkhorst. Many of the friends he made there were for life: Kenneth Clark, who would employ him during the Second World War; John Sparrow, the well-known academic; the novelists Henry [Yorke] Green and Anthony Powell; the rich Edward James, who published Betjeman's first book of poems; W. H. Auden, with whom he seems at one point to have enjoyed a brief sexual liaison; Alan Pryce-Jones, the editor and writer; the Labour politician Hugh Gaitskell; the cartoonist Osbert Lancaster; the aristocrats Patrick Balfour (later Lord Kinross), Frank Pakenham (later the Earl of Longford), Billy Clonmore (later the Earl of Wicklow); and Basil, the Marquess of

Dufferin and Ava, who was killed in the war and with whom Betjeman claimed to have been more in love than with anyone else in his life.

A word on Betjeman's sexuality: his early experiences, as with so many of his public school and university contemporaries, were homosexual. In later life, Hillier says, "John's tastes were predominantly heterosexual, but he liked to speculate about the 'percentage' of homosexuality in people's psychological make-up, including his own. He commented on a well-known Conservative politician, 'I never realized what percent he was until I saw him pouring tea.' His own 'percentage' probably remained above the average, but Alan Pryce-Jones thought that John's occasional professions of homosexuality should not be taken too literally." Late in life, he speculated on his own tastes: "I think by nature I'm masochistic. So far as the body is concerned I prefer taking orders to giving them." Hence his famous penchant for muscular, sporty girls, especially tennis players and cyclists. From "A Subaltern's Love Song":

> Love-thirty, love-forty, oh! weakness of joy,
> The speed of a swallow, the grace of a boy,
> With carefullest carelessness, gaily you won,
> I am weak from your loveliness, Joan Hunter Dunn.
> Miss Joan Hunter Dunn, Miss Joan Hunter Dunn,
> How mad I am, sad I am, glad that you won.
> The warm-handled racket is back in its press,
> But my shock-headed victor, she loves me no less.

He made a bit of a joke of this propensity (glimpsing a strapping woman one day in the Tate Gallery, he squawked to his companion, "Oh I say, wouldn't you like to be pushed in a pram by her round Hyde Park?"), but it was real enough, proved by the fact that both his wife and his longtime mistress, different though they were, belonged to the dominatrix type.

Betjeman made a strong impression at the university (his eccentric attachment to his teddy-bear Archie, for instance, was immortalized by Evelyn Waugh in *Brideshead Revisited*'s ill-fated Sebastian Flyte). But his academic career was not a success. His downfall, ironically, was persistent failure in Divinity, which at that time was required for a degree. How he managed to fail a subject in which he was already beginning to acquire an encyclopedic knowledge is something of a mystery. In Bowra's opinion, "unconsciously he wished to fail . . . He had no wish to take his finals, for which he had done very little work, and found instinctively a way out." Sent down without a degree in 1928, he followed the example of countless other Oxford failures (including both Waugh and one of his most famous creations, Paul Pennyfeather in *Decline and Fall*) and betook himself to Gabbitas and Thring, scholastic agents.

He fetched up at Heddon Court, Cockfosters. While the other masters thought him a subversive influence, he was rapturously received by the boys, as one of them recalled years later.

> The hitherto familiar and laborious hours of "parsing" and grammar were transformed into the sounds and usage and rhythms of words conveyed with such inspiration that sparks of understanding seemed to be struck from every single and different boy in the classroom. Few, if any, were insulated from J.B.'s electrifying and entirely communicable vision of literature.

Intimations, in short, of Betjeman's remarkable appeal and success as a television performer and popularizer of architecture in later years. "The great thing about John," said one of his producers, "is that he wanted you to share his love and enthusiasm." His style of didacticism did not significantly change during the course of his life. At Heddon Court he turned the school's high regard for games upside-down and promoted his own idols, literature and architecture. "He made it all such fun," recalled the former student, "and so attractive, that we readily accepted his standards."

But he never had any intention of wasting his life in an obscure boys' school. He soon procured a job as third in command at *The Architectural Review*, a magazine that had a good deal of influence in the architecture world. To be anti-modernist was then akin to sacrilege, and Betjeman toed the line with the best of them, although doubts were already beginning to simmer. But he was to prove constitutionally unable to stick to any job for long. Novelty inevitably "degenerated into routine, routine into drudgery." When Peter Quennell visited Betjeman at the *Review* office, he remembered a desk heaped with papers. "Among them," said Quennell, "I saw a huge blotting-pad, evidently quite new, on which, using a sharp pencil and decorative Gothic script, he had inscribed the now familiar couplet: "I sometimes think that I should like/To be the saddle of a bike." Betjeman brought in clever new contributors like Waugh, Lancaster, and Billy Clonmore, but he was the world's most unlikely apostle of modernism and when the chance came to edit county guides for a series that Shell-Mex was planning to put out, he grabbed it. The guides, when they appeared, were superb: Betjeman, again, brought in high-level contributors, including Quennell, Waugh, Paul Nash, and his new bosom friend John Piper, with whom he collaborated to produce the Shropshire volume.

Once liberated from the modernist party line, Betjeman was free to develop and indulge his real passions: Victorian and Georgian architecture, and churches. Nancy Mitford's light novel *Christmas Pudding* provides a good caricature of him at this period in the campy guise of Paul Fotheringay, a fey foil to the solid county characters. "John B.," commented Waugh in his diary at about this period, "became a bore rather with Irish peers and revivalist hymns and his enthusiasm for every sort of architecture." Betjeman and his cronies liked to make a bit of a game of their interests, choosing some inconsequential neighborhood, or suburb, or odd building and paying it mystifying homage. Waugh has given the best description of the routine, which Betjeman would develop and fine-tune over the years:

> The normal process of Betjemanizing is first the undesired stop in a provincial English town, then the "discovery" there of a rather peculiar police station, circa 1880; the enquiry and identification of its architect. Further research reveals that a Methodist Chapel in another town is by the same hand. Then the hunt is up. More buildings are identified. The obscure name is uttered with a reverence befitting Bernini. The senile master is found to be alive, in distressed circumstances in a northern suburb of London. He is a "character"; he has vague, personal memories of other long dead, equally revered contemporaries. In his last years he is either rejuvenated or else driven mad to find himself the object of pilgrimage.

Betjeman's first volume of poetry, *Mount Zion* (1932), and his first book of prose, *Ghastly Good Taste* (1933), were written at around the same time, and the poetry is just as truthful a reflection of his architectural and antiquarian interests as the prose. (Note some of the titles of the poems: "Croydon," "Westgate-on Sea," "For Nineteenth-Century Burials.") It is all funny, in best Betjeman style, but those with discernment could sense his underlying seriousness and even formulate it for him: as the *Country Life* reviewer of *Ghastly Good Taste* wrote, "Behind the persiflage is his conviction that good architecture is the expression of a faith, and herein lies the originality of his approach to the old story of architecture's history. He does not mind what the faith may be—mystical, rational, or intellectual; chapel, church, or State—but he believes fervently in the need for it. When it becomes self-conscious, art declines, and when it disappears, beauty vanishes with it, he declares."

It was perhaps with this sense of the necessity of faith rather than any deep personal beliefs that Betjeman eventually deviated from Quakerism and chose his own religious path, that of High Anglicanism. It was Anglicanism's historic broadness and inclusiveness that held him: "the dear old rumbling Church of England which is high, low and broad all at one . . . the Catholic Church of this country." The Roman Catholic Church, with its certainties and infallibilities, distressed him. Religion and family: traditionally sources of shelter, comfort, and certitude. Yet neither was to prove such for Betjeman. Religion for him was inextricably tied up with fear—possibly the legacy of a Calvinist nanny—and Family with guilt.

Betjeman clearly wanted to marry "up"; two of his first serious girlfriends were Lady Mary St. Clair Erskine and the Honorable Pamela Mitford. His final choice was Penelope Chetwode, the daughter of Field-Marshal Sir Philip Chetwode, the Army's Commander-in-Chief in India.

Penelope had inherited—or at any rate acquired—her father's commanding, super-assured manner. A bossy, horsy girl, apparently the quintessence of the fearsome English memsahib, she perfectly fit with Betjeman's wish for female domination. (For those who are interested, Penelope is portrayed as the title character in Evelyn Waugh's *Helena* and also figures in Lord Berners's camp classics, *The Camel* and *Far from the Madding War*; she is the model, too, for Philippa Townsend in Bruce Chatwin's *On the Black Hill*.) The German maid who worked for the Betjemans during their early days together initially assumed that John's Christian name was "Shutup," as that was how he was frequently addressed. Even Penelope's closest friends found her exhausting. Many years later James Lees-Milne reacted with panic to the idea of her coming to live nearby: "I don't think I could bear it. I love her dearly, but she is impossible to be with for more than two hours. She bulldozes one, is utterly self-centred. She overwhelms and overbears."

Youthful high spirits saw them through the first years. Their home at Uffington in Berkshire was a hive of social and domestic activity. "Penelope invented 'free range' long before anybody thought up the expression," recalled Lancaster. "The place was an animal sanctuary—and it stank." Penelope, he wrote, had "a missionary zeal for widening the cultural horizons of her rural neighbors" and "under her direction the Uffington Women's Institute became a transforming influence and its ceaseless activities demanded the full co-operation of all her friends." One evening, "the principal item on the programme was a performance of 'Summer is icumen in' sung by Adrian Bishop, Maurice Bowra, my wife and the poet himself, accompanied on the piano by Lord Berners and by Penelope on a strange instrument resembling a zither. My own contribution to the ensemble took the form of a flute obbligato. So powerful was the effect that all remained rooted to their seats."

But things are seldom as simple as they seem. The apparently ineffectual Betjeman proved to be a master of passive-aggression and had, as Anthony Powell once noticed, "a whim of iron." He immediately gained the emotional upper hand in the marriage, though it seemed to be a source of guilt rather than enjoyment to him. He and Penelope were never compatible, and his infidelities —along with her jealousy—were fatal. When he permanently transferred his affections to Lady Elizabeth Cavendish in the 1950s not only Penelope but he, too, suffered. Fatherhood was not much better. "Of all the fathers I have known, not excepting myself, he was the worst," wrote Alan Pryce-Jones. "I think he liked the idea of being a father . . . But he found that being a father was no fun at all." Relations with his daughter Candida tended to be smooth, but he teased Paul, his son, mercilessly. The boy responded by drawing as far away as possible; father and son were estranged for many years.

Betjeman's reputation as a poet rose steadily. In 1937 his new publisher, John Murray, brought out *Continual Dew*, then *Old Lights for New Chancels* in 1940 and *New Bats in Old Belfries* at the end of the war. Having started out as a coterie figure with a cultish readership, Betjeman began reaching an ever-widening group, until eventually he became the nation's best-selling and possibly best-loved poet. The feat he performed as a poet is rather extraordinary; he brought serious poetry back to the general reader. Eliot's famous dictum that contemporary poetry must be difficult had, it seemed, been at least temporarily repealed. There were complaints, like that of the American critic A. Alvarez who grumpily responded to the runaway success of Betjeman's *Collected Poems*: "the revolution called 'modern poetry,' on which all our critical standards are founded, never took place for a huge proportion of the English poetry-reading public. They are still living in some hazy pre-Prufrock Never-Never Land." What Alvarez and his ilk didn't acknowledge was that modernist poetry had stubbornly remained the business of an elite, and the contract between the serious writer and the general public had been breached. Betjeman brought them together again. The key to his achievement, perhaps, lies in a belief, as Philip Larkin pointed out, "that poetry is an emotional business, rather than an intellectual and moral one."

In a better age Betjeman would have found a rich patron. As things stood he had to earn a living, a task he found perpetually onerous. It was not that he was inefficient, though he tried hard to give that impression so as to escape tedious professional and domestic tasks: Hillier says that while he was often called "bumbling," he could be perfectly businesslike when it suited him. It was simply that he bored too easily and fatally lacked stick-to-itiveness. He worked as a film critic, a freelance book reviewer, an editor, a copywriter for Shell, assistant director of the books division at the British Council—and failed in all these jobs. During the war he worked in the films department at the Ministry of Information (as one of his colleagues remarked, "it says much for the British Civil Service that, in an hour of grave peril for the nation, it has actually been able to find something for John Betjeman to do"), as the British press attaché (some said spy) in neutral Ireland, and in the Admiralty. Again, at none of these ventures was he much use except as a dispenser of charm—not that his employers were ungrateful for this gift. Later, as the most vocal and visible architectural preservationist in England, he served on numerous committees; again, he often turned out to be less useful and successful in this field than his arch-nemesis, Nikolaus Pevsner, the apostle of *Kunstgeschichte*, whose Prussian efficiency and professionalism offended his determined sense of amateurism.

It was not until his histrionic and didactic gifts were discovered by the new medium of television that Betjeman found work that was both congenial and lucrative. He was, as producers and directors immediately observed, a natural: charm, energy, erudition, all directed full force at the audience ("our readers," as he called them) without a shade of condescension or "talking down." The programs were produced at the height of his poetic fame, in the wake of the huge sales of *Collected Poems* (1958) and his long autobiographical poem *Summoned by Bells* (1960). Among the classic television documentaries he hosted from the early 1960s on were *The ABC of Churches, Pride of Place, A Passion for Churches, Four with Betjeman*, and the hugely popular *Metroland* (1973). These shows, in the end, did far more for architectural conservation than his previous efforts. As Hillier insists, they "won over the public to Victoriana more effectively than a hundred well-researched works by Pevsner could have done."

The television appearances confirmed Betjeman in his role as, in the words of some unsympathetic observers, "teddy-bear to the nation." He was knighted in 1969. (Speaking for thousands, the writer Angus Wilson expressed his congratulations as one who had "attended your adolescent dances, your beach cricket, and wept with you at the Café Royal and the Cadogan Hotel. Long years of rhododendrons and pony clubs to you.") Three years later he was selected as poet laureate upon the death of Cecil Day-Lewis.

T he laureateship tends, like the Nobel, to be the kiss of death; the necessity for providing appropriate and, most of all, inoffensive verses upon royal events strangles creativity. "One knows poetry can't be written to order," Betjeman said. "One just waits for something to come through from The Management upstairs [God] and The Management can be very capricious." He failed his first test, Princess Anne's wedding, badly. One would have thought the courtship of two Olympic riders a natural subject for Betjeman, but of course no levity was allowed. Trying to squeeze out a poem for the Silver Jubilee was "trauma." Many began to realize that Betjeman, conservative and royalist though he was, might have been the worst possible choice as laureate.

He was also beginning to suffer the early symptoms of the Parkinson's Disease that would eventually cripple him. In the 1970s he gave up his flat in the City and moved to Chelsea to be near Elizabeth Cavendish. She, like Penelope, was an extremely controlling type, but unlike Penelope she catered to his needs and comforts. More than one friend thought that Penelope's neglect of these contributed almost as much to the breakup of the marriage as her 1947 conversion to Roman Catholicism, which had upset him deeply.

Swinging Chelsea in the 1970s was probably the least sympathetic abode Betjeman could have found, and the poet fell prey to anxiety and depression. Moreover, in his last years Betjeman was laid so low by Parkinson's, strokes, and heart attacks that his peaceful death in 1984—with Archie the teddy-bear and Jumbo

the elephant in either arm, and the cat asleep on his stomach—
came as a relief to those who loved him. Though he had proved
(like so many!) an unsatisfactory laureate, the Establishment sent
him out in style with a splendiferous memorial service at Westminster Abbey, presided over by the Archbishop of Canterbury and
with the Prince of Wales reading the lesson. Anthony Powell
recorded his impressions of the event in his journal: "One could
not help indulging in rather banal reflections about the seedy
unkempt (but never in the least unambitious) Betjeman of early
days, snobbish objections to him at Oxford, Chetwodes' opposi-
tion to the marriage, crowned at the last by all this boasted pomp
and show. It was a remarkable feat."

Bevis Hillier's task in recording this feat has not always been
easy. This is an "authorized" biography, and though it is chock-full
of marvelous gossip it is clear that Hillier was compelled to be
discreet in places; Elizabeth Cavendish, in particular, is treated
with kid gloves, and the startling appearance of a second "wife" at
Ernest Betjemann's funeral is never followed up. But Hillier has
succeeded in producing, one feels, an essentially honest portrait.
Sympathetic but not sycophantic, he communicates both Betjeman's tremendous charm and also the less agreeable sides to his
character. Wisely, he has done this not by quoting the poet's
enemies but his friends, such as Myfanwy Piper. Betjeman, she
recalled, approached all human relationships through an idea or an
invented situation. "'Approached' is perhaps the wrong expression:
'staved off' is more like it."

This concept of "staving off" was echoed by Elizabeth Jane
Howard.

> He enjoys bouts of willful rapture. There was (I thought) a
> rather unprepossessing boy/girl who provoked an
> outburst. "What a lovely girl! I thought with those trousers
> and those freckles she was a boy, but she was a girl! Didn't
> you think she was perfectly lovely? I thought she was beau-

tiful," and so on. I think this is all part of the scheme to keep affectionate laughter going. He is extremely sensitive to other people, and it is his way of having a rest from them.

Generally speaking, he was a better friend than he was a husband, a father, or a son—as so often seems the case with creative artists. The extraordinary receptivity that produces the art becomes hypersensitivity in close relationships. And Betjeman was receptive, abnormally so. It is that quality, added to his ear and glorious verbal facility, that made him not just a wonderful light poet or a wonderful minor poet but a wonderful poet, *tout court*.

(2005)

15. THE NOVELIST
UNAUTHORIZED
ANTHONY POWELL

The question of "authorized" versus "unauthorized" biographies has always been a troubled one. Authorized lives, on the one hand, tend to be too polite, too considerate of the feelings of the subject and his family—necessarily so since these people usually control access to vital materials and memories, so that their goodwill becomes essential for the success of the project. Unauthorized biographies, on the other hand, are often either scurrilous (authorization being withheld on that very account), or, if sympathetic, badly weakened by the author's lack of access to sources.

Michael Barber's *Anthony Powell: A Life* falls into the latter category. The Powell family (Powell himself died in 2000, at the age of 94) had chosen Hilary Spurling, the author of well-regarded lives of Paul Scott and Ivy Compton-Burnett, as the authorized biographer. But Barber, notable for his highly entertaining book on the disreputable novelist Simon Raven, refused to acknowledge rejection and pressed ahead with his own Powell biography.

The bad news: not only did Powell's family and friends withhold help from Barber, they seem even to have tried to hinder him: never have I read a biography that used fewer primary sources. The book contains no unpublished material, nothing that cannot be found in Powell's own four volumes of memoirs (collected under the title *To Keep the Ball Rolling*), his three volumes of Journals, or the published memoirs and journals of his friends and contemporaries. Nor will the reader find any original or even particularly thoughtful approaches to Powell's work; Barber is less interested in literary criticism than in providing a *clef* to Powell's *romans*, though even in this department he presents us with very few surprises, for *To Keep the Ball Rolling* already gave all the clues we really need to the various characters who inspired his great *roman-fleuve*, *A Dance to the Music of Time*.

The good news: the book is extremely readable. Barber, with his Rabelaisian humor and his characteristic style, brisk almost to the point of crudeness, did a brilliant job with the equally crude and Rabelaisian Simon Raven, but he might have been a very bad mismatch for the fastidious—in the subject's own words, "frightfully buttoned up"—Powell. Oddly, this has not proved to be the case, and at times Barber's plain talking, set against Powell's coy elusiveness, has a bracing effect. British reviewers (including Spurling herself in Powell's own longtime venue, *The Telegraph*) expressed pained disgust at Barber's use of vulgarisms, specifically "up your arse," but it should be noted that David Pennistone, one of the few entirely charming and sympathetic characters in *A Dance to the Music of Time*, uses the very same phrase. Powell could have a tendency to seem stuffy; Barber's breeziness undercuts this slight pomposity without ever tainting his sympathy for the man and his work.

A case in point is Powell's interest in genealogy, which he stuffed into his memoirs, tracing his family back to South Wales in the fifth century A.D. Barber would seem to be of the opinion that a taste for genealogy, like a taste for pornography, is best enjoyed in private, and he refuses to indulge Powell's little hobby in his own narrative.

Such interests—Powell claimed that Debrett's was his favorite bedside reading—and the often Blimpish, high Tory attitudes expressed in the Journals, have not helped Powell's posthumous reputation, and as we move into a century so vastly at odds, socially and technologically, with the world he wrote about, he is becoming marginalized as the specialized taste of the old-fashioned, the Tory, the aesthetically conservative. John Carey, reviewing the Barber book in London's *Sunday Times*, brutally lambasted Powell as a man with "no ideas," a second-rate Evelyn Waugh, a snob "incapable of conveying deep feeling" who "knew about only a tiny upper stratum of English society." This is so patently wrong that it deserves a thorough rebuttal, more thorough even than Barber gives us.

A snob? First of all, even if the charge were true, we must remember that snobbery has never proved a fatal handicap either to good writing or deep feeling. Proust, Henry James, Fitzgerald were all snobs of the deepest dye. But there is really nothing of the snob in Powell's narrative consciousness or in his treatment of his characters. The most deeply sympathetic characters in *Dance*, like Hugh Moreland and X. Trapnel, come from the middle classes; those from still lower strata, like Ted Jeavons, or Rowland Gwatkin, the idealistic Welsh bank clerk turned wartime officer, possess as much dignity and poignancy as anyone in the sequence. Kenneth Widmerpool's odiousness derives from his character, not his background: his unexalted origins (his father dealt in liquid manure) are structurally necessary to accentuate his rise to power, especially insofar as it serves as a foil to Charles Stringham's rapid social descent. In any case, Stringham's charm and aristocratic luster guarantee neither strength nor virtue; neither, in the end, does his very real wit. The seeds of his self-destruction are evident from the very first of the sequence's twelve volumes. And as a final argument against seeing Powell as a snob, here is one of his characters, Sir Gavin Walpole-Wilson: a true snob. No one who could write this passage could be a snob, at least not in the simple sense of the word:

> "As a matter of fact, the Wilsons are, if anything, an older family than the Walpoles—well, perhaps not that, but at least as old," he used to say. "I expect you have heard of Beau Wilson, a young gentleman who spent a lot of money in the reign of William and Mary, and was killed in a duel. I have reason to suppose he was one of our lot. And then there was a Master of the Mint a bit earlier. The double-barrel, which I greatly regret, and would discard if I could, without putting myself and my own kith and kin to a great deal of inconvenience, was the work of a great-uncle—a most consequential ass, between you and me, and a bit of a snob, I'm afraid—and has really no basis whatever, beyond the surname of a remote ancestor in the female line."

The criticism that Powell dealt with "only a tiny upper stratum of English society" is absurd. One of the most successful elements of *Dance* is the movement of the narrator, Nicholas Jenkins, beyond that tiny upper stratum—Eton, Oxford (both of which are unnamed but obvious), and the stiflingly ingrown circuit of London debutante balls—into the wider world of bohemia and the arts, and the way these worlds unexpectedly interact. The turning point comes at Milly Andriadis's high bohemian party in *A Buyer's Market*, the first such gathering Jenkins has attended. Upon arrival he is embarrassed to be seen in the louche company of Mr. Deacon and Gypsy Jones, but he soon discovers, to his surprise, that they blend quite unobtrusively into the background. It was the beginning of a new order particular to the Twenties, when "it was possible," Powell later wrote, "for the most unlikely people to meet each other in a manner which today [1951] would be, to say the least, unexpected."

What really needs to happen, but probably never will in

today's ruthlessly leveling society, is for Powell's critics to follow the advice he himself doled out to those of Evelyn Waugh: to stop talking about what a snob he was and start talking about how good the writing was. And speaking of Waugh, to call Powell a lesser Waugh makes no sense at all. They were of the same generation and used a similar cast of characters, but there the resemblance ends; Waugh's wild, powerful farce was miles away from Powell's nuanced irony. As Alan Pryce-Jones commented,

> As a young novelist, Anthony Powell had a stroke of bad luck: he happened to be just two years younger than Evelyn Waugh, so that his own *Afternoon Men* came into a world already conditioned by *Decline and Fall* and *Vile Bodies*. This . . . concealed from the public that a very unusual talent, slow to ripen, but capable of astonishing extension and modulation, had made its first appearance.

Like Waugh, Powell was a political conservative in a generation that favored the Left, but there is no need to be a Tory in order to enjoy their work, and George Orwell himself named Powell as "the only Tory I have ever liked."

One cannot be a great writer or even a passable one without ideas, and the charge that Powell lacks ideas is incomprehensible. The whole of *A Dance to the Music of Time* can be seen as the illustration of an idea, frequently articulated by Powell's friend Malcolm Muggeridge, that life amounts to a titanic struggle between the Will and the Imagination.

In Widmerpool, the abstract concept of Will takes an appropriately grotesque form, and his career illustrates the fact that while those who live by the Will profit from their single-mindedness with worldly honors, the contest, on some level, can never end: Widmerpool expires, fittingly enough, while undergoing the same sort of joyless, expiatory run that Jenkins recalls from their schooldays, when the plodding fellow seemed to be forever practicing for teams for which he would never be chosen and races he would never win.

Those who live by the Imagination tend to forego—at least during their lifetimes—the honors and prizes that a Widmerpool, or a Sir Magnus Donners, scoop up; it is the price they pay for the luxury of having an Imagination and living inside it. Moreland's musical genius makes him literally unfit for the struggle of what Jenkins thinks of as "the Acceptance World," and the same is true of the writer X. Trapnel, who can barely scrape up the price of a drink but who becomes, after his death, the subject of bitter academic turf wars. Stringham, who lives by the Imagination but is sustained by no corresponding artistic talent, undergoes an abject life but dies (unlike Widmerpool and the other power brokers) with dignity and even a species of heroism. His alcoholism is key: in Powell's books, as Barber points out, drinkers (and by extension Trapnel, a doper) self-destruct but do not impose on others; it is the abstemious control-freaks, like Widmerpool, Sillery, and Sir Magnus Donners, who are really dangerous.

Not all men of the Imagination are artists, and not all men of the Will are businessmen. The litterateurs J. G. Quiggin and Mark Members, for instance, are more driven by Will than Imagination, and their careers are accordingly successful. The trajectory of Members (loosely based on Peter Quennell) is characteristic. It is evident even on our first glimpse of him, as a precocious Oxford poet in *A Question of Upbringing*, that Members is embarked on building a reputation rather than a body of work: he emphasizes his boyishness with a floppy fringe and arranges himself in picturesque attitudes.

Just as Quiggin had dealt with the last crumb, Members rose suddenly from the sofa and cast himself, with a startling bump, almost full length on the floor in front of the fireplace: exchanging in this manner his Boyhood-of-Raleigh posture for that of the Dying Gladiator. Sillery, whose back was turned, started violently, and Members pleaded: "You don't mind, Sillers? I always lie on the floor."

Nearly half a century later he has become the old man one might have predicted. From *Hearing Secret Harmonies*: "Members, his white hair worn long, face pale and lined, had returned to the Romantic Movement overtones of undergraduate days. His air was that of an eighteenth-century sage too highminded to wear a wig—Blake, Benjamin Franklin, one of the Encyclopaedists—suitable image for a figure of his eminence in the cultural world." His collected poems—from the early "Iron Aspidistra" to the late "H-Bomb Eclogue"—have just been published, and, as we can see from their titles, they encapsulate the history of literary fashion between 1930 and 1970. He has, in other words, morphed completely into the self-important, fashion-driven "man of letters" exemplified by his former employer St. John Clarke, a hoary Edwardian relic, author of the novels *Fields of Amaranth* and *Match Me Such Marvel*, who loomed large during Members's and Jenkins' younger days and whom the young Members manipulated and patronized.

In Powell's scheme there is, I think, a third category that Michael Barber has missed: the person who lives not by the Imagination or the Will but by the senses. The prototype here is Peter Templer, who even as a boy found "no truth except in tangible things." Templer, who on his father's advice skips university to go directly into business, quickly coarsens in the constant company of men like the crude Bob Duport, but Templer's downfall is not money or power—he is not, in fact, ambitious—but women. When Sir Magnus Donners casts him in the role of Lust in the Seven Deadly Sins pageant at Stourwater, he is only stating the obvious. What is interesting, and the irony of situation is not lost on Jenkins, is that while Templer was the first of his contemporaries to be comfortable with women, losing his virginity to a London tart while still a schoolboy and later becoming a compulsive and highly successful womanizer, both of his marriages are disastrous and he dies, in wartime, in a quixotic and failed quest for a woman's love.

Templer reaps none of the rewards either of the Will or the Imagination; as a personification of Lust he gets the worst of both worlds, and his life, one feels, has been wasted. With all this in mind, it can be seen that the first chapter of *Dance* sets up the entire scheme of the novel sequence, contrasting the Will (Widmerpool), the Imagination (Stringham), and the Senses (Templer) as they begin their life's journey.

There are few factual surprises in Barber's book. The details of Powell's life are, as might be expected, very substantially the same as Nick Jenkins's. What one might have hoped was for a bit more of the self-effacing Powell to be exposed to our view, but this doesn't happen. Jenkins was not the hero of *Dance*, and Powell was not the hero of his memoirs; he is the hero of the Barber biography, but the picture we get of him is always refracted. In the absence of more personal material, in fact, Barber has sometimes had to resort to deducing Powell's thoughts and feelings from Jenkins's—a dangerous business. This only serves to prove the theory memorably formulated in *Hearing Secret Harmonies* by X. Trapnel (who, though based on Julian Maclaren-Ross, often serves as a mouthpiece for Powell), that there is more truth in fiction than in biography:

> "People think that because a novel's invented, it isn't true. Exactly the reverse is the case. Because a novel's invented, it is true. Biography and memoirs can never be wholly true, since they can't include every conceivable circumstance of

what happened. The novel can do that. The novelist himself lays it down. His decision is binding. The biographer, even at his highest and best, can be only tentative, empirical. The autobiographer, for his part, is imprisoned in his own egotism."

Or, to quote Sir Thomas Browne, "Some Truths seem almost Falsehoods and Some Falsehoods almost Truths"—"in a sense the justification," Powell remarked in his memoirs, "of all novel writing."

Jenkins is depicted primarily in negative terms. Philip Mason described him as "the almost invisible man, the universal unobtrusive confidant and observer." Mason, a longtime friend of Powell's, also said that Powell himself played that role to perfection, even as an undergraduate. James Michie, Powell's editor at Heinemann's, gives a complementary view of the subject later in life: "Like most Etonians he had superb manners, to which was added great charm and an endearing smile. You were so at ease with him that you said much more than you'd intended, particularly about something like sex. At the same time, he managed to be very oblique about himself." Oblique but not opaque; Muggeridge claimed that "for those that have eyes to see, the life story and character of Powell is unfolded with extraordinary vividness in Nicholas's narration."

Jenkins is bland; dry; prickly, but unwilling to expose himself enough to admit to taking offense; snobbish, but in the intellectual rather than the social sense. From *A Buyer's Market*:

> "Why are you so stuck up?" she [Gypsy Jones] asked,
>   truculently.
> "I'm just made that way."
> "You ought to fight it."
> "I can't see why."

And of course he is not only intellectually judgmental but

morally so as well. There is a telling throwaway line, for example, when Hugh Moreland begins secretly carrying on with Priscilla Tolland while "happily" married to Matilda Wilson: "All three persons fell in my estimation," Jenkins remarks in *Casanova's Chinese Restaurant*. Moreland and Priscilla, yes, all right, but why the apparently innocent Matilda? What does this tell us about Jenkins?

The character-sketch given by Mrs. Erdleigh, as she reads Jenkins' cards, can be taken as true, for while mysticism in *Dance* is in itself always suspect, information imparted by self-styled psychics like Mrs. Erdleigh, Scorpio Murtlock, or Dr. Trelawney always has meaning within the context of the fiction. From *The Acceptance World*:

> "You are thought cold, but you possess deep affections, sometimes for people worthless in themselves. Often you are at odds with those who might help you. You like women, and they like you, but you often find the company of men more amusing. You expect too much, and yet you are also too resigned. You must try to understand life . . . People can only be themselves . . . If they possessed the qualities you desire in them, they would be different people . . . You must make a greater effort in life."

None of this makes Jenkins (or Powell) sound a particularly likeable character, but in fact he is oddly appealing: quick to ridicule others, he just as easily sees the funny side of himself. Early in life, he reflects ruefully on his mediocre sexual score-sheet:

> [M]y interest in love was keen enough, but the thing itself seemed not particularly simple to come by. In that direction, other people appeared more easily satisfied than myself. That at least was how it seemed to me. And yet, in spite of some

show of picking and choosing, my experiences, on subsequent examination, were certainly no more admirable than those to which neither Templer nor Barnby, for example, would have given a second thought; they were merely fewer in number.

His discomfiture is equally comical some years later when he discovers that his lover Jean Duport has slept with the repulsive Jimmy Stripling and was having a secret affair with the equally disgusting Jimmy Brent at the same time that she was romantically involved with himself. Duport, Stripling, Brent: if these are the kind of men Jean finds attractive, Jenkins concludes, he had better take a very good look at himself.

I n the background is always the question, brought up by the superb General Conyers, of the "personal myth." "The General, speaking one felt with authority, always insisted that, if you bring off adequate preservation of your personal myth, nothing much else in life matters. It is not what happens to people that is significant, but what they think happens to them." Stringham, one feels, accepts his fate as part of his rather dark personal myth; General Conyers accepts the various triumphs of his life on the same level. Jenkins' personal myth is more difficult to grasp, but his role as observer and his role as artist are certainly closely linked in its construction.

That he himself might be an artist dawned on Powell only slowly. The son of an army officer, like Jenkins, he grew up within a military culture ("Stonedene," the house near Aldershot where he lived as a child, is an exact replica of "Stonehurst" in *The Kindly Ones*, where the Jenkins and Conyers families learn of the assassination at Sarajevo). As a child he planned a military career. At Eton, however, he joined the Eton Society of the Arts, whose membership at that time included Henry Green, Harold Acton,

and Robert Byron, and began to conceive of a life as some sort of
artist, possibly a painter.

Powell was not an outstanding success in any field until midlife. At Eton he was in Goodhart's, the "worst" house; at Oxford,
in spite of hard work, he got only a third. His long apprenticeship
at Gerald Duckworth & Co. Ltd., which was supposed to end with
his father putting up money for a partnership, eventually came to
nothing. His first novel, *Afternoon Men*, was promising, but it was
killed by the Depression, which dated its cast of jaded Bright
Young Things rather badly. Subsequent novels—*Venusberg, From
A View to a Death, Agents and Patients*—were pleasant but light-
weight. *What's Become of Waring*, a somewhat larger undertaking,
was published in 1939 but quickly forgotten in the countdown to
war. Powell's career as an overaged, underqualified officer in World
War II was every bit as unglamorous as Jenkins's, which reflects it
fairly faithfully. (One interesting fact, however: for a short time
Powell held the Military Assistant Secretary post at the Cabinet
Office that he gives to Widmerpool in *The Military Philosophers;*
Powell, unlike the careerist Widmerpool, failed at this job and was
thrown out after a mere nine weeks.)

After the war Powell's career as a reviewer and literary editor
flourished. He served as fiction reviews editor and chief novel
reviewer for the *Times Literary Supplement*, had a fortnightly
column in the *Daily Telegraph* for thirty years, and was the literary
editor of *Punch* during Malcolm Muggeridge's tenure, in which
post he was instrumental in adjusting the tone of the magazine,
more or less unchanged since Thackeray's day: the cartoonist Mark
Boxer, one of Powell's discoveries (and the creator of twelve brilliant covers for a collected edition of *Dance*) thought Powell
"responsible for killing the idea that everything in the magazine
had to be side-splitting."

But Powell's real achievement in life was *A Dance to the Music
of Time*, which began with the publication of *A Question of
Upbringing* in 1951. The complex scheme was a brilliant solution

to a problem that had begun to dog him, as it has dogged so many writers: "Even before the war," Barber writes, "it had become apparent to him that he would always struggle with plots and that there was a limit to the number of times he could recycle the sort of characters who interested him. The solution he hit on—to write a long novel consisting of at least six volumes—would allow him to operate on a much broader front than he could hope to cover in 80,000 words."

Barber is right, I think, to call *Dance* "one novel" rather than a series of novels, for none of them stands on its own: one must read all or none. The organization of the material was a staggering job.

"I am always torn," Powell wrote to Waugh, "between trying to emphasize the plot in order that the design should not seem woolly (and also for commercial reasons) and, on the other hand, trying to avoid too neatly contrived happenings that detract from its naturalism and may spoil the overall picture." Considering the scale of the work, he was largely successful, but it must be admitted that the naturalism does break down towards the end; the last three volumes, and particularly the Russell Gwinnett/Pamela Flitton/Widmerpool story, strain our credulity beyond endurance. The pattern is so clearly imposed, so very literary with its references to Poe and to Leslie Fiedler, that it is hard to reconcile with the sort of organic reality that has adhered to Widmerpool and all his doings through so many volumes.

Widmerpool's midlife career as a co-conspirator of Burgess and Maclean is unconvincing, too theoretical an application of Powell's Will to Power theme; even more so is his decision, in his dotage, to join a hippie cult (although as a university chancellor pandering to campus radicals he is perfectly cast). The sequence finally ends, perhaps a volume or two later than it should have; but the final pages, with Widmerpool's death and Powell's reversion to the imagery of *A Question of Upbringing*'s first chapter, are a masterstroke.

· · ·

Generally speaking, Powell's pattern is successful insofar as it imitates the repetitions and sometimes inspired coincidences of life itself: Nietzsche's "eternal recurrences," with which he was fascinated. As Waugh wrote in his review of *The Kindly Ones*, "[W]e watch [the characters] through the glass of a tank; one after another various specimens swim towards us; we see them clearly, then with a barely perceptible flick of a tail they are off into the murk. That is how our encounters occur in life. Friends or acquaintances approach or recede year by year." Close friends like Stringham and Moreland drop away, for friendship, like romantic love, appears to contain the seeds of its own dissolution. People one would never choose for a companion—Widmerpool, Odo Stevens, Pamela Flitton, Audrey Maclintick—recur, through life's mysterious rhythms, until their stories become an inextricable part of Jenkins' own. As he reflects, "certain acquaintances remain firmly fixed within this or that person's particular orbit; a law which seems to lead inexorably to the conclusion that the often repeated saying that people can 'choose their own friends' is true only in a most strictly limited degree."

"Life is full of internal dramas, instantaneous and sensational, played to an audience of one," Jenkins observes. Friendship is a way of sharing the drama, and in the last few volumes the particular drama of Widmerpool's strange career, which has amused Jenkins for so long, becomes tinged with *tristesse* since, with the passing of Stringham and Templer, he has no one left with whom to share it.

Moreland, in a disgruntled moment in *Books Do Furnish a Room*, attacks the notion of historical exceptionalism. "How bored one gets with the assumption that people now are organically different from people in the past—the Lost Generation, the New Poets, the Atomic Age." *A Dance to the Music of Time* is, among other things, a spirited affirmation of the immutability of human behavior. In the 1940s J. G. Quiggin edits a left-wing literary journal called *Fission*; twenty years later his radical daughters start a

campus rag called *Toilet Paper*, which of course horrifies their
father. Those who live long enough, like Jenkins, are privileged to
watch the drama renew itself and begin all over again. From
Hearing Secret Harmonies:

> While a dismantling process steadily curtails members of
> the cast, items of the scenery, airs played by the orchestra,
> in the performance that has included one's own walk-on
> part for more than a few decades, simultaneous derequisi-
> tionings are also to be observed. Mummers return, who
> might have been supposed to have made their final
> exit . . . The touching up of time-expired sets, reshaping of
> derelict props, updating of old refrains, are none of them
> uncommon.

Thus the mystical activities of Scorpio Murtlock and his cult,
in the sequence's last volume, directly echo those of Dr. Trelawney,
who flourished during Jenkins' childhood before the First World
War: the two even use the same nonsensical formula, "The Essence
of the All is the Godhead of the True." *Plus ça change*, in other
words: each generation has its magi, and the basic differences
between them are remarkably slight. Perhaps Mrs. Erdleigh is right
—as indeed she so often is—when she claims that Death is merely
an illusion.

But for all Powell's concern with reproducing life's patterns,
James Stern was probably correct when he stated that to Powell
"the story is not the thing: it is the place, the house, the hotel
lounge, the prevailing fashion, the people." In terms of concrete,
almost tangible imagery, he can hardly be matched, and for those
of us too young to have experienced literary pub life in the Fifties,
for example, or London during the Blitz, one feels that his descriptions carry an essential truth; this is what it was like. His affinity
with the visual and plastic arts is everywhere apparent and feeds the
immediacy of his images; where other novelists summon painterly

images as a crutch, Powell uses them to enrich, rather than to replace, the prose images. From *The Kindly Ones* and *The Acceptance World*:

> We lived on this distant hilltop, miles away from the daily activities of troops, who were to be sighted only very occasionally on some local exercise to which summer manoeuvres had fortunately brought them. Even so much as the solitary outline of a Military Policeman was rare, jogging his horse across the heather, a heavy brushstroke of dark blue, surmounted by a tiny blob of crimson, moving in the sun through a Vuillard landscape of pinkish greys streaked with yellow and silver. Among a sea of countenances, stamped like the skin of Renoir's with that curiously pink, silky surface that seems to come from prolonged sitting about in Ritz hotels, I noticed several familiar faces.

I first read *Dance* when I was in my twenties, and though I loved and treasured it, it now seems clear that I couldn't have understood half of it. Though it is a book that appeals to the young, it is not a young person's book. One has to be middle-aged, to have experienced the almost arbitrary dissolution of love and friendship, the apparently arbitrary apotheosis of some and degradation of others, to understand that Powell was not being gratuitously cruel to his characters but simply realistic. Death, for example: "As in musical chairs, the piano stops suddenly, someone is left without a seat, petrified for all time in their attitude of that particular moment. The balance-sheet is struck there and then, a matter of luck whether its calculations have much bearing, one way or the other, on the commerce conducted."

Powell's own death was not like this. Like the unkillable Sillery, he lived on, "sole survivor of his genus," missing his century by only a few years. His end, like that of so many of his characters, was an appropriate one: it is right and fitting that Jenkins should outlive his contemporaries and record the conclusion of the tale. As for Powell's own tale, Barber's biography, welcome though it is, is far from giving us the whole story or even a satisfactory part of it. Perhaps Hilary Spurling's will do the job; but somehow, one doubts it. It was Powell's style to stay backstage, and it will be very surprising if anyone, even an authorized biographer, ever succeeds in pulling him in front of the curtain for his bow.

(2004)

16. A Charmer and a User
Sybille Bedford

Part One

Sybille Bedford, a German-born writer who spent her last decades in England, was one of the twentieth century's most attractive literary curiosities. Born before World War I, she witnessed much of the tragedy, and enjoyed much of the beauty, that her volatile age had to offer.

Bedford spent her childhood and youth in her father's decrepit *Schloss* in Baden, in the stuffy and well-upholstered Berlin residence of other relatives, in Fascist Italy, in high bohemia on the Côte d'Azur in the 1920s, and in England. It was a rich and strange life, and in each of her four largely autobiographical novels she rendered its off-color luster and subtle moral gradations with humor and a remarkable tolerance that in no way implies an absence of judgment. The twentieth century displayed the human circus at its most grotesque, and Bedford had a ringside seat throughout the performance.

Bedford is not only a novelist but also the author of books on legal issues and famous trials, a biographer, and a light journalist specializing in sensual essays on food, wine, and travel, à la M. F. K.

Fisher. Her *Visit to Don Otavio: A Traveller's Tale From Mexico* (1953) is one of the most delightful travel books ever written. Her *Aldous Huxley* (1973-1974) is still, after half a century, the definitive biography of the famous polymath, whom Bedford considered her literary and moral mentor.

Bedford's publishing history has done little to promote her name or reputation in the United States, where her books have appeared intermittently, under the aegis of different publishing houses, and have often been out of print. There has been no uniform American edition of Bedford's work until recently, with Counterpoint Press's reissue of her novels: *A Legacy* (1956), *A Favourite of the Gods* (1963), *A Compass Error* (1968), and *Jigsaw: An Unsentimental Education* (1989). *A Visit to Don Otavio* will follow, along with a new collection of her essays on travel and gastronomy.

Everything Bedford has written is worth reading, but her reputation rightly rests on *A Legacy* and *Jigsaw* (shortlisted for Britain's Booker Prize), for in these she draws most fully on her own matchless experiences. Bedford's father's family were minor aristocrats from the southern German state of Baden, Catholic and agrarian, oriented toward Paris rather than Berlin; they regarded Prussia "as a barbarous menace and united Germany a new nonsense." During World War I young Sybille, nicknamed Billi, and her unhappily married parents shut up the *Schloss* and moved to Berlin to live with the parents of her father's first wife. After the Armistice, Billi's mother, a restless Englishwoman, left Germany for good. Billi spent her odd, isolated early childhood back in the *Schloss* with her newly impoverished father and one faithful servant; later, reclaimed by her mother, she shuttled for years between England, where she was sent to be "educated" (in the very loosest sense of the word), and Sanary-sur-Mer, on the by then chic Côte d'Azur, where her mother had settled with a much younger, Italian husband.

A Legacy delves into the lives of Bedford's immediate forebears, interweaving their stories as they make their various ways through the more bizarre and exotic social circles of the Kaiser's Germany. The world she depicts is, as Evelyn Waugh wrote in the review that made Bedford's reputation, "far more remote than the Athens of Pericles or the Rome of the Borgias," and it is described "with an air of authority which compels acceptance." In a letter to a friend the charmed Waugh wondered who this "brilliant 'Mrs Bedford'" could be: "A cosmopolitan military man, plainly, with a knowledge of parliamentary government and popular journalism, a dislike for Prussians, a liking for Jews, a belief that everyone speaks French in the home."

A Legacy is set at the end of the nineteenth century and the opening of the twentieth, with Germany still smarting from the birth pangs of unification. As the various German states are uncomfortably yoked together, so are the novel's three wildly different families, through marriage. The Feldens, like Bedford's paternal relations, are southern German aristocrats, anachronisms and dilettantes, relics of the eighteenth century. The French Revolution was still alive with them as a calamity, and of the Industrial one they were not yet aware. Their home was Catholic Western Continental Europe, and the center of their world was France. They ignored, despised, and later dreaded, Prussia.

Where the Feldens are detached from the world and manifestly in decline, their neighbors the Bernins, into which family one of the Felden brothers marries, are political animals who devote their energies to the quixotic and irrelevant cause of the reunification of Christendom under the Catholic banner. Added to this already highly flavored mixture is the Merz family, probably Bedford's finest creation. The Merzes are established members of Berlin's Jewish haute bourgeoisie, kind, complacent, and inconceivably narrow in their outlook and habits.

No music was heard at Voss Strasse outside the ball-room and the day nursery. They never travelled. They never went to the country. They never went anywhere, except to take a cure, and then they went in a private railway carriage, taking their own sheets . . . The Merz's [sic] had no friends, a word they seldom used . . . They did not go to shops. Things were sent to them on approval, and people came to them for fittings.

They never read.

In a turn of events just outrageous enough to be real (as so often happens in good fiction, the most apparently extravagant characters turn out to be the ones drawn most faithfully from life), a marriage occurs between a Merz and a Felden. The misunderstandings between these two families, with their mutually exclusive world views, make for very high comedy. Here are the Merzes, for example, on first hearing their daughter's name coupled with that of Julius von Felden:

"Von?" said Grandpapa Merz. "Von? Got himself baptized, eh, like poor Flora's husband?"

"Of course he didn't get himself baptized," said Sarah.

"They won't give you the von if you don't get baptized. Refused it myself three times. Once to the old Kaiser, twice to Wil'hem."

"The Barony in question was conferred by Ottomark the Bear," said Gottlieb.

"How do you know?" said Edu.

"I took the liberty of consulting the Almanach de Gotha last time I had occasion to be in your house, sir."

"We have always been Jews," said Grandmama.

And the Feldens and the Bernins in a similar powwow:

"Israelites," said Gustavus, lowering his tone in spite of himself. "Presumably a papal title."

"Converts," said Clara. "Oh Conrad!"

"No title. Not converts. I shouldn't think they were christened."

There was a silence.

"Pious Jews—" said Clara. "It is well to remember the origin of our religion."

The negotiations are predictably painful; it is a case—not so unusual even today—of "theological dead-lock between non-practising members of two religions." Habits and prejudices are, as always, flatteringly disguised as values and traditions. The connection with the larger political deadlock of Wilhelmine Germany and of Europe in general cannot be ignored.

Bedford's fine sense of justice eventually tips the balance of *A Legacy* from farce to tragedy; her special subject has always been, as she puts it, "the links between private and mass catastrophe." An old Felden family scandal is unearthed, and its reverberations shatter the ill-assembled Felden-Bernin-Merz alliance, much as the ill-assembled new Reich is soon to be shattered by the war it will help to ignite. In Bedford's canny narrative, political disaster, like the personal variety, is the inevitable result of pride and stupidity.

A Legacy is not a perfect book; Bedford is often technically awkward. Her method of narration is unconvincing, as are some of the characters; the conversations, particularly those that dominate the second half of the book, are drawn out and too obviously expository. Never mind; the source of our dissatisfaction is that Bedford's skill is not quite equal to the extraordinary nature of the material. And whose would be?

Her weaknesses are far more apparent in her next two novels, *A Favourite of the Gods* and *A Compass Error*. The first of these, though, is saved by a clever subplot in which Bedford effectively reversed the Jamesian archetype of American innocence and European experience, "the view of aristocratic Italian homelife as conveyed by high Anglo-Saxon literature—those great tales of American heiresses corrupted, exploited and deprived in cold unions and palazzi." To this end she created a high-thinking but not really very plain-living New England heiress who wears her virtue—or is it simple asexuality?—like a badge of honor, and makes life hell for her trophy husband, a malleable, good-natured Roman prince. Bedford next turned her fictional talents to the re-creation of her life at Sanary during the 1920s, first with the unsatisfactory *A Compass Error* and then, more than twenty years later, with her marvelous and explicitly autobiographical *Jigsaw*.

"As no other place in Europe, no other place in the world," Bedford has written, "France between the wars made one this present of the illusion of freedom." Although Bedford's life-long love for France never soured, the word "illusion" is nonetheless significant, and there is a distinct edge to her evocations of the apparently idyllic sensuality celebrated by her Sanary friends, a circle of artists and intellectuals that included Aldous and Maria Huxley, Thomas Mann and his family, and the painter Moïse Kisling. Here "freedom was the great thing, and it meant freedom from almost anything pre-war." As always in Bedford's fiction, there is a strong element of the travelogue. She enjoyed life's little luxuries to the fullest, and her seductive mixing of Provençal scenery with Jazz Age and modernist legend caters to the seemingly perennial hunger for all things relating to France in the twenties, and also to the more recent obsession, fueled by Peter Mayle and Frances Mayes, with the good life as lived in Mediterranean Europe. But in Bedford's world the aesthetic pleasure of the landscape and the open sexuality and affection of the bohemian newcomers to its shores are recognized as being, at least on one level, pure fantasy. Love, sex, and friendship are neither simple nor open. They are complex, treacherous, often vicious. Bedford's experiences show that her set's ethos of honesty and free love did not work on the personal level—and in the end it did not work on the political one either. Once again we are confronted with the "links between private and mass catastrophe"—in the repellent story of Billi's beautiful, intelligent, narcissistic mother and the slow movement of France toward moral and military collapse. The Sanary idyll that began so promisingly moves by stages to a grim conclusion. The uncomfortable interplay of family members and friends; the emotional education of Billi (unsentimental indeed!); the final, reluctant defection of her long-suffering young stepfather; the mother's appalling descent into drug addiction and her willful involvement of her daughter in her own degradation—all these events are described with grim exactitude and a surprising compassion.

Bedford's fictionalized memoirs come to an end at a moment of unsustainable tension between mother and daughter; the reader is left unsatisfied and deeply curious. Bedford never claimed to provide solutions; in her work the great emotional and moral questions remain unanswered. It is the oblique light she cast on them that gives her fiction its gentle, if cool, detachment and occasionally brings her close to penetrating the mystery of love and the peculiar forms it so often takes. *

2001

PART TWO

The subsequent appearance first of *Quicksands* (2005) and of Selena Hastings' *Sybille Bedford: A Biography* reveals hoped-for new layers to her story. With the passing of the Nuremberg Laws in 1935 and a French parliamentary act restricting the movement of refugees, the part-Jewish Sybille ran the risk of being deported. What was to be done? "We must get one of our bugger friends to

---

marry Sybille," announced Maria Huxley. In the end one Walter Bedford, attendant at a gentlemen's club in London, was induced to marry her for the sum of one hundred pounds, giving her a British name and passport. By this time she had determined to become an Englishwoman in substance as well as name: "The fact that I had any connections with this terrible country"—Germany —"became a cause of guilt, and for some time I tried desperately to Anglicize myself entirely."

B edford spent much of World War II in the United States (re-encountering the Mann and Huxley circles in Los Angeles, where they had taken refuge) and spent eight months traveling through Mexico in 1946-47; for the rest of her life she moved between England, France and Italy with a motley series of women lovers. "I wish I'd written more books and spent less time being in love," she admitted late in her life, and her fans can only agree. Bedford wrote with great difficulty: "I sit before my hostile type-writer and sicken before the abnormal effort. What is this blight I have suffered from all my life that makes trying to write . . . such tearing, crushing, defeating agony." It was far preferable to go to parties and dinners, and to cook spectacular meals for her friends. "Remember," one friend prodded her when she had shirked work for too long, "you are a writer, not other people's cook."

But Bedford's busy social and romantic life nearly always took priority. Hastings calls her existence a "sexual carousel" and has clearly had quite a job keeping track of the constantly shifting part-nerships. Here is a typical sentence: "Returning to Normandy, Sybille was prepared for the tensions surrounding Allanah's affair with Eda; what she had not expected was Esther's sudden infatua-tion with Joan." Much of this material is not especially interesting. What is interesting is that Bedford so often had the upper hand in her own relationships. Her partners seemed to take it for granted that they should bear the brunt of the dirty work (housekeeping,

gardening, bill paying, etc.), and they often supported her financially too.

Lots of people supported her financially. Indeed, she stands
revealed in this biography as a world-class freeloader, with generous
friends like Martha Gellhorn subsidizing her travels and writing
periods and offering her deluxe accommodation in beautiful spots
like Provence, Rome, the Alps. She was, in short, a user—though
her compensatory qualities were such that ex-lovers, even those
who had been most thoroughly used, happily stayed in her orbit
years after their liaisons had ended.

Bedford was an eccentric writer and not a perfect one; many
readers are annoyed by her refusal (or inability?) to draw a line
between biography and fiction. And her overriding obsession with
gastronomy and wine can get tedious and, as Jan Morris
commented, "may drive readers of less urbane gourmandise all the
more readily to the deep-freeze Ocean Pie." But her works are
dense, exotic, rich with historical hindsight. In a life that spanned
most of the twentieth century, she lived that century in all its high
drama and delivers it to the twenty-first in idiosyncratic, textured
prose.

(2021)

17. SMALL IS BEAUTIFUL.
SOMETIMES.
ANNE TYLER IN MID-COURSE

Is Anne Tyler's place so near the top of the literary heap merited? Tyler is a good writer, to be sure, on occasion a very good one. Yet there doesn't seem to be much recognition that the quality of her work varies tremendously from novel to novel. The books for which she received the National Book Critics Circle Award and the Pulitzer Prize, *The Accidental Tourist* and *Breathing Lessons* respectively, are hardly her best, while her best books often have not been singled out for special notice. Her showier tricks have been much touted, her truer, subtler gifts often overlooked. Tyler herself, more astute than most of her critics, prizes *Celestial Navigation* (1974) above all her other work and has confessed to a wish that the four novels which preceded it might quietly disappear.

Tyler's novels, in fact, can be divided into three categories: the downright bad—a category that includes *If Morning Ever Comes* (1964), *The Tin Can Tree* (1965), *Searching for Caleb* (1975), and *Morgan's Passing* (1980); the worthwhile but extremely flawed—*A Slipping-Down Life* (1969), *The Clock Winder* (1972), *Earthly Possessions* (1977), *The Accidental Tourist* (1985), and *Breathing Lessons* (1988); and the good—*Celestial Navigation* (1974),

Dinner at the Homesick Restaurant (1982), and *Saint Maybe* (1991). I would place the recent *Ladder of Years* in the last group; it is one her most accomplished and least self-indulgent pieces of work to date.

Tyler is a popular novelist, but one who, however well she writes, will never appeal to everyone. She is doggedly determined to celebrate the clutter and mess of domestic life. She speaks with a very feminine voice, and sees things from a feminine (though not necessarily "feminist") point of view. She is regional—all her novels except the first three have been set in or around Baltimore, where she has lived since 1965—and resolutely untimely: her characters are old-fashioned in the way they live and in the way they define themselves.

Conventional husbands and wives, parents and children: these are Tyler's only true subjects. Her fascination with family life is rooted, she states, in the fact that it is "horrific at times" while remaining "the one situation that we are generally forced to go on with, even so, picking ourselves up and trying again in the morning. And that is valuable in itself."

A more formidable barrier to an appreciation of Tyler's work is that, while she is capable of conceiving powerful characters, she has a special interest in misfits, an interest which unfortunately is sentimental rather than analytical. Drifters, dreamers, Southern eccentrics: the very mention of such ghastly stock figures is enough to send this reader running the other way, and it's even scarier when an author resorts to symbol-loaded characters like fortune-tellers, carnival workers, or, God forbid, puppeteers. Tyler does so often, and she has added to this assortment another stereotype peculiarly her own: the dizzy housewife with the repressed husband, who for all her scatterbrained impracticality can be seen to represent the richness of connected life against isolation and sterility.

Even putting aside her unpromising novels of the 1960s, which can most generously be described as soggy imitations of Carson

McCullers, Tyler has produced rather too many books which depend for both theme and structure upon nonsensical clichés. *Searching for Caleb* tells the story of two cousins, Justine and Duncan Peck, who escape the stuffy bourgeois world of Baltimore's Roland Park and take up a grotty itinerant life which Tyler constrains us to view as free-spirited (many Tyler characters chafe at the oppressiveness they perceive in upper-middle-class life, and the rapid descent from high respectability to the trailer park is a recurrent theme in her work). Justine, rather sickeningly warm and impulsive, becomes a fortune teller; Duncan, a typical "drifter," flits passively from job to job spouting the jargon of the intellectual manqué: "'I am fascinated by randomness. Do you realize that there is no possible permutation of four fingers that could be called absolutely random?'"

Morgan's Passing, written five years after *Searching for Caleb*, was hardly an improvement on it. Morgan Gower, a middle-aged, middle-class father of seven, has an irrepressible urge to wander out of his own orbit and see what other lives are like; he poses around Baltimore now as a doctor, now as a sailor—not with any sinister intent but in the most benign, not to say adorable fashion. (His wife, Bonny, voices the reader's own reservations about his character: "Oh, from the outside he seems so comic and light-hearted, such a character, so quaint, but imagine dealing with him." Tyler, however drowns this cool assessment in her own warm sea of love for Morgan.) In all honesty the reader must agree with James Wolcott, who in a review of the novel in *The New York Review of Books* cruelly and correctly pegged the insufferable Morgan as "a scruffy, king-size Life Force—Henderson the Rain King's slightly retarded brother."

These are all boring people, and they make for boring characters and boring books. Here, as in her later novels *Breathing Lessons* and *The Accidental Tourist*, Tyler makes a fatal mistake: she confuses being eccentric with being interesting. Eccentric characters often make for very dull reading, especially when they are predictably eccentric, as Tyler's tend to be. Thus Elizabeth, the girl-handyman in *The Clock Winder*, is for all her flouting of convention much less compelling as a character than her employer, the bourgeois Mrs. Emerson—a bossy, humorless matriarch for whom "the world was made up of people forever happy, wastefully happy, laughing at something too far away for Mrs. Emerson to see even when she stood on tiptoe."

And yet Tyler's weakness is also her strength. Her focus upon people who are unreflective, inarticulate, either intellectually or emotionally limited has produced her finest characters as well as her silliest. Tyler has stated that the single piece of fiction that has influenced her the most is Eudora Welty's "The Wide Net," which she read as a teenaged student in Reynolds Price's writing class at Duke University. "I can even name the line," she says. "It's the one where she says Edna Earle is so dim she could spend all day pondering on how the little tail on the 'C' got through the 'L' in a Coca-Cola sign. I knew many Edna Earles. I didn't know you could write about them."

The first intimation that Tyler could in fact write about Edna Earles with anything like Welty's truth was in her 1974 novel *Celestial Navigation*, a work of beauty and skill. In that book Tyler put aside her penchant for the lovable and the poignant and told a bleak, strong story of an agoraphobic man who creates, in the fastness of his Baltimore row house, masterly collages. Jeremy Pauling conquers his crippling shyness and proposes marriage to one of his boarders, Mary Tell; the story of his marriage and its breakup, his failure as a husband and his genius as an artist, is narrated with a balance and restraint that is as good as anything that Tyler has yet produced.

All of the characters in this novel are hobbled by their own limitations, and the opening pages, which are narrated by Jeremy's sister Amanda, are a tour de force. Amanda is an ordinary, unintel-

ligent woman, someone who senses that life has treated her cruelly
and takes her revenge in being tough and self-reliant, and in
scorning the weaknesses of others, thereby pushing away the only
people who might possibly love her. Here are her feelings after
returning from her mother's funeral:

> When I got to the bedroom Laura was already stepping
> out of her dress. "Don't let the wrinkles set in that," I told
> her. (She tends to be careless in her personal habits.) "I
> suppose we'll just have to sleep in our slips and make the
> best of it," I said, all energy. And I took my own dress off
> and hung it up neatly. But then, just as I was sitting on the
> edge of my bed to roll my stockings down—oh, I can't
> explain what came over me. Such heaviness, such an
> exhausted feeling. As if there were no point to moving any
> more . . . I know what I am. I'm not blind. I have never had
> a marriage proposal or a love affair or an adventure, never
> any experience more interesting than patrolling the aisles
> of my Latin class looking for crib sheets and ponies—an
> old maid schoolteacher. There are a thousand jokes about
> the likes of me. None of them are funny.

It is no wonder that Tyler felt *Celestial Navigation* to be a
personal breakthrough. How to explain, then, her reversion to
type with the next three novels? It is not until *Dinner at the Homesick Restaurant* that we find a book to compare with her earlier
favorite. *Dinner at the Homesick Restaurant* is a family portrait,
but its central, most real and moving figure is a woman not unlike
Amanda Pauling, a stupid, plodding person who wages perpetual
war against a world she cannot understand.

Pearl Tull is a genteel lady, born in the early part of the twentieth century, who had more or less resigned herself to being a spinster when a jaunty, handsome salesman several rungs down the
social ladder came along. The couple produced three children,

Cody, Ezra, and Jenny, and then, after some fifteen years of marriage, Beck Tull walked out; his name was never mentioned again, either by Pearl or the children. Pearl, with very little money and very few wits about her, was left to bring up her family on her own.

Pearl is a loving if rigid and humorless mother, but occasionally she cracks and exposes a violent, Mr. Hyde aspect that terrifies her children.

> Which of her children had not felt her stinging slap, with the claw-encased pearl in her engagement ring that could bloody a lip at one flick? Jenny had seen her hurl Cody down a flight of stairs. She'd seen Ezra ducking, elbows raised, warding off an attack. She herself, more than once, had been slammed against a wall, been called "serpent," "cockroach," "hideous little snivelling guttersnipe." But here Pearl sat, decorously enquiring about Julia Carroll's weight problem.

It is to Anne Tyler's credit that she never once descends to proselytizing about "child abuse" or the "dysfunctional family": she writes fiction, not sociology, and her characters are far more complex than the cardboard figures of "abuser" and "victim." The fact is that the terrible and pathetic Pearl, with all her faults, tries her best; she is quite simply as good a mother as she is capable of being, and though she herself believes that her family has failed, the reader, finally, cannot agree. Pearl is unexpectedly moving as, looking at her middle-aged sons and daughter, she grieves for the tiny children of thirty years before, when she used to take them to the beach on holidays from which she had always been far too worried and joyless to take any pleasure. Only as she slips gently from life to death is she finally able, at least in her own mind, to connect with them:

She remembered a country auction she'd attended forty years ago, where they'd offered up an antique brass bed complete with all its bedclothes—sheets and blankets, pillow in a linen case embroidered with forget-me-nots. Two men wheeled it onto the platform, and its ruffled coverlet stirred like a young girl's petticoats. Behind her eyelids, Pearl climbed in and laid her head on the pillow and was borne away to the beach, where three small children ran toward her, laughing, across the sunlit sand.

But *Dinner at the Homesick Restaurant* is finally kept from being a first-rate novel by its corny use of metaphor—the celebratory dinners at Ezra's restaurant that the family is never able to finish together are obtrusively symbolic—and by the upbeat ending which Tyler seems to have tacked on in accordance with her own tendency to dreamy optimism rather than with the book's own, much darker, truth. Several years ago, John Blades in *The Chicago Tribune* wondered whether "Tyler, with her sedative resolutions to life's most perplexing problems, can be taken seriously as a writer." This indeed seems to me to be the real question when dealing with Tyler: only in *Celestial Navigation* does she allow that some family relations must be permanently severed, that some differences must ever be irreconcilable, that sometimes the darkness in human nature blots out any hope of redemption or renewal.

Tyler's next two books, *The Accidental Tourist* and *Breathing Lessons*, were significantly less impressive than *Dinner at the Homesick Restaurant*, and it seemed for several years that in middle age she had settled for a lucrative niche as a crowd-pleasing, middlebrow writer—with a gift, certainly, for evoking the brilliant detail, but a fatal wish to impose a wishy-washy glow of optimism over everything.

Yet having reached this plateau of mediocrity Tyler unaccountably began to be called a major American talent, and was generously rewarded with prizes and kudos. People were being asked to take Anne Tyler very seriously, far more seriously than her current work warranted.

The Accidental Tourist is the story of Macon Leary, a repressed near-recluse whose ever-so-symbolic job is to write travel guides for those who hate to leave home. His twelve-year-old son has been killed; grief and self-reproach have ended his marriage, and Macon slips into a depression he isn't clued-in enough to recognize. He is rescued by another of Tyler's Life Force characters in the person of Muriel, a young woman who is noisy, clinging, and abrasive, but spunky—excruciatingly spunky. Tyler's theme, not unpromising in itself, is explained by Macon as he muses over his reasons for turning his back on the appropriate mate—his wife, Sarah—and aligning himself with the wildly inappropriate Muriel. "He felt a mild stirring of interest; he saw now how such couples evolved. They were not, as he'd always supposed, the result of some ludicrous lack of perception, but had come together for reasons that the rest of the world would never guess." Interesting in theory, yes: but in reality the only sympathy the wooden Macon inspires in the reader is due to the terrible loss he has suffered, while Muriel sets one's teeth on edge every time she opens her mouth. It's hard to give a damn what happens to either of them.

Breathing Lessons is the story of a marriage told, with the aid of flashbacks, in the course of a single day's drive. Ira and Maggie Moran, in their late forties, have reached a turning point. Their son has grown up and left home, their daughter is about to go away to college, and they are suddenly confronted with the fact that they will spend the rest of their lives alone together. During the day in question they drive to an old friend's funeral, where they see for the first time in many years all the friends of their youth and, on the way home, they visit their son's estranged wife and try to re-establish relations with her and with the grand-daughter they are never allowed to see.

The book is neat and skillful like all of Tyler's later work, but empty at the center, for Ira and Maggie, upon whom everything depends, are nothing but the same old stock figures dug up out of Tyler's familiar bag of tricks. Ira is Mr. Still-Waters-Run-Deep, "a closed-in, isolated man," "most comfortable, Maggie thought, when he could act tolerant and long-suffering." Maggie is Tyler's version of the eternal feminine, her Molly Bloom: disorderly, fecund, maternal, impulsive, ordinary, "special." In actuality she's sub-ordinary: an infuriating woman who stupidly indulges her own eccentricities at the expense of her family.

In 1991 Tyler broke this mold and produced another really good novel, *Saint Maybe.* "All I knew at the start," Tyler has said, "was that I wondered what it must be like to be a born-again Christian, since that is a kind of life very different from mine." An intriguing idea, since despite the enormous role they play in our culture, born-again Christians are as beyond the pale as subjects for serious art as they are in higher social spheres.

Saint Maybe begins with the attractive, indeed picture-perfect upper-middle-class Bedloe family. Daniel, the adored elder son, marries Lucy Dean, a young divorcée several steps down the social scale; after they have been married about a year his younger brother, Ian, angry at Lucy and obscurely jealous of his brother, tells Daniel that Lucy has been unfaithful to him. This leads to Daniel's suicide and to Lucy's own death soon afterward. The family is shattered: Ian, paralyzed with remorse, joins a fundamentalist church, leaves school, and devotes his life to raising Lucy's three children.

This is perhaps Anne Tyler's most adult work, in its acknowledgment that guilt, remorse, and atonement might be concrete realities and not fallacious psychological states. Though Tyler is herself an agnostic, she gives real validity to Ian's religious development, taking it beyond the range of theology into that of practical ethics. Mrs. Bedloe, distressed at the change in her son, gives the usual WASP argument against fervent piety: "Of course we have nothing against religion; we raised all of you children to be Christians. But our church never asked us to abandon our entire way of life," to which Ian responds, "Well, maybe it should have."

I an's conversion leads inevitably to his social ostracism. Speaking to him, people's smiles would glaze over whenever "the bald, uncomfortable sound of God's name was uttered in social surroundings." Ian "seemed slightly out of step, so often— his jokes just missing, his churchy language setting strangers' eyes on guard, his clothes inappropriately boyish and plain as if he'd been caught in a time warp." Ian's mother exposes her own wrong-headedness when she defines her grief over her son's death and Ian's metamorphosis in terms of social class (though she doesn't use those words): "Our lives have turned so makeshift and second-class, so second-string, so second-fiddle . . . We're not a special family any more." "Special," of course, is in fact just what the family has become; and as a nice touch of irony, Lucy's little waifs grow up to become highly successful adults—successful in terms that Mrs. Bedloe herself would understand.

Tyler's most recent novel, *Ladder of Years*, starts with an unpromising hodgepodge of echt-Tyler ingredients: a twenty-year marriage, a charmingly scatter-brained wife, a saturnine husband, a flight, a journey, a return. Delia Grinstead is one of the tribe of Tyler women that John Updike described as being "admirably active in the details of living yet alarmingly passive in the large curve of their lives—riders on male-generated events." Though only forty years old, Delia is strangely anachronistic, seemingly belonging more to the generation brought up on Doris Day and Rock Hudson than on the Rolling Stones—to Tyler's own generation, in fact. The youngest of three sisters, and fifteen years younger than her husband, Sam, Delia has played the child all her life and now, in middle age, still affects a frilly, baby-doll look.

Tyler traces the novel's conception to a moment some twenty years ago.

> Back in 1975 or so, while I was on a family beach trip, I went to the local produce stand in a T-shirt that said One Hundred Years of Solitude—the title of my favorite book. I was waiting in the cashier's line when a woman told me, "I would love that."
>
> Considering she was surrounded by children, all of them clamoring for different flavors of Sno-Cones, I knew right away what she was referring to. It wasn't my cantaloupe, or even the book; it was the hundred years of solitude.
>
> Who hasn't had an urge to up and leave at some point, packing no more than a toothbrush? I have been fascinated all my life by the tension between the wish to fly and the resolve to stay earthbound.

Delia, then, the ordinary, slightly ridiculous Roland Park doctor's wife, is to fulfill this not-uncommon female fantasy and abandon her cluttered existence for a stark, clean one. But her flight is not joyful or comical, as Tyler's comment, above, might suggest, for events have united to bring about a crisis in Delia's life. Her children, in late adolescence, have reached the age where they no longer really need her, and the fifty-five-year-old Sam has had his first glimpse of mortality in the form of a brand-new heart condition.

More obscurely, the comfortable continuity of Delia's life is being badly shaken: the favored youngest, Delia had in fact never left home; she married her father's junior partner and the young couple continued to live with the old man. Now Delia's adored father is dead, and while she is shattered, Sam blandly goes about the business of remodeling the house and office as though he had been waiting for years to usurp his father-in-law's place. One day in the supermarket Delia has a rather absurd encounter with Adrian Bly-Brice, an attractive young man who asks her to pose as his girl-friend in order to make his ex-wife jealous. This leads to other, more romantic encounters with him; Delia is not tempted to fall in love, but she is startled to realize that someone else sees her not merely as someone's wife, mother, or daughter but as an attractive, even interesting person in her own right. Almost subconsciously Delia begins to reassess the marriage she had always taken for granted, to feel sure that Sam married her out of self-interest rather than for love, to believe that her children scorn her and that even they, whom she has always loved so unreservedly, had somehow in growing up "become just a bit less overwhelmingly all-important to her."

Delia understands that her experience is not unique. "Didn't it often happen, she thought, that aged parents die exactly at the moment when other people (your husband, your adolescent chil-dren) have stopped being thrilled to see you? But a parent is always thrilled, always dwells so lovingly on your face as you are speak-ing." But Delia has lived her life by her instincts; she does not have the intellectual resources fully to understand, or solve, the prob-lems in her marriage, which are certainly far from unusual: over the years Sam and Delia have slipped ever further into the sort of defensive role-playing that so many couples indulge in, each even-tually coming to define himself purely in terms of the other's difference. Delia reflects that Sam "always got to be the reasonable one, the steady and reliable one; she was purely decorative. But how had that come about? Where had she been looking while that state of affairs developed?"

Marriage as a trap—it is a theme that has cropped up in many Tyler novels, but never with such dark implications as in this one. One of Delia's friends complains about her own situation in words with which any number of Tyler characters would heartily agree:

"Funny how men always worry ahead of time that marriage might confine them . . . Women don't give it a thought. It's afterwards it hits them. Stuck for life! Imprisoned!" Delia, a startlingly old-fashioned woman who might never have heard the word "feminist" in her life, went into marriage believing that it would be perfect, and it has taken her twenty years to realize that it is not.

This raises an interesting question in relation to Anne Tyler: what effect has the feminist movement, which played so large a role in the story of her own generation, had on her work? On the surface, astoundingly little. Katha Pollitt has noted that, with very few alterations, any of Tyler's stories could take place in the 1920s or 30s—not only because they are not topical but because their characters seem eerily untouched by any of the revolutions, be they sexual or feminist, of the years since then. Not only do none of Tyler's wives see themselves as feminists, they apparently do not even acknowledge that such a creature exists, or that there might be any alternative to conventional marriage save shameful spinsterhood or, as in Delia's case, rather dramatic flight.

Nor does there seem to be any more covert feminist statement in Tyler's novels. Her subject is not the bid for independence but the bridging of gaps; her characters struggle, more or less successfully, not so much to free themselves from repressive relationships as to find ways of communicating within those bonds. There are permanent separations, to be sure—Mary takes the children and leaves Jeremy in *Celestial Navigation*, Jenny flees her first husband in *Dinner at the Homesick Restaurant*—but the norm is represented by Charlotte in *Earthly Possessions*, or Elizabeth in *The Clock Winder*, both of whom finally shoulder the burdens imposed on them by their respective families and accept the claustrophobia of married life along with its rewards. Even the absconding Beck Tull is reincorporated into the family circle he had left, so definitively as he thought, thirty years earlier.

Delia Grinstead, a creature of impulse like so many of Tyler's characters, never makes a conscious decision to leave; she simply veers off down the beach while her family is swimming and sunbathing, gets a lift in a repairman's van, and disappears not only in space but in time, for the destination she picks almost at random, Bay Borough, is a small town straight out of Norman Rockwell: "Look west as you crossed an intersection, and you'd see pasture, sometimes even a cow." Here Mrs. Grinstead takes a room in a boardinghouse and becomes Miss Grinstead, a "sombre, serious-minded woman" utterly unlike anything Delia herself has ever been; she gets a job as a secretary, spends her evenings reading in her room, and her nights in violent fits of weeping. Yet Miss Grinstead is not entirely unhappy. She takes pride in her new-found efficiency, her detachment, her intelligence. Most of all she enjoys her solitude: "She had noticed that Miss Grinstead was not a very friendly person. She hadn't developed the easy, bantering relationships Delia was accustomed to."

Tyler is very skillful at establishing a delicate balance between fantasy and reality. For the early Bay Borough scenes take the story into an anti-realistic mode: Bay Borough, as Miss Grinstead first experiences it, is a dreamscape just as Miss Grinstead herself is not a person but a fantasy of Delia's, and there are conscious echoes of *The Wizard of Oz* and *Alice in Wonderland* in these pages. But though Delia has undergone a breakdown of sorts, she has kept her sanity, and little by little Bay Borough loses its elements of fantasy, just as Miss Grinstead and Delia begin to coalesce. Indeed, Delia starts to gather "an impression of Bay Borough as a town of misfits. Almost everybody here had run away from someplace else, or been run away from. And no longer did it seem so idyllic."

The human responsibilities that Delia thought she could leave begin to pile on again, as she acquires friends and, eventually, takes a job caring for a small boy and his recently divorced father. Old worries and responsibilities begin to reassert themselves—"It was so easy to fall back into being someone's mother!"—and finally

Delia becomes so enmeshed with this new family that she must make a decision: to let Joel and Noah Miller become *her* family, or to return to the one she had left, with such unresolved anger, a year earlier.

Tyler's pattern of escape and return is so well established that Delia's choice should come as no surprise. Yet there is a significant difference here: for the first time, it strikes me that Tyler herself doesn't believe in her own happy ending. There are plenty of clues planted in the text to make the reader suspect that Joel and Noah are meant to be simply another version, another face, of the Grinstead family, but there is no question that Tyler has made the Millers kinder, more attractive, and more emotionally necessitous people than the Grinsteads. Delia obviously loves Sam, but his lovableness is not readily apparent to the reader.

He is a familiar, and not very appealing, type: "I'm glad to hear it was one of Sam's favorite responses. Along with If you say so, Dee, and Have it your way. After which he might serenely turn a page, or he would start talking with the boys about some unrelated subject." Similarly, the loutishness of adolescence doesn't go far enough to explain the singular coldness of the Grinstead children, while Noah Miller is affectionate, eager to love his surrogate mother.

Ladder of Years is essentially about facing and coming to terms with grief: in Delia's case, grief for her father, long-ago and deeply repressed grief for her mother, grief for the ideal marriage she never had and for the husband and children she will soon lose. Delia finds a way of coping with the grief, but it doesn't abate. And never before has Tyler seemed so ambivalent about the neat resolution she has imposed on her story. As in *Saint Maybe*, Tyler shows a new maturity in being content to leave some central questions unanswered: why does Delia so fiercely repress any memory of her mother? Will Sam and Delia meet on a better-informed level, or will their marriage continue to limp unsatisfactorily along?

To sum up a writer's life and work at what is essentially mid-career can be only a tentative business, especially since Tyler has demonstrated that, while there is a rather predictable aesthetic and subject matter to which all of her books conform, she is quite capable of transcending her norm and confounding our expectations. Capable, but not always convinced of the necessity, and her weak spots are only too obvious. "As far as I'm concerned," she has said, "character is everything. I never did see why I have to throw in a plot, too." Well, sometimes she doesn't—or at least, not enough of one. Instead, she lets her characters talk on and on, in the naïve expectation that the reader will find them as irresistible as she does herself.

Yet Tyler has given us four excellent books, and may well do more. In her last two novels she has attempted to go honestly to the heart of the matter, without succumbing to the temptation of local color, histrionic characters, or easy optimism. There is every reason to suppose that she will continue to improve.

(1995)

18. DEADEYE DICK
RICHARD BURTON, DIARIST

L iz and Dick. It was, for a while at least, the romance of the century. In 1962, when Burton and Taylor dodged their respective spouses while filming *Cleopatra* in Rome and began their melodramatic liaison, which included a suicide attempt (Elizabeth's) and a condemnation from the Vatican, there ensued a paparazzi feeding frenzy the likes of which would not be seen again until the death of Princess Diana thirty-five years later. Even Brangelina had nothing on Liz and Dick. Burton was devastatingly attractive and virile, and was widely acknowledged as a great actor, the natural successor to Gielgud and Olivier. And Taylor was, according to popular opinion, the most beautiful woman in the world. Even as a small child, hardly able to read, I was somehow made aware of the brouhaha.

Their elopement was romantic but the long-term picture was not pretty. The Burtons turned out to be not only the most glamorous couple in the world but one of the most self-indulgent: alcohol, food, yachts, private jets, diamonds as big as the Ritz. They treated drinking as a competitive sport, and booze spawned unseemly brawls. Paparazzi shots from the later years of their partnership show a puffy, degenerate-looking couple. Their careers suffered. They divorced in 1974, then remarried a year later, but it was only a few months before the marriage's final meltdown.

The exploits of Liz and Dick, as revealed by the tabloids, made a singularly unedifying spectacle. Richard and Elizabeth, the human beings behind the tabloid stories, seem to have been rather different. The recently published *Richard Burton Diaries* shows us a couple whose habits were as undisciplined as those of Liz and Dick but whose humor, intelligence, and family feeling made up for a great many of their failings. Richard Burton himself is the greatest surprise here: the diaries reveal a man of considerable intellectual abilities who was tormented by a feeling that he had ended up in the wrong life. If he had followed his own inclinations, he would have been a writer or a professor of literature, but his rise to stardom was so meteoric and its rewards so lavish that he hadn't the willpower to change directions. In 1969, irritated after an interview with a fatuous journalist, he went on a characteristic rant in his diary:

> I think Mr. Thompson was deeply shocked when I told him that acting on stage or films, apart from one or two high moments of nervous excitement, was sheer drudgery. That if I retired from acting professionally tomorrow I would never appear in the local amateur dramatic society for the sheer love of it. Could he not understand the indignity and the boredom of having to learn the writings of another man, which nine times out of ten was indifferent, when you are forty-three years old, are fairly widely read, drag yourself off to work day after day with a long lingering regretful look behind you at the book you're interested in . . . They will never understand that E and I are not "dedicated" and that my "first love" (God how many times have I read that?) is not the stage. It is a book with lovely words in it. When I retire which I must do

before long I shall write a screaming diatribe against the whole false world of journalism and show business.

Burton was not exaggerating his love of reading: he went through about three books a day, everything from *Ulysses* to *The Murder of Roger Ackroyd* to nature books to biographies of J.B.S. Haldane, George Custer ("Unreadable. It is as if the writer was not only bad but a homosexual madly in love with Custer"), and Queen Victoria ("To my astonishment I find the book written very racily, and the subject, absolutely absorbing . . . There was more, obviously, to the dwarf Queen than met the eye"). His great passion was poetry. A man whose university education extended to a six months' short course program at Oxford University during World War II, Burton was avid for intellectual stimulation; he admitted that his greatest pipe dream was to be a fellow at All Souls, and when he was invited to spend a term at Oxford teaching English poetry to undergraduates he went mad with excitement.

But despite these literary ambitions Burton was fatally hooked on the celebrity culture he claimed to scorn. He reveled in having landed the world's top girl and he gloated at the attention Elizabeth got when bedecked in the jewels he had bought her, baubles that included the Krupp Diamond, the La Peregrina Pearl (a wedding gift from Philip of Spain to Mary Tudor), and the famous Taylor–Burton diamond, weighing in at more than sixty-nine carats. He was dazzled by his luxurious yacht, the Kalizma (named for three of the Burtons's children, Kate, Liza, and Maria):

The Monet is in the living room or salon, the Picasso and the Van Gogh are in the dining room. The Epstein bust of Churchill is brooding over the salon and there is a Vlaminck on the wall of the stairwell to the kids' cabins . . . We didn't go to bed until 3:30 because we were so excited at the joy of the boat. I can't as 'twere stop touching it and staring at it, as if it were a beautiful baby or puppy-dog. Something you can't believe is your very own.

You can hear the distinct tones of the poor boy who made good; this was a rags-to-riches story that rivals any. For Burton was the twelfth child of a coal miner in a Glamorgan valley; only his unusual intelligence and talent, and the interest and support of a teacher, Philip Burton (whose name the young Richard Jenkins eventually took), kept him from following his father and older brothers into the mines. As the bright cynosure at the center of the celebrity whirlwind, Burton viewed its frenzy with the jaundiced eye of an outsider and, while he never forgot his origins, he had no wish to return to obscurity. "I like being famous," he reflected in 1970. "I wonder how I'll feel when I'm not. After twenty years of it now and a further few years I suppose it will feel very strange to be Richard Jenkins again as it were."

The gossip in these diaries, for those of us who are still interested in the stars of that era, is spectacular. Rex Harrison, at premieres and other special events, "always wears a toupée and makes up with 'Man Tan.'" Mrs. Rex Harrison, the actress Rachel Roberts, "who is always pretty good value for a diary, showed everybody her pubic hairs, and as a dessert lay down on the floor in a mini-skirt and showed her bum to anyone who cared to have a glance." Lucille Ball, who in the wake of the great diamond ring purchase of 1970 had persuaded the Burtons to appear on her sitcom *Here's Lucy*, gets a particularly brutal drubbing: "Those who had told us that Lucille Ball was 'very wearing' were not exaggerating. She is a monster of staggering charmlessness and monumental lack of humor . . . Milady Balls can thank her lucky stars that I am not drinking." (I was inspired by this diatribe to track down the episode in question on YouTube and am here to say that in this case Burton was wrong: Milady Balls knew what she was doing and the schtick she concocted was very funny, to the point where it seemed to me that Taylor might have had a career in farce had she chosen to go in for it.)

For an actor of his caliber, Burton seemed surprisingly uninterested in the craft of acting. Mostly he complained about the exertions of his trade: while filming *The Taming of the Shrew* with Elizabeth, for example, he describes a week in which "we waded through wool, ran through bats, swung on trapezes, threw each other around." A gig in the 1971 film *Raid on Rommel* was even more punishing: "climbing in and out of tanks and lorries and running across the sand and diving into various holes when explosions are supposed to be going off." On the rare occasions when Burton did expound on acting techniques, his observations tended to be amusing if not terribly enlightening:

I do not wish to compete with Olivier or Gielgud and Scofield and Redgrave etc. as they are too "actory" for my liking. Apart from occasional performances, few and far between, I don't believe a word they say. Larry is the past-master of professional artificiality. A mass of affectations. So is Paul. John is always the same and when it fits the part he is very watchable, but when it doesn't it can only be described as regrettable. They have splendid presences and are very hard-working and genuinely love their jobs. I cannot match the two latter qualities. And do not wish to.

Or, when acting the part of Henry VIII in *Anne of the Thousand Days*:

Oh, blessed relief, I had to work with Tony Quayle and Michael Hordern. Marvelous pair of pros and no rubbish and cunning as snakes. I held my own I think. They have every shrug, nod, beck, sideways glance and shifting of eyes ever invented. I said to the director that it was somewhat akin to playing between the frying-pan and the fire. All Michael Hordern had to say was "Yes, your Grace." He must have said four hesitant "yours" and the three words, uttered in his inimitable way became slightly longer than Hamlet. Uncut. They both varied the time of their readings in an unconscious effort to "throw" each other off, and me. But I'm too old a hand. I "threw" them a couple of times too. None said a word to each other about it but all three old bastards knew bloody well that when that camera is purring it's every man for himself. Of course if you are the "star" or the "money" as the technicians call it you can afford to be magnanimous because the "money" is almost automatically protected but it's as well to know what the hell you're up to. And to let them know that you know what they are up to.

Burton did not enjoy the filming process and seemed happiest when living a quiet life with Elizabeth on the Kalizma or in their home in the Swiss Alps where, although there was—as always—plenty of booze, their amusements were simple and even innocuous; during one period in 1965 they spent several hours a day playing Yahtzee, of all things. (In fact during one of their frequent arguments Burton angrily told Elizabeth that the only thing they had in common was Yahtzee.) Food was also a pleasure and, all too often, a trap.

Both E and I went mad last night and started eating Callard and Bowsers Liquorice Fingers. I must have eaten a pound or so and E somewhat less. The results were evident this morning. I had put on 3½ lbs and E 2 lbs. Today we are unrepentant but determined to redress the balance. E longs to be 129 lbs and I to be 170. It can be done. But not perhaps by us.

One of the more appealing characteristics of the Burtons is the time and trouble they took over their children, which was unusual for showbiz parents of the era. Between them they had six: Kate and Jessica Burton, daughters of Burton with his first wife Sybil; Michael and Christopher Wilding, sons of Elizabeth and her second husband, the British actor Michael Wilding; Liza Todd Burton, daughter of Elizabeth and the deceased Mike Todd, whom Richard adopted; and Maria, a German orphan Richard and Elizabeth had adopted together. The children, their education, and their complicated comings and goings were a constant focus of concern, as were the doings and needs of the members of Burton's extended family back in Wales, many of whom he supported.

Chris Williams, the editor of this volume, has done an astounding amount of research, tracking down every reference to even the most obscure acquaintances. When it comes to Burton's early associations in Wales, this could not have been at all easy. Williams is a professor of Welsh history at Swansea University, and in the manner of most academics he piles on the footnotes with too much gusto; there is no reference, however obvious, that Williams doesn't feel the need to explain. Agatha Christie, Montgomery Clift, Cary Grant, Barbra Streisand, Leonardo da Vinci: one wonders why a reader who needed to have all these people identified would be interested in ploughing through 600 pages by an actor who, by now, is less well known than any of them. But really important references are unaccountably absent; there is no mention, for instance, that Jessica Burton was autistic—a great and haunting tragedy in Burton's life.

For it is among his family that Burton is shown to his best advantage. He was not always a perfect parent and not always— God knows!—a perfect husband. But he was a fond one, and it is the little domestic details, in the end, that stick with the reader.

Both E and I did our going to bed exercises last night together. It is difficult to keep a straight face when she is doing her numbers as she goes at it with a solemn ferocity which is hilarious. It is especially droll when we do running on the spot as she has to hold her breasts—one hand on each—for firm as they are, really like a thirty-year-old's more than a nearly forty-year-old's, they are pretty big and the resultant wiggle-waggle would be pretty odd as well as bad for her. It's a very fetching sight and were it open to the public would fetch a lot of people. Like ten million.

During the time they were married Richard left his diary lying about for Elizabeth to read whenever she liked, so we can take flattering little asides, such as the one about the firmness of Elizabeth's breasts, with a bit of cynicism. But even without the sweeteners, the picture we find here of the famously volatile Burton marriage is an affectionate one. Nothing in the post-Liz entries comes close to this sort of domestic contentment—and Burton continued the diary, sporadically, until his death. Life went on, but with less love, it seems, and considerably less humor.

(2013)

19. The Art of Exile
Horton Foote's Staying Power

Like Eugene O'Neill, the playwright Horton Foote essentially had two careers. During the first, which lasted from the early 1940s until the late 1960s, he established a reputation as a fine regional writer with a homespun flavor, occasional flashes of brilliance, and a flawless ear for the dialogue of his native East Texas. The one-act plays Foote wrote for live television in the early 1950s (*The Oil Well*, *The Trip to Bountiful*, and *Death of the Old Man*, among others) were immediately recognized as works that lifted the new medium to a higher level. His Oscar-winning screen adaptation of Harper Lee's *To Kill a Mockingbird* (1962) put him at the top of Hollywood's A-list.

But the downward slope from that pinnacle is famously precipitous, and by 1968 the world seemed to have lost interest in what Foote had to offer. Sex and violence now ruled at the Hollywood box office. Original television drama was no longer being produced. Broadway, in the era of *Hair*, deemed Foote non-commercial. With four children to support, the playwright considered giving up writing altogether. He retreated with his family to New Hampshire and thought about opening an antique shop. It was only at his wife's insistence that he continued doggedly to pursue his vocation, with no guarantee that the plays he was turning out in his backwoods study would ever be produced. As his colleague Alan J. Pakula would later say, Foote did not "cut his talent to the fashion of the time." He continued to work his particular vein, which was the multilayered society of his hometown, Wharton, Texas—usually called Harrison in his plays.

And yet, qualitatively, the works that grew out of Foote's New Hampshire exile (like those of O'Neill's exile in the California hills) were something entirely new, indicating that the playwright had achieved a level of artistry of which, to judge from his earlier pieces with their neatly tied ends and generally satisfactory outcomes, one might not have thought him capable. There were dark comedies like *The Blind Date* and *The One-Armed Man*. And within two years of moving to New Hampshire, Foote had written eight of the nine plays that make up the *Orphans' Home Cycle*, an epic work based loosely on the lives of his parents, fictionalized as Horace and Elizabeth Robedaux. (The eight he wrote were *Roots in a Parched Ground, Convicts, Lily Dale, Courtship, Valentine's Day, 1918, Cousins,* and *The Death of Papa; The Widow Claire* was written later and inserted into the series.) Before long, these were being produced in the new off-Broadway theaters that had begun to flourish during Foote's absence from the scene.

More wonders ensued. Foote's original screenplay *Tender Mercies* (1983) won Oscars both for him and for his star, longtime Foote performer and devotee Robert Duvall. The new plays were much darker and more complicated than previous ones. There was *The Habitation of Dragons* (1988), Foote's version of Sophoclean tragedy. There was *Dividing the Estate* (1989, first performed in New York in 2007), the play Marx and Engels might have written if they'd had a sense of humor: a hilarious excoriation of the rentier class as worked out through the fortunes of a disintegrating family of Texas landowners. There was *The Young Man from Atlanta* (winner of the 1995 Pulitzer Prize for Drama), a masterpiece of reading and writing between the lines: a play largely about homosexuality in which the word homosexuality, and even the concept of it, are never actually mentioned. There were emotionally complex and unsettling pieces like *The Roads to Home* (1982) and *The Day Emily Married* (1996). No more happy endings or even conclusive ones: whatever tragic events might have occurred on stage, we are always made aware that the next day, and the next, and the next, the spent characters will have to go back to uttering the banal niceties and enduring the prying curiosity that make up life in their unforgivingly conventional society.

I was impressed by all these achievements, but it wasn't until I saw the full three-evening production of the *Orphans' Home Cycle* at the Signature Theater Company in 2010 that I experienced one of those artistic epiphanies that the modern theater all too rarely provides. This is clearly a very great work of art, and Foote (who died in 2009 at the age of ninety-two) has proved a very great playwright, in my opinion the greatest American playwright of the last century.

His work suffers from none of the limitations that have marred even the best of his peers. O'Neill had no ear for language and was unforgivably self-indulgent in his refusal to edit; Foote seldom misplaced a phrase or an intonation. Arthur Miller delivered solid melodramas with neatly packaged moral messages, all totally lacking in humor. A view of life that does not include humor is an incomplete one. In Foote, as in Chekhov (with whom he is often compared), tragedy and comedy are not separate entities but are inextricably blended through all of life's trials. And where Miller was heavily didactic Foote was the opposite: nowhere in all his sixty plays and screenplays can one find a line as obvious or as nakedly declarative as Mrs. Willy Loman's famous "Attention must be paid . . . Attention, attention must finally be paid to such a person." Foote knew that nobody talks like that. Tennessee

Williams, a longtime friend and admirer of Foote's, knew it too, but his plays examined the pathological where Foote's turned to the universal.

For a long time I have privately agreed with Mary McCarthy's unkind assessment of "the cave-world of the American school playwrights, who have accustomed us to a stage inhabited by inarticulate, ape-like individuals groping for words":

> The typical character of the so-called American realist school belongs to the urban lower middle class sociologically, but biologically he is a member of some indeterminate lower order of primates. This creature is housed in a living-room filled with installment-plan furniture, some of which will be broken before the play is over. The sound of breakage and the sound of heavy breathing will signify "theatre." As directed by Elia Kazan, the whip-cracking ringmaster of this school of brutes, the hero is found standing with clenched fists, stage left, yelling at some member of his family, stage right, until one of them breaks into hysterical weeping and collapses onto a chair by the stage-center table, his great head buried in his hands. The weeping character is confessing to being alcoholic, homosexual, a failure.

Foote, even from his earliest days, was so very different. His plays contain countless alcoholics, homosexuals, and failures, but these characters are subtly self-revealing rather than crudely confessional.

Yet Foote is not a household name and is ignored, it seems, in the academy. Flipping through the SAT Literature Review book recently, I was struck by its summary of late twentieth-century drama: "Important English-language playwrights of the era," it said, "included Eugene O'Neill, Tennessee Williams, Arthur Miller, and Thornton Wilder in the United States." Mention is then made of verse plays and theater of the absurd. The author(s) go on to opine that, "Perhaps the most important English-language playwright of the present day is Tom Stoppard. Other major contemporary playwrights include David Mamet, Edward Albee, Peter Shaffer, and August Wilson." No mention of Foote.

W hy should he have slipped beneath so many people's radar? Some, like his biographer Wilborn Hampton, have suggested that Foote's relative obscurity might be due to his quiet middle-class lifestyle. He bedded no movie stars, imbibed only Dr. Pepper, had no nervous breakdowns. He was married to the same woman for nearly fifty years and enjoyed happy relationships with all his children. (His daughter Hallie, now a distinguished actress, has proved the preeminent interpreter of her father's work.) He was also an unassuming man, and the public has shown us again and again that it accepts artists' own valuation of themselves: portentousness and self-importance have never hurt any writer's reputation. Then too, as Martin Benson, the director of Foote's play *Getting Frankie Married—and Afterwards* (1995), once pointed out, "Maybe one reason he's not produced as much as he should be is that sometimes his plays seem simplistic on the page. You can think, 'Oh, rural America,' and that it's oversimplified and a cliché. But when you get up to act them, they're incredibly rich, with enormous depths."

Rural America. Yes, Foote was a regional writer, but—at least in the great later plays—regional only in the sense that Jane Austen was a regional writer: he shared with Austen, that is, the conviction that a provincial backwater offers as full a panoply of human folly, nobility, tragedy, and absurdity as any great metropolis does. Just as Austen's characters occasionally repair to Bath to take the waters, Foote's sometimes seek greener pastures in nearby Houston, but their inner lives are always lived back in Harrison. And of all the major Southern writers Foote relied the least on "South-

ernisms." His plays contain no redeye gravy or fried green toma-
toes; his characters seldom venture to the Piggly Wiggly. His earlier
plays have a few colorful regionalisms, but as he matured artistically they dwindled, and by the time he wrote the *Orphans' Home
Cycle* they had all but disappeared. Instead, local flavor is
embedded in the rhythms and music of the dialogue (Reynolds
Price called Foote "unquestionably the supreme musician among
our great American playwrights"), as well as in the telling
euphemisms and circumlocutions required to be cruel, to be
pointed, to be direct in a society that prides itself on gentility and
politesse. How often, while visiting my own Texan relatives, have I
not heard barbed little exchanges like the following?

Roberta [speaking of her son, Tommy]: Did you know
Julia and Tommy were engaged, Mrs. Nelson?

Mrs. Nelson: Yes, I heard.

Roberta: We think she's mighty sweet. She isn't the prettiest girl in the world, but she's mighty sweet.

Tommy: I think she's the prettiest girl in the world.

Roberta: I'm glad you do, Sonny. Anyway, Daddy and I
think she's mighty sweet.

— *THE OLD BEGINNING*, 1952

Foote was a master of this sort of thing. He was a master, too,
at rendering the inconsequential chit-chat that makes up the background noise of all our lives:

Frankie: What was the name of her first husband? I can't

remember and Mrs. Willis is about to drive me crazy asking me to remember his name.

Laverne: Ross. Ross something. He was with an oil crew. I don't think they were married more than eight months.

Constance: Ross Matthews?

Laverne: I think so. (Isabel comes in) Was the name of Georgia Dale's first husband Ross?

Isabel: No, Billy.

Laverne: Billy?

Isabel: Yes, don't you remember? She was a little taller than he was and so she stopped wearing high heels whenever she went out with him.

Laverne: It wasn't Billy. It was Ross.

Constance: Ross Matthews.

Isabel: Well, maybe so, but who was Billy?

Laverne: God knows.

Isabel: Don't you remember how she stopped wearing high heels when she met him? I thought she married him.

Laverne: No, it was Ross.

Constance: I think so, too. Ross Matthews.

— *GETTING FRANKIE MARRIED—AND*
AFTERWARDS, 1995

Critics have usually classified Foote as a realistic playwright, but as such dialogue indicates his "realism" was always stylized, and as he got older it became more so, with startling whiffs of Samuel Beckett rising from Harrison's banal street corners. Three of the *Orphans' Home* plays—*Convicts*, *Valentine's Day*, and *Cousins*—attain an absurdism worthy of Ionesco, with dramatic and even tragic events occurring in a context of farcical mayhem. One of Foote's favorite techniques along these lines was to make use of a character who is in some way impaired—drunk, senile, or, in Harrison parlance, "not quite bright"—and who has to have everything explained to him over and over, so that while laughing at the comic reiteration the audience is given a painless dose of exposition. It was a device the playwright used again and again, always to advantage. In *Valentine's Day*, he compounded the effect with a madman, a drunk, and a simpleminded girl, so that the pivotal events of the play—Elizabeth and Horace's moving reconciliation with Elizabeth's parents, Mr. and Mrs. Vaughn, and the eventual suicide of the madman—are played out against a disconcerting background of low farce.

Foote was not in any conventional sense of the word a political playwright, but he never lost sight of the often dreadful political and social realities of the Texas he knew, where the scars of slavery and Reconstruction were still raw. As mentioned above, *Dividing the Estate* carries an almost Marxist message, and when the matriarch Stella Gordon boasts that the family estate "has taken very good care of us all these years," the audience readily understands the opposite to be the case: the existence of the estate and its promise (false, as things turn out) of unearned income for life has in fact ruined each and every one of the Gordons.

Well, not quite every one, after all. There are always a few people who rise above circumstances just as there are those who sink inexplicably beneath them, and the question of why "some men amount to something and some men don't," as one of Foote's characters remarks, remains a mystery. As a boy, Foote was faced with that question on a daily basis in the persons of his three maternal uncles, every one of them a drunkard and a wastrel. How had this happened when their parents were so very respectable? Foote explored the issue in the *Orphans' Home Cycle*, for whose purposes he rolled up all three of his uncles into the single character of Brother Vaughn. (The very young Matthew Broderick's portrayal of Brother in early productions of *Valentine's Day* and *1918* made an indelible impression on those who saw it, so much so that Foote delayed production of the cycle's final installment, *The Death of Papa*, until Broderick was old enough to play the by-then-thirtyish Brother.)

The issue of race relations is never front and center in Foote's plays, but neither is it ever forgotten. Just as Jane Austen did not presume to write a scene in which two men speak alone, Foote did not presume to write one in which two black characters speak alone. But such characters hover most significantly at the fringes of his plays and sometimes step in to steal the scene. In his *Farewell: A Memoir of a Texas Childhood*, Foote mused on the mysterious lives of Wharton's black citizens, wondering at their silent stoicism.

[The population of Wharton] was three thousand then, with almost as many blacks as whites. I knew all the whites, at least by sight, and I knew many of the blacks by their given names: Stant, Baby Clegg, Delia, Celleste, Little Bit, Willie, Dee and Walter. Walter was Stant's cousin, and looked almost white. I wondered about that, but never asked why it was so . . .

Walter and his sister Eliza each had a one-room house in my grandparents' backyard. I wonder now how they endured their lives without complaint.

Eliza had to be up every morning (seven days a week) at seven and cook breakfast, dinner and supper. For all this she was paid three dollars a week, and a furnished one-room house and food. Walter worked in the yard, and after my grandfather died, chauffeured my grandmother on trips to the farms, the cemetery to visit my grandfather's grave, around town or to Houston. I never knew what he got paid, but I feel sure it was only three dollars too.

The grim lives of such domestics in these plays is never dwelt on too obviously, but they serve to put the white characters' carping into proportion. In *Dividing the Estate* the Gordon family's hysterical wailing over their financial losses is set in unflattering relief against the joy of the two black servants when they are told of their modest five-thousand-dollar bequests from matriarch Stella: "Didn't I tell you she was going to generously remember us?"

But in this area as in every other, nothing could make Foote a didactic writer, and some audiences have been offended by his apparently brutal manner of telling it like it is rather than as it should be. The dark farce *Convicts*, set in 1904, features a broken-down, paranoiac landowner who has thought to save money by contracting black convicts to work his decrepit plantation in conditions not essentially different from the slavery their forebears endured on the same spot half a century earlier. That a violent and exploitative man should nonetheless be portrayed as pitiable and human, even comical, offended the sort of critics who like their moral lessons unadulterated. And yet—looking at this illiterate, drunken old creature decked out in his Confederate officer's blue coat, by now faded and unraveling—well, what clearer metaphor could anyone want?

In 1991 an excellent film version of *Convicts* appeared, directed by Peter Masterson and starring Robert Duvall as Soll Gautier and James Earl Jones as Ben, his long-suffering retainer. As with most of Foote's original movies it was low-budget and had a limited release. Only two have escaped this fate: *Tender Mercies* and *The Trip to Bountiful* (1985, also directed by Masterson). *The Trip to Bountiful* was a fine movie, undoubtedly, but it has always bothered me that, of all Foote's dramas, this one should be the most widely known. For it is an immature work, originally written for live TV in the 1950s when Foote's writing had not yet begun to achieve what John Lahr has called his characteristic "rhapsody of ambivalence." *The Trip to Bountiful* could almost have been written by Arthur Miller. There is too clear a differentiation between "good" and "bad" characters, with the warm, earthbound Carrie Watts set against her ragingly narcissistic daughter-in-law, Jessie Mae. Jessie Mae is a memorable character, especially as portrayed in the film by the brilliant Carlin Glynn, but she is too coarse-grained. Over the course of his career Foote would greatly refine his narcissists, so that the later specimens—Josie Weems of the chilling *Night Seasons* (1993), for instance, or Horace's sister Lily Dale of both the *Orphans' Home Cycle* and *The Young Man from Atlanta*—are far more subtle and ultimately more insidious examples of the type. In a single line from one of these ladies, Foote could open whole vistas of self-regard:

Josie: I wish I had never permitted that marriage. I blame myself for giving my consent.

Laura Lee: I think they would have married anyway, Mother.

Josie devours the life of her daughter, Laura Lee, preventing her from marrying the man she loves and from having the home of her own that she longs for. But by the time Foote wrote *Night Seasons* he had come to understand that characters like Laura Lee (and by extension Carrie Watts) are not pure victims; they play a definite role in their own subjugation. There were to be no more pure victims in his work, and no more pure villains.

This is why the cozy Grandma Moses view of Foote is so very wrong. The playwright's obituary in the *Houston Chronicle* stated that "in an increasingly confused and rootless world, he was a voice of certitude and continuity—yes, like a grandfather or uncle imparting basic yet invaluable life lessons." But no—that is exactly what Horton Foote was not. Confusion and rootlessness are at the heart of all his best work, and the longer he wrote the less certitude and continuity he seemed to find in anything. No one ever wrote more truthfully of the speed with which the waters close over the heads of the recently deceased, or of the social changes that casually obliterate ways of life and even the memories of them: the transition, which Foote experienced firsthand, from an aristocratic plantation economy to a mercantile one; the coming of oil and the social retrenchments it imposed; the greedy spurt of development in which Wharton/Harrison's lovely tree-lined Richmond Street began, as he said, a "slow but steady descent into a metaphor for all the ugly, trashy highways that scar a great deal of small-town America." Nothing is permanent; the only way we can experience even the illusion of continuity is to cling to it for dear life.

Ben's final speech in *Convicts* says it all:

Ben: Says she's gonna let the weeds and trees and the cane get this land. Six months from now you won't know where anybody's buried out here. Not my people, not the convicts, not Mr. Soll. The trees and the weeds, and the cane, will take everything. "Cane land" they called it once, cane land it will be again. The house will go, the store will go, the graves will go, those with tombstones and those without.

"The world's an orphan's home," wrote Marianne Moore in the poem from which Foote took the title for his masterpiece. We are all orphans wandering alone through life, and the consolations of community and family are fleeting at best.

(2004)

20. A Newby Abroad
The English Travel Writer

I n his 1982 autobiography *A Traveler's Life*, the delightful travel writer Eric Newby, who died in 2006 at the age of eighty-six, expressed his thoughts on human existence.

In his writings, the Venerable Bede compared the span of human life to coming out of darkness into a lighted hall and, having reached the end of it, finding oneself under the necessity of setting off once more into the all-embracing gloom. To me life has been more like one of those sections of autostrada on the Italian Riviera, on which there are lots of tunnels, some long, some short, with sunlit open spaces of varying lengths between them for which the darkness leaves one temporarily dazzled and often unprepared.

Few writers of his generation matched Newby's felicitous gift for describing life's sunlit open spaces. His series of travel narratives began with *The Great Grain Race* (1956), a description of his experiences as an eighteen-year-old apprentice aboard a four-masted Finnish grain ship bound for Australia, and include *Slowly Down the Ganges* (1966), in which Newby and his redoubtable

Slovenian wife Wanda navigate the entire length of India's sacred river; *The Big Red Train Ride* (1978), an account of a trip on the Trans-Siberian Express during the Soviet era; and his most popular book, *A Short Walk in the Hindu Kush* (1958), a classic in the bumbling-Englishman-abroad genre.

Newby had much in common with fellow-travel writers and compatriots like Peter Fleming, Patrick Leigh Fermor, and Evelyn Waugh. As Waugh himself wrote in his preface to *A Short Walk in the Hindu Kush*, Newby approached travel in a peculiarly English manner: "The understatement, the self-ridicule, the delight in the foreignness of foreigners, the complete denial of any attempt to enlist the sympathies of his readers in the hardships he has capriciously invited": all these characteristics, Waugh felt, placed the young Newby squarely within "a whimsical tradition."

This is all true, but something set Newby slightly apart from his peers. Perhaps it was inferior social class: Newby defined himself as "middle-middle class," born in a "first-floor flat—facing the Metropolitan Water Board's reservoirs and filter rods by the Thames on the Surrey side of Hammersmith Bridge." Unable to make a living from writing until he reached middle age, he toiled away for two decades in uncongenial jobs in the garment trade, first in the family business of Lane and Newby Ltd., Wholesale Costumiers and Mantle Manufacturers, later for other companies. (His amusing memoir, *Something Wholesale*, gives a picture of these years.) Unlike England's other great travel writers, he did not receive a university education: when it looked as though he would fail the School Certificate in mathematics, his father removed him from St. Paul's and put him into business. "I was sorry about the decision," Newby wrote, striking an entirely uncharacteristic note of regret. "I was good at English, History, even Divinity, and I had dreamed of reading History at Oxford."

Perhaps it is this background that accounts for his steadfast refusal to lapse into the occasional mandarin riffs that Waugh, Fermor, and Wilfred Thesiger indulged in, and even occasionally

Fleming. Newby's commentary is characterized by a Chaucerian earthiness that provides a piquant contrast to his often spectacular surroundings. He writes glowingly, for example, of "the pleasure of looking down a railway lavatory pan and seeing the permanent way rushing past beneath me, something that has never ceased to fascinate me, whether on the Orient Express, the Trans-Siberian Railway, the 12:15 to Ernakulam Junction, or the 16:30 to Penzance." His literary references, when he indulges in such things, are not to high-flown travelers like Lawrence or Doughty, but to nursery staples like Hilaire Belloc and Kenneth Grahame. Metaphors and similes are frequently of the homeliest variety. The Volga in spring resembles "Brown Windsor Soup." Elephant dung in Africa is "four dollops of what looked like Old Auntie Mary's rich Dundee cake still steaming from the oven."

Newby took a perverse pleasure in the myriad hassles and hazards that exotic travel involves—as indeed all serious travelers must do: "The overcoming of insuperable difficulties is, of course, one of the unspoken reasons for traveling in remote places," he admitted. His setting off to climb the daunting peak of Mir Samir in Afghanistan's Hindu Kush seemed particularly suicidal, for as he readily admitted in the book he had never in fact climbed anything. "It was true that I had done some hill walking and a certain amount of scrambling in the Dolomites with my wife, but nowhere had we failed to encounter ladies twice our age armed with umbrellas. I had never been anywhere that a rope had been remotely necessary." Neither, as it turned out, had his companion for the voyage, Hugh Carless. The two spent a mere four days in Wales learning the basics, coached by some jolly hiking waitresses —a scene charmingly described in the book—and then set off with foolish optimism. Finally face-to-face with the mountain, Newby found that Mir Samir's "imminence gave the scene an air of unreality, like a stage set on which a piece is about to be enacted—as indeed it was. I only hoped it would be a comedy."

This hope was richly fulfilled, with the comedy frequently

descending into pure slapstick, such as the moment when Newby glissades twenty feet down a chimney of ice on his behind. "Very stupidly I was wearing my crampons attached to a sling round my middle and I sat on them for the full distance, so that they went in to the full length of the spikes, scarring me for life in a most interesting manner." And yet Newby was able to turn, on a dime as it were, to convey a scene of lyrical loveliness—in this case, Afghanistan's Panjshir Valley:

> But it was the river that dominated the scene. In it boys were swimming held up by inflated skins and were swept downstream in frightening fashion until the current swirled them into deep pools near the bank before any harm could come to them; while in the shallows where the water danced on pebbles smaller children splashed and pottered. On its banks, too, life was being lived happily; a party of ladies in reds and brilliant blues walked along the opposite bank, talking gaily to one another; poplars shimmered; willows bowed in the breeze; water flowed slowly in the irrigation ditches through a hundred gardens, among apricot trees with the fruit still heavy on them, submerging the butts of the mulberries, whose owners squatted in their properties and viewed the scene with satisfaction. Old white-bearded men sat proudly on stone walls with their grandchildren, grave-looking little boys with embroidered pillbox hats and little girls of extraordinary beauty. This evening was like some golden age of human happiness, attained sometimes by children, more rarely by grownups, and it communicated its magic in some degree to all of us.

In view of what has happened in Afghanistan since then, this breaks one's heart.

Newby defined "travel" broadly, and approached even the

most banal voyages with a zest that raised them to the level of adventure. A childhood trip through Harrods with his mother, a former model and compulsive shopper, takes on, in the telling, the perilous aura of an African safari.

> Get lost in Harrods and you had every chance, I believed, of ending up in the equivalent of that undiscovered country from whose bourne no traveler returns, which when I became a grown-up with an account of my own I located somewhere between Adjustments and Personal Credit (which comprehended Overdue Accounts) and the Funeral Department, for those whose shopping days were done but whose credit was still good, both of which were on the fourth floor.

And what about the truly harrowing Journey, a twice-yearly odyssey through Scotland and the north of England, undertaken by Newby and various other employees of Lane and Newby to show their wares to potential department-store buyers? On the first morning of his first Journey—Edinburgh, 1946—Newby eyed the coming day's schedule with some trepidation:

> 9:30 Mrs. McHaggart, Robertson's, Edinburgh 10:30 Mrs. McHavers, Lookies, Dundee 11:30 Miss McTush, Campbells, Edinburgh 11:45 Mrs. McRobbie, Alexander McGregor, Edinburgh 2:30 Miss Wilkie, McNoons of Perth 4:30 Miss Reekie, Madame Vera, Edinburgh

"To me," he remarked, "it sounded more like a gathering of clans in some rainswept glen than a series of assignations to buy dresses in the sub-basement of a railway hotel."

If I am giving the impression that Newby stressed the comedy of travel at the expense of its romance, that would be wrong. There is no doubt that on his train journey across Russia and Siberia he took special note of ridiculous details—the female deputy station-master in Omsk, for instance, in a dreadful gray skirt "which made her look as if she was embedded in a block of concrete" or, still more frighteningly, the "most terrible of all torments devised for visitors behind the Iron Curtain, an extended tour of a wire-making factory"—but he conveys with some power the epic scale of every landscape and every undertaking in that vast country, and compares his own impressions with those of earlier travelers like Chekhov to trace the persistence, through a series of wildly different political regimes, of a recognizable national character. In the Shetland Islands he derives some humor from the instructions he is given on how to get to the remote island of Taransay. ("Tarbert to Horgabust—twelve miles. Taxi. Try to hire the Rev. Macdonald's rowing boat. If he won't lend it light bonfire on headland and hope that the Campbells will pick you up.") But his description of the place's unearthly beauty, and of how the few remaining islanders cling to their dying way of life, is haunting.

Newby's most romantic book is possibly his best: *Love and War in the Apennines* (1971), in which he relates his dramatic experiences as an escaped prisoner of war in the Italian mountains during World War II. Serving in a special boat unit, Newby was captured off the coast of Sicily in 1942 and sent to a prison camp. With the Italian armistice in 1943 and the subsequent German invasion of Italy, a group of local partisans helped him escape from his captors and hide in the Apennines through that bitter winter. He survived, thanks to the bravery and generosity of the area's *contadini*, until his eventual and probably inevitable capture by German troops the following spring. Decades later Newby decided to write the book, he said, "because I felt that comparatively little had been written about the ordinary Italian people who helped prisoners of war at great personal risk and without thought of personal gain, purely out of kindness of heart.

The sort of people one can still see today working in the fields as one whizzes down the Autostrada del Sole and on any mountain road in the Apennines."

The elderly schoolmaster and partisan leader who helped spirit Newby out of his prison hospital in 1943 was a Slovene who happened to have a beautiful daughter. Wanda's "strangely melancholy" accent would become a subject for humor in Newby's later writings—she pronounced his name "Hurrock," for instance—but in early days he found it distinctly romantic, "a triple distillation of the essence of middle Europe." The two fell in love, and Wanda, like her father, risked her own life to save his, for the Germans had announced that anyone who helped prisoners of war would be sentenced to death. They brought him into the remote farms and villages of the mountains for safety, leaving him to the charity of the locals.

Love and War in the Apennines lovingly recalls a stark, primitive, yet beautiful and oddly innocent life that would disappear forever in the immediate postwar years. Here is Newby's description of a farmhouse in which he took temporary refuge:

> I shall never forget the moment when Signor Zanoni led me through the boiling slush in the yard and into the kitchen. It was more like a cavern than any room I had ever been in. One wall of it was part of the mountain, a great, smooth, shiny protruding rock which had been partly hollowed out to form the fireplace, itself a cave within a cave, as black as the outside of the copper pot which was suspended over the fire on a long chain, and the other three walls were made of rough blocks of undressed stone, some of them boulders, which heightened the illusion that this was an excavation rather than a room. In it the hot embers of the fire gave everything a reddish tinge and lamps hung on hooks on the walls which were nothing more than iron dishes filled with oil in which the wicks floated, the sort of

lamps the Etruscans might have used while digging their tombs . . .

I climbed up into the bed and burrowed down into it between the rough, white sheets. It was the best bed I have ever slept in before or since. It was as warm and soft as a woman and almost equally alive. I was almost tempted to talk to it but instead I fell asleep laughing with sheer joy while the thunder rolled and the rain beat down on the roof overhead. At this moment, about seven o'clock on the night of the twenty-fifth of September, 1943, there could have been few people in the whole of Fortress Europe more contented or fortunate than I was.

He eventually fetched up in the isolated Pian del Sotto with a family consisting of middle-aged parents, a teenaged daughter, a hired girl, and a hired man. Newby, who could not speak fluent Italian, was to pose as a deaf-mute relation in case any German officers showed up. He was nonplussed to discover that so far from being the idyll of *dolce far niente* he had imagined, the lives of the Italian *contadini* consisted of backbreaking labor beginning before dawn and ending long after dark. Newby himself was put to work digging large stones out of a field, loading them into a wheelbarrow and dropping them off a cliff, a task which took him many months. "When the last meal of the day was over, we used to sit in a half circle round the fire in our stockinged feet toasting them and talking about all sorts of subjects, except the war in which no one seemed to have any interest whatsoever, except that it should finish." A favorite activity was the interpretation of everyone's dreams with the aid of a volume called *I Miei Sogni*. Newby did his best to provide interesting material for this symposium, but had to admit that he dreamed only one dream, night after night after night: that he was picking up stones on the Pian del Sotto.

A heady combination of high romance and low comedy, *Love and War in the Apennines* reads like a farcical—and more truthful

—version of *The English Patient*. Best of all, the reader knows it will have a happy ending, despite Newby's recapture, for he eventually marries Wanda and their long life together sounds very much like "happily ever after." Although he spent hard years in the rag trade, Newby later became travel editor of *The Observer*, a job he held from 1964 to 1973.

At the end of *A Traveler's Life* Newby reveals his reasons for leaving *The Observer*.

In the nine years I had been its travel editor the mechanisms of travel had changed out of all recognition. The great majority of travelers, myself included, were now moved around the world *en masse*, rather like air freight, and just like freight when they reached their destinations they were lifted out of the bowels of the aircraft and delivered to their hotel rooms.

And those hotel rooms, once they were attained, too often turned out to be interchangeable and homogenized units in anonymous cement boxes.

Entombed in such places I thought with nostalgia of Japanese inns in which some of the pleasures were decidedly unexpected. The silence of the Pera Palace [in Istanbul], shattered only once it is said by a Bulgarian whose suitcase, full of bombs, blew up in the hall as he was registering; the romantic decrepitude of the Bela Vista at Macau; the sleaziness of the Cavendish in the days of Rosa Lewis; the inspired improbability of the Oloffson at Port-au-Prince; and the friendliness of a certain pub on the estuary of the Kenmare River. I felt, too, and I felt myself responsible having for years written about lonely places, that the time was not far off when there would be no place on earth accessible to ordinary human beings in which they would be able to feel themselves alone under the sky without hearing the noise of machines.

His gloom might have been well-founded, but it was out of character. Newby was a cheerful soul whose enthusiasm could not be damped for long. He kept traveling, and kept writing: later books include *On the Shores of the Mediterranean* (1984), *Round Ireland in Low Gear* (1987), and *A Small Place in Italy* (1994).

The passing of Eric Newby is a sad thing, but I cannot be as pessimistic as Waugh was when he observed the young Newby half-a-century ago and feared that he might turn out to be the last of his genus. Several younger versions of the English amateur traveler have come along since then, including William Dalrymple and Nigel Barley, a.k.a. the Innocent Anthropologist. We have even produced a few in America: readers who enjoy Newby will find Tony Horwitz and Eric Hansen to be his kindred spirits. The England that produced Newby may have changed beyond recognition, but the restless, game, endlessly amused spirit that inspired him has not yet died. And in spite of globalization, mass tourism, increasingly unfriendly natives, and other hazards, it seems that there are still distant and exotic places to which the intrepid can repair.

(2007)

21. Updike's Farewell
A Writer Comes to the End

Many artists who keep working into their old age find themselves developing in new and sometimes unexpected directions. In fact the phenomenon is so common that critics have developed the term "late style" to account for it. The concept of late style is a loose one, for artists of course are different from one another and their aesthetic ideas can only unfold in ways determined by their previous careers, but these elderly writers, painters, and musicians have enough in common that some rather rough generalizations have been attempted. Kenneth Clark, in an essay entitled "The Artist Grows Old," isolated several common characteristics of what he called "old-age style": "its pessimism, its *saeva indignatio*, its feeling of hermetic isolation; and on the formal side its anti-realism, and its accumulation of symbolic motives"; also "the feeling of imminent departure" and "a mistrust of reason, a belief in instinct." Edward Said, whose meandering thoughts on the subject were collected in book form after his death, wrote: "This is the prerogative of late style: it has the power to render disenchantment and pleasure without resolving the contradiction between them. What holds them in tension, as equal forces straining in opposite directions, is the artist's mature subjectivity, stripped of hubris and pomposity, unashamed either of its fallibility or of the modest assurance it has gained as a result of age and exile."

Did John Updike, who died in 2009 at the age of seventy-six, have a "late style"? On the surface, at least, the answer would seem to be No. Despite the frequent turbulence of his domestic life he seems to have been an unusually happy man (for a major writer, that is), even "well-adjusted," ridiculously inadequate as that term might be. One searches in vain through his autobiographical writings (and almost all of his writing is, in one form or another, autobiographical; the examples that are not tend to be among his less successful fiction) for signs of the artist's traditional "alienation." A much-loved only child, he was made to feel safe and protected throughout his small-town Depression-era childhood. He even seems to have been happy in high school, acting as senior class president and enthusiastically maintaining old friendships and attending class reunions through the fifty-fifth, his last. Though his first marriage (to Mary Pennington) contained plenty of angst, chronicled in detail in his novels and short stories of the 1960s and 70s, he found much joy in it—joy that is also evident in his fiction, right up to his 1994 story "Grandparenting," the last installment of the eighteen "Maples" stories that describe a marriage very, very much like his own first one. His second marriage (to Martha Bernhard) was clearly a success. He faced old age with relative equanimity, pointedly refraining from airing the usual masculine anguish over fading potency, whether professional or sexual. He once wrote with approval of "the widely-met responsibility to make the best of each stage of life, including the last," a responsibility he met manfully, maintaining the diligent habits and prodigious output he had adhered to throughout his life—a book a year, and then some. Keeping pace right up to the end, he even left us two posthumous volumes: one of short stories, *My Father's Tears*, and another of poems, *Endpoint*.

There is little of Clark's *saeva indignatio* in Updike's late work; what *indignatio* there is tends to be controlled and rueful. Neither does one find the pessimism Clark mentioned. The infinitely beautiful physical world Updike celebrated throughout his career is not cheapened by the fact that it is receding from his grasp, and there is no sign of the sour-grapes, all-is-vanity rage that consumes so many old men. Updike knew he was leaving the world—for nearly all of the stories and poems in these two collections are imbued with that awareness—but this knowledge seemed to inspire not rage but a sort of rapturous appreciation for the many joys that were still on offer. Then there was the incredulity (which will be instantly recognizable to many older people) that this could be happening to *him*. The experiences of Martin Fairchild (one of numerous authorial surrogates in *My Father's Tears*) in "The Accelerating Expansion of the Universe" are characteristic. "Fairchild had not hitherto really believed in his own aging. He could see in the mirror his multiplying white hairs, his deepening wrinkles, and feel his shortness of breath after exertion, his stiffness after sitting too long in a chair or a car; but these phenomena took place a safe distance from the center of his being. His inmost self felt essentially exempt from ruin."

I think the key is in the last sentence; Updike wrote, in the final few years of his life, like a man who felt his inmost self to be essentially exempt from ruin. Even on his deathbed, in the hospital with terminal lung cancer—and despite some rather dark preceding verses—he didn't quite seem to believe it.

> The sky is turning that pellucid blue
> seen in enamel behind a girlish Virgin-
> the doeskin lids downcast, the smile demure.
> Indigo cloud-shreds dot a band of tan;
> the Hancock Tower bares a slice of night.
> So whence the world's beauty? Was I deceived?

One suspects that these qualities were simply gifts; Updike's nature, or brain chemistry, or whatever you want to call it, was predisposed to happiness and pleasure. Some might ascribe it to his religion, but then we have the usual problem of the cart and the horse. Did Updike's religion inform his attitudes or did his natural attitudes direct him towards his particular brand of Protestantism, fuzzy on dogma but affectionate toward ritual and stubborn in its refusal to doubt the existence of some sort of guiding Providence, despite much evidence to the contrary?

The story "Varieties of Religious Experience," written in reaction to the September 11 attacks, provides a few clues— at least if we are to associate Updike with one of the story's characters, which I think is unavoidable. Dan Kellogg, a sixty-four-year-old Episcopalian, abruptly loses his faith when, from the close vantage point of the Brooklyn Heights Promenade, he sees the World Trade Center towers topple. "No hand of God had intervened because there was none. God had no hands, no eyes, no heart, no anything." Dan's "revelation of cosmic indifference thrilled him, though his own extinction was held within this new truth like one of the white rectangles weightlessly rising and spinning within the boiling column of smoke. He joined at last the run of mankind in its stoic atheism."

"In his previous life, commonsense atheism had not been ingenious enough for him, nor had it seemed sufficiently gracious toward the universe. Now he had been shown how little the universe cared for his good will." Of course the very fact of waiting sixty-four years to realize the universe's indifference to human suffering displays a failure of imagination: what made the attack on the Trade Center any worse, in cosmic terms, than well-publicized events that occurred during Dan's lifetime in Europe, in Japan, in Russia, in Rwanda? Is enormity only really comprehensible when it is perpetrated on one's own turf? Dan is disgusted, suddenly, with the feeble consolations of his church: "like dogs, we creep back to lick the hand of a God Who, if He exists, has just given us a vicious kick. The harder he kicks, the more fervently we cringe and creep forward to lick His hand."

But predictably, the conversion to atheism does not last; the mental and spiritual habits of a lifetime are not sloughed off so easily.

> The Episcopal church, high in Cincinnati but not evangel-ical, presented a stream of Cranmer's words in which the mind could lose itself. Dan would have missed the mild-mannered fellowship—the handshakes under the vaulted ceiling, the awkward passing of the peace. Why punish with his non-attendance, in protest of something God and not they had done, a flock of potential probate clients for whom periodically chorusing the Nicene Creed was part, and not the very least part, of getting along, of doing their best, of being decent citizens? . . . He was alive, and a shadowy God with him, behind him. Human conscious-ness had curious properties. However big things were, it could encompass them, as if it were even bigger. And it kept insisting on making a narrative of Dan's life, however nonsensically truncated the lives of others—crushed in an instant, or snapped off on the birthing bed—had been.

As the narrator of the story "My Father's Tears," another Updike stand-in, remarks, "I had been conditioned to feel that there could be no joy in life without religious faith, and if such faith demanded an intellectual sacrifice, so be it." If none of this made for a very passionate creed, it was at any rate one that pulled the worshiper out of the centrifugal force of his own ego. It also connected him with the community—something that was very important to Updike, in whose work domesticity and community are so central. And then there was the matter of thanksgiving: as Updike said once (I can't remember when or where), you have to thank someone for the party. One suspects, too, that Updike got a bit of a contrarian kick out of being an unregenerate mainline Protestant in a literary world dominated by Jewish and atheist intellectuals. "I somehow wasn't Jewish, which made me/minority and something of a pet," he confessed in his poem "The Author Observes His Birthday, 2005."

U pdike believed in the Eliotic dictum that "In my beginning is my end," and his late stories (though not his poetry) hover almost obsessively over the hunk of 1930s small-town Pennsylvania that is already so familiar to his readers. The painter Francis Bacon once expressed the opinion that "artists stay much closer to their childhood than other people. They remain far more constant to those early sensations. Other people change completely, but artists tend to stay the way they have been from the beginning." The example of Updike would seem to support this view. His alter ego Jim Werley in "My Father's Tears" thought that one of the reasons his second marriage had lasted was that his wife, "knowing me in my old age, recognizes that I have never really left Pennsylvania, that it is where the self I value is stored, however infrequently I check on its condition."

Jim Werley may not check on its condition very often, but Updike certainly did, to the point of repetitiveness. Shillington, Pennsylvania (which often appears as Olinger in his fiction), in the manner of Winesburg, Ohio, and Grover's Corners, New Hampshire, provided its son with a comprehensible world that enriched his nascent understanding of humanity's variety. Updike's poem "Peggy Lutz, Fred Muth 12/13/08" is worth quoting at length:

> Dear friends of childhood, classmates, thank you,
> scant hundred of you, for providing a
> sufficiency of human types: beauty,
> bully, hanger-on, natural,

twin, and fatso—all a writer needs,
all there in Shillington, its trolley cars
and little factories, cornfields and trees,
leaf trees, snowflakes, pumpkins, valentines.

To think of you brings tears less caustic
than those the thought of death brings. Perhaps
we meet our heaven at the start and not
the end of life. Even then there were tears
and fear and struggle, but the town itself
draped in plain glory the passing days.

The town forgave me for existing; it
included me in Christmas carols, songfests
(though I sang poorly) at the Shillington,
the local movie house. My father stood,
in back, too restless to sit, but everybody
knew his name, and mine. In turn I knew
my Granddad in the overalled town crew.
I've written these before, these modest facts,

but their meaning has no bottom in my mind.
The fragments in their jiggled scope collide
to form more sacred windows. I had to move
to beautiful New England—its triple
deckers, whited churches, unplowed streets
to learn how drear and deadly life can be.

Can the town really have been the Eden of prelapsarian innocence Updike remembers? Probably not, but that is not important;
what was important to him is that it nourished him. Throughout
his life Updike was self-involved in the pleasant manner of a child;
he was aware of others' pain but happy, most of all, to be cocooned
in their love and approval. Lee, the little boy in the best of the

childhood stories in this volume, "The Guardians," lives out a boyhood very similar to the author's: an only child, he shares a modest home with his parents and grandparents, who have been compelled by the exigencies of the Depression to set up house together. He knows his value to the adults: "It did occur to Lee, though not in words he could say, that he was a bright spot in a demoralized household"; he revels in their attention. "He felt the four adults as sides of a perfect square, with a diagonal from each corner to a central point. He was that point, protected on all sides, loved from every direction." Updike drew nourishment that would last a lifetime from this idyll, so productively that it comes as a bit of a shock to realize that he denied such security to his own children, leaving his family for another woman when all four of them were still in their teens. Not that he ever attempted to justify his behavior. "I drank up women's tears and spat them out/as 10-point Janson, Roman and ital" he admitted in "The Author Observes His Birthday, 2005":

My life, my life with children, was a sluice
that channeled running water to my pan;
by tilting it, and swirling lightly, I
at end of day might find a fleck of gold.

What of remorse? The elderly Craig Martin in "Personal Archaeology" looks back from a distance of three or four decades at his traumatic divorce: "In abandoning his family, a man frees up a bracing amount of time. Craig found himself projected into novel situations—dawn risings from a strange bed, visits to lawyers' offices, hotel stays hundreds of miles from home—and reacted like an actor who had rehearsed the lines he spoke, who had zealously prepared for this unsympathetic role, and played it creditably, no matter what the reviewers said. So why the stage fright now, in his sleep? It had been there all along, and was rising up into him, like his death."

There were undoubtedly memories that made Updike feel unease and remorse, but these were not sentiments he chose to dwell on; throughout his career he resolutely refused to countenance the tragic, though everyone's lives contain tragedies, even his. Yet tragedy pops up, sometimes in the most surprising places, as in the beautiful poem "Bird Caught in My Deer Netting":

> . . . The panicky
> thrashing and flutter, in daylight and air,
> their freedom impossibly close, all about!
>
> How many starved hours of struggle resumed
> in fits of life's irritation did it take
> to seal and sew shut the berry-bright eyes
> and untie the tiny wild knot of a heart?
> I cannot know, discovering this wad
> of junco-fluff, weightless and wordless
> in its corner of netting deer cannot chew through,
> nor gravity-defying bird bones break.

The bird's death was preventable, terrifying. Updike's own, as he knew before finishing *Endpoint*, would come from inevitable decrepitude, "on a bed." His reaction to his impending demise, if these poems and stories are any indication, was to hold fast to memory. Looking back at childhood—his beginning and his ending—he found poignancy in the thought that his consciousness was the last repository for so many of these once-concrete realities, and the thoughts he gave to the adult Lee in "The Guardians" were undoubtedly his own:

> Now all were gone. Of that early mid-twentieth-century household, only Lee was left. The coal bin in the cellar, the shelves of homemade preserves, the walnut icebox, the black stone sink, the warping kitchen linoleum in the

pattern of little interlocking bricks, the stained-glass dining-room chandelier shade, the front-hall newelpost with ribs around it like the rings of Saturn or Plastic Man's telltale stripes, the narrow back stairs that nobody used and that became a storage space choked with cardboard boxes and appliances to be repaired some day, the windowless stair landing where they had huddled in the pitch dark during mock air raids, the long side porch where hoboes had knocked for handouts, the pansy-faced calico cat that came to the porch to be fed but was too wild to come into the house, the tawny wicker lawn chair where Grampop would sit in the twilight with his cigar, watching the fireflies gather—only Lee was left to remember any of this.

It is an unremarkable litany; each one of us has such a list somewhere in our long-term memory. But to Updike each item was sacred because it was his, a part of his life, evidence of the benign providence that cushioned his existence. A charmed life, indeed. His resolute turning from darkness to light has annoyed some critics who demand a more tortured, agonistic approach from their great writers. And perhaps Updike was not a great writer. But he was an artist of tremendous gifts who gave an inordinate amount of pleasure over a career of more than half a century; and these wonderful last offerings live up to his highest standards.

(2009)

22. Capote Reconsidered
After Notoriety

When Truman Capote died in 1984, just before his sixtieth birthday, his life had been a shambles for years. The phenomenal success of *In Cold Blood* (1966) fulfilled all his dreams, but just at that moment he began inexplicably to implode. His crack-up was as public and spectacular as any in recent history. Suffering from what is known as free-floating anxiety, he ingested heroic amounts of alcohol and patronized all the pill-pushing Dr. Feelgoods who flourished in New York during the 1960s and 70s. He derived no benefit from his frequent stays in clinics and hospitals, often returning to the bottle the very evening of his release. Increasingly detached from his longtime partner, Jack Dunphy, who had been a stabilizing force, he embarked on a series of inappropriate relationships, culminating in one with a suburban heterosexual bank official, John O'Shea: this was an insane mésalliance that turned into an orgy of mutual abuse.

The 1975 publication in *Esquire* of a chapter from his work in progress, *Answered Prayers*, made him a social pariah: the rich and beautiful friends he had long cultivated went mad with rage when they read the thinly disguised, deeply hurtful descriptions of themselves by the adorable little man they had come to think of as a favorite household pet, an *ami de la maison*. How could he ever have thought he would get away with it? What demon of perversity, what layers of self-delusion could have persuaded him that he could write such things without causing offense?

During his last few years, Capote's appearances in the gossip columns and magazines were pathetic, featuring pictures of him being led off the stage incoherently drunk at a reading, being carried comatose from his apartment after an overdose, snorting coke with Steve Rubell and Bianca Jagger at Studio 54. He had become a grotesque to the younger generation, a terrible example for their elders, who could remember the great talent of the young Capote and comprehend the tragedy of its destruction. "Something in my life has done a terrible hurt to me," he said, at a loss to explain his own despair, "and it seems to be irrevocable."

In honor of what would have been Capote's eightieth birthday, Random House and its subsidiary, the Modern Library, have done an important service for their troublesome but lucrative author by bringing out a collection of his letters, edited by his biographer Gerald Clarke, and by producing new editions of his first novel, *Other Voices, Other Rooms*, and *The Complete Stories of Truman Capote*. It is a stunning experience to reread this fiction— mostly written when he was in his early twenties—and to realize how very golden this golden boy was. The image of the unhappy middle-aged clown dissolves; we are in the presence of a tremendous talent, and a fully mature technique as well. Norman Mailer's judgment that Capote was the most perfect writer of their generation—"he writes the best sentences word for word, rhythm upon rhythm"—seems true and just.

Capote decided upon his literary vocation in early childhood and never looked back. "How did it happen? That's what I ask myself," he said to his biographer. "My relatives were nothin', dirt-poor farmers. I don't believe in possession, but something took over inside me, some little demon that made me a writer." Capote is the perfect illustration of his own belief that education can neither make nor break a novelist. His own was sketchy, to say the least: he barely finished high school, with grades so bad that some teachers considered him subnormal.

Though Capote never wrote an autobiography, parts of his childhood are quite faithfully recorded in his novel *The Grass Harp* and his stories "A Christmas Memory," "The Thanksgiving Visitor," and "One Christmas," and also in his childhood friend Harper Lee's novel *To Kill a Mockingbird*, in which he appears as the strange little Dill. He was the progeny of a small-town con-man, Arch Persons, and Lillie Mae Faulk, an ambitious girl itching to get out of Monroeville, Alabama. Their marriage was brief, its break-up stormy. Southern Gothic, as so many examples have proved, is not a literary affectation so much as a literal representation of local life, and one of Capote's most outrageous pieces of fiction, the short story "My Side of the Matter" (1945), is not in fact an imitation of Eudora Welty's "Why I Live at the P.O.," as one might think at first, but a perfectly truthful portrait of Arch and Lillie Mae's absurd honeymoon.

The custody battle over little Truman was ugly and prolonged, but in truth neither parent really wanted the responsibility of caring for him. Eventually Lillie Mae won the tussle; she was a marginally more responsible person than the hopeless Arch. She embarked on a series of jobs, adventures, and love affairs, dragging the child along for the ride; his earliest memories were of being locked in hotel rooms while she went out on the town or slept with various transient boyfriends. "I had an intense fear of being abandoned," he later said, "and I remember practically all of my childhood as being lived in a state of constant tension and fear." Finally, just before his sixth birthday, his worst fear came true when his mother dumped him with the eccentric Faulk family in Monroeville: an elderly brother and his three sisters. When, if ever, would Lillie Mae come back? "Imagine a dog, watching and waiting and hoping to be taken away. That is the picture of me then." His emotional state, if not the literal circumstances that created it, is reproduced in that of the young Joel Harrison Knox in *Other Voices, Other Rooms*.

The years in Monroeville were blighted by his feelings of abandonment, but the small town, and the unchanging Faulk family, provided a stability that was sadly lacking in his earlier and subsequent life, and it is no accident that so much of his best fiction revolves around that quiet place. The Faulks loved the precocious little boy—"He is the sunshine of our home," said one of the old cousins—and he formed a strong bond with the odd Miss Sook Faulk, who was later to make an unforgettable appearance as "my friend" in "A Christmas Memory." Capote later acknowledged that it would probably have been better for him if his mother had simply let him spend the rest of his childhood there.

Lillie Mae had moved up in the world: married to a Cuban businessman, Joe Capote, she had changed her name to Nina and now lived on Park Avenue. Truman left the Faulks to become a part of the Capote household, at least on sufferance. Joe was a kind stepfather, adopting Truman and giving his name, but Nina never really loved or accepted him: she was disgusted by Truman's effeminacy, already evident in childhood, his affected manner, and his almost dwarfish stature (his adult height was only 5'3"), and she was evidently immune to his charm.

After Truman spent a spell at Trinity School in New York, Nina conceived the idea of sending him to military school, perhaps with the idea of making a man out him. The project proved disastrous: Truman, as might have been predicted, made irresistible sexual prey for older, rougher boys. Eventually the Capotes moved to Greenwich, Connecticut, and Truman attended the upscale Greenwich High, where he began to grow into the unconventional and decidedly attractive "character" that would soon ravish literary New York. "Truman brought happiness into our lives," remembered one Greenwich friend. "He said, 'Let's do it! Don't be afraid!' He created the fun, and if we got bored, he would come up with an idea of how we could get unbored."

Truman had too many other interests to bother with school-work; he failed to graduate with his class and, since the Capotes were returning to Manhattan, he was enrolled in a school that catered to students who couldn't make the grade elsewhere. That same year (1942) he took a job as a copyboy at *The New Yorker*. The magazine's editors expected their copyboys to perform their tasks silently and invisibly so that the resident geniuses could get on with their work in peace. Hiring the likes of Truman, surely the least silent and invisible copyboy in *New Yorker* history, was (as Gerald Clarke has said) truly an act of wartime desperation. "For God's sake! What's that?" the ultra-masculine Harold Ross demanded, catching a glimpse of Truman drifting down the hall.

He had begun writing short stories, some of which he submitted to *The New Yorker*, but they were not considered: "Very good. But romantic in a way this magazine is not," said the rejection slip. They found a warm welcome, however, at *Harper's Bazaar* and *Mademoiselle*, which, hard as it is to believe today, published some of the best and most innovative new fiction of that period. The first of Capote's stories really to make a hit was "Miriam" (1945: Capote was twenty years old), a creepy little tale about an aging spinster whose life is taken over by an evil, controlling child who just might be a projection of her own mind or soul. "Miriam" made a huge impression (at that time in New York, new short stories were as eagerly gobbled up and discussed as movies are today) but now it seems the least interesting of his early tales: his own later judgment that it was "a good stunt and nothing more" is probably correct.

But the general level of these early stories is remarkably high, and the magazines were soon avidly competing for his favors. "*Harper's* and *Mademoiselle* turned into temples which the cultist[s] entered every month with the seldom fulfilled hope that the little god would have published a new story there," recalled the critic Alfred Chester. Howard Doughty, a new friend, described the stories as showing "uncanny talent—almost frightening. He seems to have had practically no education except the back-files of the little magazines and is almost entirely unencumbered with ideas except on the practice of his art, but a mediumistic voice speaks through him in the most impeccable of accents. It's a long time since I've read anybody with such a specific gift for writing—like a musician's for music." Ideas that Capote were to articulate a decade later in his *Paris Review* interview are well illustrated by even his earliest stories: "Writing has laws of perspective," he said, "of light and shade, just as painting does, or music." He also expressed his belief that a story "can be wrecked by a faulty rhythm in a sentence—especially if it occurs toward the end—or a mistake in paragraphing, even punctuation."

At this magic moment of his life, Capote carried all before him. He was already adept at the art of publicity, to be sure, but his charm, by now legendary, was very real. It was based on an entirely original wit and eccentricity, his tiny stature and "baby seal's voice," his enveloping warmth. He had a puppyish desire for love—surely a result of his parents' emotional neglect—that most people found irresistible.

Christopher Isherwood, meeting him at about this time, remembered that "Something happened which one wishes occurred far more often in life: I loved him immediately." Humphrey Bogart said, "At first you can't believe him, he's so odd, and then you want to carry him around with you always."

At Yaddo, where he spent several weeks during the summer of 1946 working on *Other Voices, Other Rooms*, Capote cut a swath that has never quite been equaled. As one fellow-guest recorded in his diary:

Spontaneous when others are cautious, he has a child's directness, a child's indifference to propriety, and so gets to the heart of matters with an audacity strangers find outrageous, then delightful. Yet nothing he says or does accounts for the magnet somewhere in his makeup that exerts itself like a force beyond logic; he's responsible for turning the summer into a dance of bees. His slightest movements throughout the mansion, about the grounds, or on the side streets of Saratoga are charted and signaled by sentries visible only to one another. Schemes to share his table at dinner are laid at breakfast, sometimes by single plotters, sometimes by teams united in shamelessness. There's always laughter at his table, echoing across the moat of silence in which the tables around it are sunk.

Not everyone responded with such enthusiasm. It was back in the 1940s, for instance, that he and Gore Vidal began their lifelong feud; Vidal bitterly resented Capote's easy usurpation of a role he believed was rightfully his, that of Most Promising Young Novelist in America. ("How can you call anyone talented who's only written one book at twenty-three?" Vidal spluttered. "I've written three books, and I'm only twenty-two!") And Capote had uneasy relations with various other southern writers who jealously guarded their literary turf, as indeed he did himself. He and Carson McCullers, who had started out a close friend, soon drifted apart. Tennessee Williams forgave him for countless transgressions, even *Answered Prayers*, where he was depicted as a washed-up, squalid queen reduced to hiring call-boys to walk his dog.

Other Voices, Other Rooms was one of those books that seemed almost to write itself. "It is unusual, but occasionally it happens to almost every writer that the writing of some particular story seems outer-willed and effortless; it is as though one were a secretary transcribing the words of a voice from a cloud. The difficulty is maintaining contact with this spectral dictator." The final pages had not gone quite as smoothly as the rest, presaging a difficulty he would have with endings throughout his career. "But these last few pages!" he moaned. "Every word takes blood, I don't know why this should be, especially since I know exactly what I'm doing."

The novel's publication was almost upstaged by its jacket photo, which showed Capote, who appeared barely pubescent, lolling provocatively on a sofa like some male Lolita. Still, its reception was everything—or almost everything—he could have hoped for. Orville Prescott in *The New York Times* pronounced the young writer "gifted, dangerously gifted," and urged him to "ponder long on how he intends to use his exceptional talents."

He used them, for the next decade and more, well. Many consider that Capote squandered his gifts, but he devoted his youth and early middle age to hard and sustained labor, holing up for months in quiet spots in both Europe and America to work on whatever project he was embarked upon. Jack Dunphy, with whom he joined forces in 1948, was also a writer and shared his commitment to his art.

Capote's second novel was to be a story of contemporary New York, but he dropped this project, which he had come to see as rather brittle and artificial, when old Alabama memories began to resurface. He started *The Grass Harp* in 1950 and worked on it with steady focus. "It is very real to me," he wrote to his Random House editor, Robert Linscott; "[I]t keeps me in a painful emotional state: memories are always breaking my heart, I cry—it is very odd, I seem to have no control over myself or what I am doing. But my vision is clear, and if I can half execute that vision it will be a beautiful book."

Communicating intense emotional states was always Capote's strong suit, and readers of *The Grass Harp* (1951) were as affected by the material as he was himself. When a Broadway producer suggested that it be turned into a play, Capote responded with an enthusiasm that eventually proved misguided. His adaptation flopped on Broadway but garnered enough enthusiasm to keep him plugging away at theater and films; over the course of the next few years, he wrote another play (a musical based on his story "House of Flowers," also a failure) and worked on the scripts for several movies. All this work was respectable and even rather good, but it proved to be a misdirection of his energies, as Linscott tried to persuade him: "It's my hunch that a talent, delicate and evocative as yours, would illuminate more deeply from the printed page than in a theater, where coarser effects are perhaps essential and where you are at the mercy of the interpreters." This was undoubtedly true, but Capote's showbiz moonlighting and the new world it revealed led him into what we now call the "new" journalism, of which he was to be one of the foremost practitioners. Two *New Yorker* pieces from this period, a profile of Marlon Brando ("The Duke in His Domain") and a long account, subsequently published in book form, describing a black American theatrical troupe's tour of the Soviet Union (*The Muses are Heard*) are among the finest pieces of writing Capote ever produced.

Breakfast at Tiffany's was published in 1958. Probably the best-read and loved of all Capote's books, it strikes me as the least interesting as well, and not even original: character by character, situation by situation, it is a nearly exact imitation of Isherwood's "Sally Bowles," although no one ever mentions this fact—including Isherwood himself, who stayed more or less pals with Capote for the rest of their lives. Holly Golightly remains, however, a more synthetic creation than Sally, perhaps because while Sally was based on a real character, Holly was an idealized composite of a number of girls-about-town Capote knew, an abstraction—and an idealization, which Sally was not—rather than a human being.

In November, 1959 Capote noticed a newspaper item about the murder of the Clutter family of Garden City, Kansas. This was the beginning of a six-year creative odyssey and, ultimately, a mental ordeal. It would send Capote straight to the top of the literary heap while simultaneously upsetting his emotional equilibrium, which had never been anything but shaky.

Artistically, he knew he was doing something quite new. "Journalism," he commented, "always moves along on a horizontal plane, telling a story, while fiction—good fiction—moves vertically, taking you deeper and deeper into character and events. By treating a real event with fictional techniques . . . it's possible to make this kind of synthesis." Since then, many others have adopted this idea of the "nonfiction novel," but few have crafted it with Capote's integrity: while he performed painstaking research, meeting and corresponding with the drama's participants until every detail of the events was familiar to him, subsequent imitators have tended to treat facts as though, being "fictionalized," they are changeable and dispensable.

Capote immersed himself in the grisly material until it tainted every part of his life—the more so since he found himself powerfully identifying with one of the killers, Perry Smith. (Norman Mailer called Capote's Smith one of the great characters of American fiction, a plausible judgment.) "Every morning of my life I throw up because of the tensions created by the writing of the book," Capote said. "But it's worth it; because it's the best work I've done." While the murderers were swiftly convicted, their execution dates were postponed again and again as various appeals worked their way through the legal system. Capote found himself in an unhappy position; he could not finish the book until Smith and Hickock were executed, but he dreaded the actual event, and correctly: it haunted him forever, he said, like the echo in the Marabar Caves in Forster's *Passage to India*.

"Before I began [In Cold Blood], I was a stable person, comparatively speaking. Afterward, something happened to me. I just can't forget it, particularly the hangings at the end. Horrible!" But his demons were temporarily suppressed with the ecstatic reception of *In Cold Blood*, which in 1966 appeared in four consecutive issues of *The New Yorker*, breaking all sales records for the magazine. There had in fact been nothing like it since, over a century before, New York readers of *The Old Curiosity Shop* waited at the piers and shouted to a ship arriving from England, "Is Little Nell dead?" "My wife and I read each *New Yorker* as it came, tearing it out of the postman's hand," wrote one representative reader, a Lutheran minister from California. "Now we will re-read all of them; the first time we gobbled them down, glub-glub!"

Capote was the cynosure of literary New York and of worldly New York as well, when the famous black-and-white ball he threw at the Plaza late in 1966 was dubbed the party of the century. (Its guest book read "like an international list for the guillotine," joked Leo Lerman.) But the signs of instability were more evident. When *In Cold Blood* failed to win the Pulitzer Prize or the National Book Award, Capote let the snub bother him much more than he should have done—for how often have the best books ever won the big prizes?

His sense of self, always frail since the insecurities and aban-donments of his childhood and further harmed by the suicide of his unloving mother in 1954—the ultimate withdrawal—began slipping dangerously. For years he had been obsessed with wealth and glamour. "Style is what you are," he said, and he appeared really to believe this. His deepest friendships, as he entered middle age, were with café-society types like Babe and Bill Paley, Lee Radziwell, and Slim Keith. Capote's confusion was nowhere more evident than in his sincere worship of these peacocks (as the dyspeptic Dunphy called them) and their values, or lack thereof, and then in his apparently unconscious attack on them in *Answered Prayers*. While he claimed that the ultra-rich led charmed lives, and certainly toadied to them as though he thought that was the case, he portrayed them in the segment of *Answered Prayers* that appeared in *Esquire* as lost souls. That he could have been unaware of this double-think—unaware even that, in writing, he had done anything to offend—shows the true degeneration of his mental state. As John O'Shea said time and again, it was not a drying-out clinic he should have been taken to when he began drinking, but a really serious psychiatric hospital. His 1984 death was probably the result of an overdose—essentially a suicide, like his mother's.

Too Brief a Treat, a collection of Capote's letters, is a disappointment. Capote turns out to have been a surprisingly mediocre letter-writer; perhaps wisely, he saved his best efforts for his fiction. One feels that his natural medium of communication was the telephone rather than the pen, and when he did write he tended to do so swiftly and carelessly and to reuse his material when he could. Another problem is that the letters in this volume are addressed to only a few recipients, a small portion of his circle of acquaintance. There are hardly any letters to Jack Dunphy and few or none to the Paleys, Lee Radziwell, Carson McCullers, Nina Capote, Joanne Carson, Christopher Isherwood, or his old pals from their teenage years—Oona O'Neill Chaplin, Gloria Vanderbilt, and Carol Marcus Saroyan Matthau.

Clarke's explanatory footnotes are maddeningly inadequate. One is constantly running up against some intriguing item like "poor Greta [Garbo]—but a great deal of it is her own fault" or "Darling, isn't this ironic about Christopher [Isherwood]? I told you so" without any explanation whatsoever, so that the reader is continually frustrated. And yet Clarke explains other things needlessly, for example adding "[Williams]" after a reference to "Tennessee" (has there ever been another Tennessee?). Also, he has appended no cast of characters, which would have been easy to do and extremely useful. All of this is especially surprising in light of Clarke's previous achievement: his 1988 *Capote: A Biography* is one of the finest biographies in recent decades—superbly written and well documented.

But while the letters will only appeal to true enthusiasts, *Other Voices, Other Rooms* and *The Complete Stories of Truman Capote* should be as widely distributed as possible. Nowadays most people know Capote only through *Breakfast at Tiffany's* and *In Cold Blood*, which are fine, but Capote started out as a different type of writer who might have developed in a different, and equally exciting, way.

The appearance of Capote's early books in Modern Library editions led me to hope that his work has definitively entered the canon. This morning my hope was fulfilled when, as I strolled through my Brooklyn neighborhood, I noticed a large banner for the benefit of tourists that read: "Brooklyn Heights: Home of Truman Capote." This is fame indeed: fame, one hopes, that will outlive the mere notoriety of his final years.

(2004)

ABOUT THE AUTHOR

Peter Aaron

Brooke Allen has published two previous essay collections. Her work has appeared in *The New Criterion, The Wall Street Journal, The Hudson Review, The New York Times, The Nation, The Atlantic,* and elsewhere. With a PhD from Columbia University, she has taught literature at Bennington College and history of thought in its prison program. She and her husband, the photographer Peter Aaron, have two daughters and live in New York's Hudson Valley.

ACKNOWLEDGMENTS

I owe a debt of gratitude to the publications where these essays, often under different titles, were first published, and which graciously allowed me to reprint them here. "Love and Separateness," "Into Africa," "The Novelist Unauthorized," "Capote Reconsidered," "Whim of Iron," "The Poet in his Dungeon," "A Newby Abroad," "The Mot Juste," "The Strindberg Variations," "The Art of Exile," "Deadeye Dick," "Small Is Beautiful," "The Gay Blade," and "The Devil's Disciple" appeared originally in *The New Criterion.* "Updike's Farewell" and "A Life as Theater" appeared in *The Hudson Review.* "Another Day, Another Dolor" appeared in *Christianity Today.* Part One of "A Charmer and a User" was published in *The Atlantic;* Part Two was in *The New York Times Book Review,* also the source of "Without Peer" and "The Old Parrot." "The Man in Full" combines two essays from *The Wall Street Journal.* "Servant of the People" was published in *Barnes & Noble Review.*

In particular I want to thank Michael Anderson, Alida Becker, the late Christopher Carduff, Paula Deitz, Erich Eichman, Robert Erickson, David Kelly, Roger Kimball, Ron Koury, James Mustich, James Panero, Benjamin Riley, Katherine Seger, Isaac Sligh, William Tipper, and Zachary Wood.

Also by Brooke Allen

- Twentieth Century Attitudes: Literary Powers in Uncertain Times (2003)
- Artistic License: Three Centuries of Good Writing and Bad Behavior (2004)
- Moral Minority: Our Skeptical Founding Fathers (2006)
- The Other Side of the Mirror: An American Travels Through Syria (2011)
- Benazir Bhutto: Favored Daughter (2016)